Issues in Curating Contemporary Art and Performance

Edited by Judith Rugg and Michèle Sedgwick

Issues in Curating Contemporary Art and Performance

Edited by Judith Rugg and Michèle Sedgwick

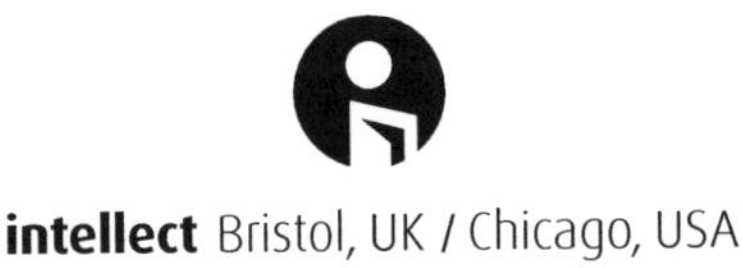

intellect Bristol, UK / Chicago, USA

Acknowledgements

The editors would like to thank all the contributors and acknowledge the financial support of the University College for the Creative Arts; the University of the Arts, London; the University of Plymouth; the University of Surrey and the University of Northumbria.

First Published in the UK in 2007 by
Intellect Books, PO Box 862, Bristol BS99 1DE, UK

First published in the USA in 2007 by
Intellect Books, The University of Chicago Press, 1427 E. 60th Street, Chicago, IL 60637, USA

A catalogue record for this book is available from the British Library.

Cover Design: John McCabe
Copy Editor: Holly Spradling
Typesetting: Mac Style, Nafferton, E. Yorkshire

ISBN 978-1-84150-536-7

Printed and bound by 4edge Limited, UK

CONTENTS

Introduction

Judith Rugg

The impetus for this book came from a series of symposia hosted during 2004 and 2005 by the University College for the Creative Arts at Canterbury on issues of curating as a form of critical intervention into ways of comprehending contemporary culture. The contributors to this book and to that debate are artists, academics, writers, theorists and curators whose activities overlap several of these categories, who examine varied perspectives on curating contemporary art and performance and the relationships between them. The book as a collection of chapters, proposes that the concept of curating is a complex field of enquiry. By drawing together writers from different academic backgrounds, *Issues in Curating Contemporary Art and Performance* initiates new paradigms and critical thinking about this increasingly expanding field.

Part 1: Forms of Thinking in Contemporary Curating proposes a mapping of various issues in approaches to contemporary curating and their implications for the reception of contemporary art. In 'The Curatorial Turn: From Practice to Discourse', Paul O'Neill proposes a short history of contemporary curating by examining some of the issues that have emerged in curatorial discourse over the last ten years, including the ritualizing of the experience of art through exhibitions, the rise of 'biennale culture', the expansion of the artist as a meta-curator and the large-scale curated exhibition as the new autonomous artwork. By articulating the inter-dependent relationship between academic research into the discursive field of contemporary curating and his own curatorial practice, O'Neill proposes an inter-related, performative position as a means of critiquing current issues of contemporary art curating.

In 'Curatorial Strategy as Critical Intervention: The Genesis of *Facing East*', Liz Wells proposes that curation is essentially a research process, involving investigation, discovery and critical reflection. Through discussion of the curatorial elements of her curated exhibition on contemporary photography from the Baltic, *Facing East*, she argues that the essential mechanisms and processes of curating parallel those of more established academic models of enquiry, involving the definition and refining of particular research questions. Wells asserts that research underpins the curatorial 'voice' through a process which is composed of a careful definition of the field, rigorous contextualization of the work and consideration of the 'theatre' of the exhibition. Curatorial strategy becomes most effective as critical intervention when it opens exploration and debate, invoking a range of issues and emotions for the viewer.

In 'No Place Like Home: Europa', Sophia Phoca discusses how concepts such as that of the shifting perception of Europe through its expansion eastwards, and the collapse of the Soviet Union, informed the approach to her co-curated *Europa: Film and Video from the Centre of Europe* held at Tate Modern in 2004. She also examines issues of co-curatorial practice and authorial ideologies inscribed in this form of curatorial practice and the implications for curating film and video. She explores the significance of curatorial methodology in generating debate about the moving image in an expanding geographic and curatorial context.

Part 2: Curating and the Interdisciplinary: Encounter, Context, Experience looks at concepts of the editor-curator, and the relationships between curating, reception and encounter. In 'Critical Spatial Practice: Curating, Editing, Writing', Jane Rendell outlines her interests over the past few years in exploring interdisciplinary fields through the curation of texts. Her chapter draws on some of those projects where she has been involved as editor and curator, as well as participant, in order to investigate the role of the editor/curator, artist/architect and critic/theorist. She explores methods of engagement with artworks which she proposes are 'sites', which can be perceived differently through various tools of investigation. Critical spatial writing, she argues, questions terms of reference that relate the critic to the artwork within the terms of 'critique'.

In 'Exhibitions and their Prerequisites', Chris Dorsett argues that art-science collaborations have become a familiar concept within funding initiatives such as those of the Arts and Humanities Research Council and the Welcome Trust. For Dorsett (an artist-curator), such collaborations are forms of interdisciplinary ventures that arise out of the 'expanded field' of arts practice which has shaped the visual arts for several decades. In this chapter, the interdisciplinary nature of the arts/science collaboration is explored via the author's botanical research in a field station at the National Institute for Amazonian Research and its dissemination at the Royal Botanic Gardens, Kew. Dorsett explores the possibilities of the reception of such arts/science curations where the context of the reception of the exhibition of work, informed by forest field station, studio and ethno-botanical archive, is in non-art museums.

Part 3: The Role of the Curator: Contestation and Consideration looks critically at the role of the curator of contemporary art. In 'Curating Doubt', JJ Charlesworth proposes that the relatively recent dialogue around curating has been generated by curators and critics. Curators function practically as well as being reflexive of their own practice and there is a need for the aspect of self-justification that may inflect the discussion as a creative force. Charlesworth considers how art has been 'bureaucratised' over the last ten years, creating a new art managerial class where artist has been displaced by the claims of the curator as the core legitimizing role in the institutions of art. He contemplates a relativism of cultural values, which proposes no special status for any privileged cultural activity but which nevertheless continues in a privileged institutional form.

In 'A Parallel Universe: The "Women's" Exhibitions at the ICA, 1980 and the UK/Canadian Film and Video Exchange 1998–2004', Catherine Elwes discusses how the early years of feminist art saw a struggle against institutional invisibility which prompted three major exhibitions of women's art at the Institute of Contemporary Arts, London, in 1980. She describes the internal and external problems that arose when a 1970s artists' collective attempted to work within the major art institution of the ICA. Elwes compares this event with another curatorial project she was involved with twenty years later: the UK/Canadian Film and Video Exchange, which similarly was concerned to make visible groups of artists neglected by history. These initiatives form the basis for a discussion of the role of the curator deriving from a tradition of collaborative decision-making set down in the 1970s and perpetuated in the contemporary UK/Canadian exchanges. A controversial plea is made by Elwes as both curator and artist, for the burgeoning 'army' of today's curators to follow James Lingwood's advice and 'understand their position in the food chain'. The visibility of art, she argues, should be the goal of curating, not the aggrandizement of what is, in essence, a 'service' trade.

In 'Thoughts on Curating', Richard Hylton sets out candidly to explore the nature of curating at a time when art in Britain enjoys an unprecedented visibility and popularity. He assesses how changes in public funding coupled with current concerns with conceptual access and inclusion have influenced the notion of 'critical' or 'interventionalist' practice. Using his own personal testimony and experience of curating over the past fifteen years as a background, and discussing a number of key projects which traverse both the public and private sector, involving artists such as Janette Parris, Donald Rodney and David Hammons, Hylton asks if the significance attached to the role of the curator is itself misleading. With the professionalism of curating (typified by the expanding numbers of curating courses in the 1990s) and the growth of newly built or converted spaces for the display of art, Hylton questions that, rather than expanding access to contemporary art, curators and institutions are merely supporting an increasingly regulated visual arts terrain beholden to both market (private) and government (public) agendas.

Part 4: Emergent Practices: Subverting the Museum looks at how curating may be a form of critical intervention when it considers the 'space' of the exhibition. In 'Oscillating the "high/low" Art Divide: Curating and Exhibiting Animation', Suzanne

Buchan, as curator, film festival director and academic, explores the problematics of curating animation in a range of exhibition spaces from festival to cinema programming to gallery installation to museum exhibitions. Historically, curatorial practices have limited understandings of animation, and this chapter poses questions relating to changing concepts of animation as an art form and how it relates within an interdisciplinary sense to other art forms.

In 'Generator: The Value of Software Art', Geoff Cox uses an example of approaches to curating software art and the challenges it presents to the curator. He discusses how *Generator*, a touring show he co-curated with Spacex Gallery (2002), was an attempt to historicize (contemporary) artist-programmers with more established (historic) forms of conceptual art approaches using instruction-based practices.

In 2000, Kate Lawrence was a recipient of a Year of the Artist Award and in 'Who Makes Site-specific Dance? The Year of the Artist and the Matrix of Curating' she considers four other site-specific dance projects in this Arts Council-funded programme. Referring to concepts of site-specificity in the visual arts, she investigates the relationship of these works to their places of performance. An examination of the writings of choreographers and producers involved in the case studies leads to her contention that site-specific dance is curated and created by a matrix of bodies, including artists, producers, landowners, community participants, funding bodies and businesses. Recognition of the labour of this diverse range of producers as creative, expands notions of the function of art and artists in society, since site-specific projects are revealed to be made by a web of co-dependent authors.

Issues of the museum and its governing processes of selection, presentation and display are discussed by Alun Rowlands in 'The Movement Began with a Scandal', which investigates how curators can develop structures and models of thinking which are sensitive to emergent practices, both in curating and in art. Rowlands examines how the exhibition, in adopting activist methods, can be allied to institutional critique. Shifting between disparate venues, subjects and forms, a 'relational curatorial strategy' argues for the re-consideration of the exhibition as a specialized space for communication, presentation and interpretation. It is within these interpretative structures that the discourse of art is fashioned and regulated, and where such a strategy seeks to intervene. The intention is to piggyback institutions (art and non-art) temporarily, subverting conventions of thinking and introducing different rhythms and narratives that promote a continual questioning of both the nature of contemporary art and of curating practices.

PART 1: Forms of Thinking in Contemporary Curating

THE CURATORIAL TURN: FROM PRACTICE TO DISCOURSE

Paul O'Neill

Introductory context:
It was in the late 1960s that Seth Siegelaub used the term 'demystification' in order to establish the shift in exhibition production conditions, whereby curators were beginning to make visible the mediating component within the formation, production and dissemination of an exhibition.

> I think in our generation we thought that we could demystify the role of the museum, the role of the collector, and the production of the artwork; for example, how the size of a gallery affects the production of art, etc. In that sense we tried to demystify the hidden structures of the art world. (O'Neill, P. and Siegelaub 2006)

During the 1960s the primary discourse around art-in-exhibition began to turn away from forms of critique of the artwork as autonomous object of study/critique towards a form of curatorial criticism, in which the space of exhibition was given critical precedence over that of the objects of art. Curatorial criticism differed from that of traditional western art criticism (i.e. linked to modernity) in that its discourse and subject matter went beyond discussion about artists and the object of art to include the subject of curating and the role played by the curator of exhibitions. The ascendancy of the curatorial gesture in the 1990s also began to establish curating as a potential nexus for discussion, critique and debate, where the evacuated role of the critic in parallel cultural discourse was usurped by the neo-critical space of curating. During this period, curators and artists have reacted to and engaged with this 'neo-criticality' by extending the parameters of the exhibition form to incorporate more discursive, conversational and geo-political discussion, centred within the ambit of the exhibition. The ascendancy of this 'curatorial gesture' in the 1990s (as well as the professionalization of contemporary curating) began to establish curatorial practice as a potential space for critique. Now the neo-critical curator has usurped the evacuated place of the critic. As Liam Gillick pointed out:

> My involvement in the critical space is a legacy of what happened when a semi-autonomous critical voice started to become weak, and one of the reasons that happened was that curating became a dynamic process. So people you might have met before, who in the past were critics were now curators. The brightest, smartest people get involved in this multiple activity of being mediator, producer, interface and neo-critic. It is arguable that the most important essays about art over the last ten years have not been in art magazines but they have been in catalogues and other material produced around galleries, art centres and exhibitions. (Gillick 2005: 74)

Accompanying this 'turn towards curating' was the emergence of curatorial anthologies. Beginning in the 1990s, most of these tended to come out of international meetings between curators, as part of curatorial summits, symposia, seminars and conferences, although some of them may have taken local curatorial practice as their starting point. Without exception, they placed an emphasis on individual practice, the first-person narrative and curator self-positioning – articulated through primary interviews, statements and exhibition representations – as they attempted to define and map out a relatively bare field of discourse.

Alongside this predominantly curator-led discourse, curatorial criticism responded with an assertion of the separateness of the artistic and curatorial gesture – when such divisions are no longer apparent in contemporary exhibition practice. I would argue that such a divisive attempt to detach the activity of curating from that of artistic production results in resistance to recognition of the interdependence of both practices within the field of cultural production. Moreover the mediation of hybrid cultural agents through the means of the public exhibition is overlooked.

The curatorial turn

'Exhibitions have become *the* medium through which most art becomes known.'
(Ferguson, Greenberg & Nairne 1996: 2)

Exhibitions (in whatever form they take) are always ideological; as hierarchical structures they produce particular and general forms of communication. Since the late 1980s, the group exhibition has become the primary site for curatorial experimentation and, as such, has generated a new discursive space around artistic practice. The group exhibition runs counter to the canonical model of the monographic presentation. By bringing a greater mix of people into an exhibition, it also created a space for defining multifarious ways of engaging with disparate interests, often within a more trans-cultural context. Group exhibitions are ideological texts which make private intentions public. In particular, it is the temporary art exhibition that has become the principal medium in the distribution and reception of art; thus, being the principal agent in debate and criticism about any aspect of the visual arts.

Exhibitions (particularly group exhibitions, art fairs, temporary perennial shows and large-scale international art exhibitions) are the main means through which contemporary art is now mediated, experienced and historicized. Just as the number of large-scale, international exhibitions increased since the 1990s, so has the respectability of the phenomenon of curating been enhanced. Similarly, writing about exhibitions has further reinforced the merit of curatorial practice as a subject worthy of study. As a tactic: 'This may either be a compensatory device, a politicized attempt to consider works of art as interrelated rather than as individual entities, or a textual response to changes in the art world itself' (Ferguson, Greenberg & Nairne 1996).

The critical debate surrounding curatorial practice has not only intensified, but as Alex Farquharson has pointed out, even the recent appearance of the verb 'to curate', where once there was just a noun, indicates the growth and vitality of this discussion. He writes: 'new words, after all, especially ones as grammatically bastardised as the verb "to curate" (worse still the adjective "curatorial"), emerge from a linguistic community's persistent need to identify a point of discussion.'(Farquharson 2003)

Indicative of a shift in the primary role of curator is the changing perception of the curator as carer to a curator who has a more creative and active part to play within the production of art itself. This new verb, 'to curate...may also suggest a shift in the conception of what curators do, from a person who works at some remove from the processes of artistic production, to one actively "in the thick of it".' (Farquharson 2003) Ten years previously, when writing about cultural production, Pierre Bourdieu noted that the curator (*inter alia*) added cultural meaning and value to the making of art and artists:

> The subject of the production of the artwork – of its value but also of its meaning – is not the producer who actually creates the object in its materiality, but rather the entire set of agents engaged in the field. Among these are the producers of works, classified as artists...critics of all persuasions...collectors, middlemen, curators, etc.; in short, all those who have ties with art, who live for art and, to varying degrees, from it, and who confront each other in struggles where the imposition of not only a world view but also a vision of the art world is at stake, and who, through these struggles, participate in the production of the value of the artist and of art. (Bourdieu 1993: 261)

As cultural agents, curators and artists participate in the production of cultural value, exhibitions are intrinsic and vital parts of what Theodore Adorno and Max Horkheimer termed the 'cultural industries' associated with: entertainment; mass culture; the communications enterprise of mass reception; and as part of the consciousness industry (see Adorno and Horkheimer 1997: 120–167). Exhibitions are, therefore, contemporary forms of rhetoric, complex expressions of persuasion, whose strategies aim to produce a prescribed set of values and social relations for their audiences. As such exhibitions are subjective political tools, as well as being modern ritual settings, which uphold identities (artistic, national, sub-cultural, 'international', gender-or-race-specific, avant-garde, regional, global etc.); they are to be understood as institutional 'utterances' within a larger culture industry. (See Ferguson 1996: 178–9.)

Biennial culture and the culture of curation

One of the most evident developments in contemporary curatorial practice since the late 1980s has been occurring on an increasingly inter-national, trans-national and multi-national scale, where the 'local' and the 'global' are in constant dialogue. In *Contemporary* magazine's special issue on curating, published in 2005, Isabel Stevens produced a substantiative list of 80 official Biennials/ Triennials throughout the globe to be held between 2006 and 2008. Terms such as 'biennial', 'biennale', or 'mega-exhibitions' no longer refer to those few exhibitions that occur perennially, every two years or so: they are now all encompassing idioms for large-scale international group exhibitions, which, for each local cultural context,, are organized locally with connection to other national cultural networks (Stevens 2005). Biennials are temporary spaces of mediation, usually allocated to invited curators with support from a local socio-cultural network. They are interfaces between art and larger publics – publics which are at once local and global, resident and nomadic, non-specialist and art-worldly.

In what Barbara Vanderlinden and Elena Filipovic call the 'biennial phenomenon' such 'large-scale international exhibitions' reflect the cultural diversity of global artistic practices and call into question the inertia of public art institutions that are unwilling or too slow to respond to such praxis (Filipovic & Vanderlinden 2005). Biennials have become a form of institution in themselves; their frequency has resulted in an index of comparability. In a rather prophetic essay, written in the early 1990s, Bruce Ferguson, Reesa Greenberg and Sandy Nairne had already begun to question the fundamental idea of international survey exhibitions. Their collective essay ended with the paragraph:

> However progressive the political or economic intentions behind them, international exhibitions still invite a presumption that the curators have access to an illusionary world view, and that spectators may follow in their wake. But a more specific and sustained engagement with communities and audiences, creating meanings beyond the spectacular and mere festivalising of such occasions, may produce a new genre of exhibition. It seems that in order to accommodate both artist's needs and audience demands, the new exhibition must have reciprocity and dialogue built into its structure. How successfully this is accomplished will determine international exhibition maps of the future. (Ferguson, Greenberg & Nairne 2005: 3)

As was predicted, these event-exhibitions have shaped new social, cultural and political relations in a more globalized world, where the traditional biennial model is maintained through discourse on cultural policy, national representation and internationalism, thereby enabling cultural travel, urban renovation and local tourism. Alternately, it is arguable that they have become polarizing spaces to legitimize certain forms of artistic and curatorial praxis within the global culture industry.

Very few *biennials* are of the scale of *Documenta, Johannesburg, Venice* or even *Istanbul*. Many tend to be improvisatory, localized and modest in their aims. Here I am interested in the general-specific homogeneity produced by the institution of the biennial, not the heterogeneity of the myriad of localized cultural statements. The populist perception of the activity of curating has changed in large part due to the spread of biennials in the 1990s, whereby new degrees of visibility and responsibility were placed upon the curator. Apart from the particular issues of scale, temporality and location, the activity of curation made manifest through such exhibitions is articulated as being identity-driven; therefore, an overtly politicized, discursively global and fundamentally auteured praxis prevails, in spite of the many variable forms they have taken on. The biennial form as a global exhibition model has driven much of the art world's global extension since 1989, when *Les Magiciens de la Terre* began the process. Biennials have become the vehicle through which much art is validated and acquires value on the international art circuit. Now such 'global exhibitions' often have as their main theme, 'globalization', whilst questioning the ideological underpinning of the exhibition itself as a product of that process.

Despite any curatorial self-reflexivity in recent large-scale exhibitions that may exist towards the global effects of 'biennialization', the periphery still has to follow the discourse of the centre. In the case of biennials, the periphery comes to the centre in search of legitimization and, by default, accepts the conditions of this legitimacy. Charles Esche suggests that the globalization of art within large-scale exhibitions has, through a process of standardization, absorbed the difference between centre and periphery. According to Esche, the 'centre first' model of global art, largely begun in 1989, still holds sway over much of the museum and biennial culture. It requires 'the key institutions of contemporary culture officially to sanction the "periphery" in order to subsume it into the canon of innovative visual art.' (Esche 2005: 105). Even though many of the artists in each exhibition may have developed their practice on the fringes of the recognized art world, 'their energy is validated and consumed by the centre and therefore the relationship between rim and hub remains in place. This is, of course, how globalisation generally operates – sometimes to the economic benefit of the patronised but rarely in the interests of maintaining their autonomy and sustainability.' (Esche 2005: 105).

The exhibition's ritual of maintaining a given set of power relations between art, display and reception is particularly true of, what John Miller called, the 'blockbuster exhibition', which tends to incorporate anachronistic elements whilst recuperating any dissent from viewers as part of the totality of the overall event. In consequence, a 'cycle of raised expectations and quick disillusionment' is both predictable and over-determined. Miller argues that the 'mega-exhibition' is an ideological institution that reifies social relations between artworks and spectator. As the explicit purpose of these shows is to offer a comprehensive survey of artworks on a demographic basis, the terms of discourse are treated as pre-determined, rather than being 'transformed in the course of art production and therefore subject to contradiction and conflict.' (Miller 1996: 270)

According to Miller, a critique of these exhibitions on the basis of curatorial choices made within the established framework would be to ignore the ideologies underpinning the institutions that are responsible for them. He suggests that such institutions often treat and address audiences as a concrete social constituency, whereby artworks are relegated to mere 'raw material' within the 'total artwork' of the exhibition (Gesamtkunstwerk), thus privileging the curator's subjectivity, so that the outcome of the exhibition-form is naturalized as an organic inevitability within the organization's institutional framework producing an illusion of curatorial inspiration and genius (Miller 1996a: 272).

I would argue that during a period of transformation since 1989 the notion of exhibitions as authored subjectivities produced dominant discourses around 'mega-exhibitions'. Although more recent biennials have moved away from the single-author position towards more collective models, a globally configured exhibition market has persisted with a curator-centred discourse. Discussions, lecture programmes, conferences, publications and discursive events are also now a re-current and integral part of such exhibitions, or in the case of some exhibitions, such as *Documenta X* and especially *Documenta 11*, discursive events formed the very foundation of the project. As Elena Filipovic suggested:

> This striking expansion goes in tandem with curatorial discourses that increasingly distinguish the biennial or mega exhibition as larger than the mere presentation of artworks; they are understood as vehicles for the production of knowledge and intellectual debate. (Filipovic 2006: 66)

In many ways the expanding network of biennials has effectively embraced art and artists from the peripheries beyond a dominantly Western European and American internationalism, but as Jessica Bradley argued, they function as a more responsive and spectacular means of distribution:

> [O]ne that can efficiently meet the accelerated rate of exchange and consumption parallel to the global flow of capital and information today…while curatorial aspirations are frequently concerned with addressing cultures in flux and eschew cultural nationalism, the motives for establishing these events may nevertheless reside in a desire to promote and validate local, culturally specific production within a global network. (Bradley 2003: 89)

It is the inter-relational attributes of both culture and location that are the most obviously marketable aspects of global tourism upon which they depend. Locality embodied in the promotion of tourist spots, local specialities, sites, culture and produce are actually the most reliable economic revenues for local communities. It has also been argued that during these times of 'culture as spectacle', artistic production is a catalyst for culture to be globalized, attracting financial investments as well as audiences. Ivo Mesquita also argues that during these times of 'culture as spectacle', artistic production acts as a catalyst for globalized culture, attracting financial investments and audiences. Biennials (and art fairs) are happening in more and more cities, which have adopted cultural tourism as a means of securing a place in the international arena of economy and culture, wherein artists, curators, critics, art dealers, patrons and sponsors nurture a clearly defined production system, through labour division, which produces hierarchical roles for the participants (Mesquita 2003: 63–68).

As an important agent within the global cultural industry, a new kind of international curator was identified by Ralph Rugoff as a 'jet-set *flâneur*' who appears to know no geographical boundaries, and for whom a type of global-internationalism is the central issue (Rugoff 1999). In particular, the role of the nomadic curator within large-scale exhibitions is to select and display "international" art through a visible framing device: a subjective (curatorial) system of mediation that has the notion of inclusivity as one of its central thematics. The rise of the global curator has less to do with embedded power structures within the art world and more to do with inherited cultural significance (and capital), where practice has long been prioritized over discourse within the culture industry as a whole, where practice is in turn dependent on being translated back into discourse in order to facilitate more equivalent practice, which enables the maintenance of the existing superstructure. As Benjamin Buchloh identified in 1989, there is an urgent need for articulating the curatorial position as part of art discourse, where practice as 'doing' or 'curating' necessitated a discourse as 'speaking' or 'writing', in order for the curator's function to be acknowledged as part of the institutional superstructure at the level of discourse:

> The curator observes his/ her operation within the institutional apparatus of art: most prominently the procedure of abstraction and centralisation that seems to be an inescapable consequence of the work's entry into the superstructure apparatus, its transformation from practice to discourse. That almost seems to have become the curator's primary role: to function as an agent who offers exposure and potential prominence – in exchange for obtaining a moment of actual practice that is about to be transformed into myth/ superstructure. (Buchloh 1989)

This interest in discourse, as a supplement or substitute for practice, was highlighted in Dave Beech and Gavin Wade's speculative introduction to *Curating in the 21st Century*, 2000, in which they stated that 'even talking is doing something, especially if you are saying something worthwhile. Doing and saying, then are forms of acting on the world.' (Wade & Beech 2000: 9–10). So, it seems fair to characterize the discursive as an ambivalent way of saying something *vis-à-vis* doing. This may seem a somewhat optimistic speculation, as Mick Wilson argues in his assessment of the productive powers of language, which have been part of the stock assumptions of a wide range of experimental art practices and attendant commentary (Wilson 2007). This tendency has been given further impetus by what he calls 'the Foucauldian moment in art of the last two decades, and the ubiquitous appeal of the term "discourse" as a word to conjure and perform power', to the point where 'even talking is doing something', with the value of the discursive as something located in its proxy for actual doing within discourses on curatorial practice (Wilson 2007: 202).

The 'rise of the curator as creator', as Bruce Altshuler (1994) labeled it, has also gathered momentum. The ever-increasing number of global biennials has provided what Julia Bryan-Wilson claims to be prestigious 'launching pads for the curatorial star system' in 'the age of curatorial studies', in which the 'institutional basis of art is taken as a given, and the marketing and packaging of contemporary art has become a specialized focus of inquiry for thousands of students.'(Bryan-Wilson 2003: 102–3). If the 1990s were all about a new professionalization during a period of globalization, they now seem to represent acceleration in the global art exhibition-making market followed by a settling down period. Only now can we begin to evaluate the processes of translation that accompanied these productions and recognize that curating as distinct moments of practice is significantly divergent from curatorial discourse.

Beatrice von Bismarck provided an example of this bifurcation between curatorial practice and discourse, so that professionalization and differentiation within the art world have turned curating into a hierarchically arranged job description, whereby "internationally networked service providers" offer their skills to a diverse exhibition market, when curating as practice is understood in discourse as something that is distinct from its understanding as a job title:

> Of the tasks originally associated with the fixed institutional post, curating takes only that of presentation. With the aim of creating an audience for artistic and cultural materials and techniques, of making them visible, the exhibition becomes the key presentation medium. In contrast to the curator's other duties, curating itself frees the curator from the invisibility of the job, giving him/her an otherwise uncommon degree of freedom [...] and a prestige not unlike that enjoyed by artists. (von Bismarck 2004: 99)

Within curatorial discourse, the figure of the curator operates at a level previously understood as being the domain of artistic practice, where in Foucauldian terms, such discourse is 'the general domain of all statements, sometimes as an individualisable group of statements, and sometimes as a regulated practice that accounts for a certain number of statements...' (Foucault 2003: 30). Thus, curating-specific discourse engenders a requisite level of prestige, necessitated by the dynamics of contemporary curating. Practice alone does not produce and support such esteem, rather distinct moments of practice translate into a hierarchical 'common discourse' of curating as it is understood through its discursive formations. While internationalism is now at the core of practice with the biennial industry, its accompanying curatorial discourse functions to maintain the superstructure of the art world on a much wider scale than ever before. Where the biennial curator is a well-travelled subject, the curators of exhibitions are already engaging in a complex network of global knowledge circuits that traverse and overlap the other: each 'biennial' is 'in conversation' with the next, providing yet another momentary place of exchange of curatorial discourse across exhibitions; each exhibition speaks with one another as well as to the world they claim to reflect.

Curator as meta/artist, artist as meta/curator
Since the late 1980s, the shift away from curating as an administrative, caring, mediating activity towards that of curating as a creative activity more akin to a form of artistic practice was indicated by Jonathan Watkins' polemic on curating written for *Art Monthly* in 1987. Using Oscar Wilde's idea that objects were transformed into art by the critic through writing, Watkins provocatively argued that curating was a form of artistic practice and that curated exhibitions were likened to Marcel Duchamp's 'Readymade Aided' artworks, where the display or exhibition is aided by the curator's 'manipulation of the environment, the lighting, the labels, the placement of other works of art.' (Watkins 1987: 27)

Watkins' loose description of what role curators/artists/critics take on within an exhibition context may no longer be completely in synchrony with the development (over the last eighteen years) of curatorial practice beyond the parameters of gallery or museum exhibition displays. Yet Watkins' belief that curating is a 'necessary, if insufficient, medium through which the communication between art and its audience takes place' (Watkins 1987) seems in tune with the way in which the cross-fading of individual positions within our cultural economy has aided the transformation of artistic practice. Its slight shift away from an author-centred cultural hierarchy towards a post-productive discourse, in which the function of curating has become another recognized part of the expanded field of art production.

Almost twenty years after Watkins' polemic, the issues inherent to the "curator as artist" question remains one of the key debates within curatorial discourse: it is still being discussed within many contemporary art magazines such as *frieze* and *Art Monthly*. In 2005, writing for his monthly column in *frieze*, curator Robert Storr expresses his fears about the notion of the curator as an artist by refusing to call curating a medium since it 'automatically conceded the point to those who will elevate curators to the status critics have achieved through the "auteurization" process.' Storr also situates the origins of the idea of the curator as artist in Oscar Wilde's 1890 essay 'The Critic as Artist' (where it is the eye of the beholder that produces the work of art) rather than in Barthes' post-structuralist analysis of authorship. Storr's conclusive response, 'No I do not think that curators are artists. And if they insist, then they will ultimately be judged bad curators as well as bad artists' ends up reiterating 'the artist/ curator divide and inadvertently returns the power of judgement to the critic.' (Storr 2005: 27).

Storr's rejection of the notion of curating as a form of artistic practice and his refusal to call curating a medium represents one of the ongoing tensions within critical debate surrounding curatorial discourse since the late 1980s. Yet, as John Miller has argued, the spectre of the curator as meta-artist began to haunt large-scale international exhibitions since Jan Höet's *Documenta 9* in 1991, when Höet put himself forward as a curatorial artist who used a diverse range of artworks as his raw material. For Miller, the momentum of artist-curator, or the artist as meta-curator, had already been building up from the work of artists linked to institutional critique, who had taken curatorial prerogatives and the works of other artists into their own practice, such as Group Material, Julie Ault, Louise Lawler, Fred Wilson, Judith Barry and others working in the US in the 1980s. Miller argues, however, that Höet's technique of 'confrontational hanging' was less about the exposure of 'non-reflexive assumptions about what makes up an exhibition and what that might mean' (Miller 2004b: 59) associated with these artist's curatorial interventions and more about 'the wilfully arbitrary juxtaposition of works, equates artistry with free exercise of subjectivity.' (Miller 2004b: 59).

The idea of the curator as some type of meta-artist became prominent in the1990s, where, according to Sigrid Schade, 'curators [now] sell their curatorial concepts as the artistic product and sell themselves as the artists, so the curators "swallow up" the works of the artists, as it were. In such cases, the curators claim for themselves the status of genius traditional in art history.' (Schade 1999: 11) Dorothee Richter echoed this view when she stated:

> Since the eighties, we can see another shift in the roles ascribed to artists and curators: It seems perhaps as if a shift in power in favour of the curator has taken place, especially since the role of the curator increasingly allows for more opportunity for creative activity. Thus, the curator seems to employ the artistic exhibits in part as the sign of one text, namely, his or her text. (Richter 1999: 16)

Richter suggests that the presentation of an exhibition is a now a form of curatorial self-presentation, a courting of a gaze where an exhibition's meaning is derived from the relationship among artistic positions. This, she argues, is represented by the co-dependent idea that the curator and artist now closely imitate each other's position (Richter, 1999: 16).

In 1972, the artist Daniel Buren wrote 'Exhibition of an Exhibition', where he claimed that: 'More and more, the subject of an exhibition tends not to be the display of artworks, but the exhibition of the exhibition as a work of art.' (See Buren 2004: 26.) At the time, Buren was referring both specifically to the work of curator Harald Szeemann and his curation of *Documenta 5*, and to the emergence of the idea of exhibition organizer as author. Buren was suggesting that works were mere fragments that make up one composite exhibition, and, although having not changed his position, he later updated his initial thoughts in 2004:

> ...[art works are] particular details in the service of the work in question, the exhibition of our organiser-author. At the same time – and this is where the problem has become pointed enough to create the crisis in which we find ourselves – the 'fragments' and other 'details' exhibited are, by definition and in most cases, completely and entirely foreign to the principal work in which they are participating, that is, the exhibition in question. (Buren 2004: 26)

Buren's disdain for the tendency towards large-scale exhibitions to acquire the status of quasi-artwork where the work of the curator transforms the work of the artist into a useful 'fragment' in his or her own work of exhibition as art still prevails. Buren claimed that this can and has taken on many guises in the more recent past:

> The organisers/ authors/ artists of large-scale exhibitions provide results we already know: Documenta transformed into a circus (Jan Höet) or even as a platform for the promotion of curators who profit from the occasion in order to publish their own thesis in the form of a catalogue essay (Catherine David) or as a tribune in favour of the developing politically-correct world (Okwui Enwezor) or other exhibitions by organiser-authors trying to provide new merchandise to the ever voracious Western market for art consumption, which, like all markets, must ceaselessly and rapidly renew itself in order not to succumb [...] (Buren 2004: 26).

But the great irony of Buren's statement is that it is a published response to the question as to whether the *Next Documenta Should be Curated by an Artist* (2003) proposed by curator Jens Hoffmann as a part of his own curatorial project/exhibition/publication. By enabling Buren's text and other artists, Hoffman's intention was to pass to artists the critical and curatorial voice and to include them in the discussion around the effectiveness of an artist-led curatorial model, but Mark Peterson states, '...[it] ultimately uses a similar curatorial strategy as the one he is criticising, namely to invite artists to illustrate his thesis.' (Peterson 2004: 80) Peterson goes on to argue that Hoffmann's position only appears as one of self-reflexivity, as the curator attempts to involve artists in questioning, not only his own practice, but the various mechanisms and dynamics of his medium and his profession and how exhibitions gain form, yet ends up deflecting attention away from his own curatorial trap. This may in part be true, but Peterson's position, not unfamiliar as a general viewpoint, again places the curator and artist in opposition to one another.

According to Zygmunt Bauman, it is precisely because of an absence of a single, universally accepted authority within contemporary culture that curators are becoming 'scapegoats [...] because the curator is on the front line of a big battle for meaning under conditions of uncertainty.' Bauman adds the term 'scapegoat' to a long list of ingredients for a curator's role which he lists as animator, pusher, inspirer, brother, community maker and someone who makes people work and things happen and someone who inspires artists with ideas, programmes and projects. He also adds that 'there would be an element of interpreting, of making sense of people, of making them understand, giving them some sort of alphabet for reading what they see, but cannot quite decide about.' (Bauman 1998: 31)

From the late 1980s, – a period of crisis – according to Bauman, who perceives art as being re-centered around what he calls 'the event of the exhibition' where the experience of art is generated primarily by short-lived temporal events and only secondly, if at all, by the ex-temporal value of the work of art itself. It is mostly the work of art exhibited in a widely publicized event that meets the standards set for the proper object of consumption, that stand the chance of maximizing the shock while avoiding the risk of boredom, which would strip it of its 'entertainment value'.

As well as their temporal and transient nature, large-scale international group exhibitions have tended to lend themselves towards thematic shows. It has been argued that such projects prevent artists from realizing their 'true potential' and even that this emphasis on the curatorial project has quite serious implications for the status and roles of art and artists. For example, Alex Farquharson questions exhibitions that foreground their own sign-structure, which pose the risk of using art and artists as constituent fibres or pieces of syntax subsumed by the identity of the whole curatorial endeavour. He argued that we are more likely to remember who curated *Utopia Station*, ongoing since 2003, than which artists took part, forgetting that Rirkrit Tiravanija (an artist) was one of the curators. For Farquharson, projects such as Hans Ulrich Obrist's *Do It* (1993 onwards, www.e-flux.com) and *Take me (I'm yours)* (Serpentine Gallery, London, 1995) or *A Little Bit of History Repeated* (Kunst-Werke Berlin, 2001), curated by Jens Hoffmann, result in the relegation of artists to deliverers of the curators' conceptual premise, while curatorial conceit acquires the status of quasi-artwork (Farquharson 2003). This more than common opinion seems to yearn after an upholding of the cultural value of the artist over curator within contemporary art exhibitions and has serious problems for the overall question of advocacy within the art world. As Gertrud Sandqvist has warned, the curated exhibition is not intended merely to reinforce the identity of the artist or of the curator. Instead of seeing curating as one of the rare, more intellectual, positions in the processes of art-circulation, there is a danger that curators may become mere agents for the artists and risk as a type of trademark. So, if the exhibition is a producer of meaning, then its purpose is different from the art market's, and possibly also from the artist's (Sandquist 1999: 43–44). Finally, as Maria Lind has pointed out reverence towards the work of art has its own problematic: it is suspiciously close to resting upon ideas about art as detached from the rest of our existence; and it often conceals the concept of a curator as 'pure provider' who simply supports an artist without affecting the exhibition and its reception (Lind 1998).

The same old story of repressed histories: by way of concluding the beginning
Prior to the 1990s, few historical assessments or curatorial paradigms existed, let alone a discourse specific to contemporary curatorial practice. As an historical discourse, curating still has yet to be fully established as an academic field of enquiry. In *The Power of Display: A History of Installation at MoMA*, 1998, Mary Anne Staniszewski proposed that western art history had forgotten to take into account the functions performed by curating, exhibition design and spatially arranged exhibition forms. For Staniszewski, our relationship to this past is not only a question of what art is now seen to have been part of this history, but what kind of documentation and evidence of its display has survived. She writes: 'What is omitted from the past reveals as much about a culture as what is recorded as history and circulates as collective memory.' (Staniszewski 1998: xxi)

Visual effect, display and narrative are central to any curated exhibition. The exhibition remains the most privileged form for the presentation of art; thus, display may be understood as the core of exhibiting. Staniszewski suggests that the history of the exhibition is one of our most culturally 'repressed' narratives. The contextualization of space and its rhetoric have been overshadowed by the context of art in terms of epochs and artists' *oeuvre*, despite the fact that exhibition installations have had such a crucial significance for how meaning is created in art. One of the key factors in the production of artistic posterity is the dominance of the modernist' 'white cube', which eliminated the context of architecture and space as well as of institutional conditions. According to Thomas McEvilley, the endurance of the power structures inherent to the white cube centres on that

> [...] of undying beauty, of the masterpiece. But in fact it is a specific sensibility, with special limitations and conditions that is so glorified. By suggesting eternal ratification of a certain sensibility, the white cube suggests the eternal ratification of the claims of the caste or group sharing their sensibility. (McEvilley 1999: 9)

Hans Ulrich Obrist is one of numerous curators to have mirrored Staniszewski's assessment, by stating: 'seeing the importance of exhibition design provides an approach to art history that does acknowledge the vitality, historicity and the time and site bound character of all aspects of culture' (Obrist 2001a). He has claimed that this amnesia 'not only obscures our understanding of experimental exhibition history, it also affects innovative curatorial practice.' (Obrist 2001b) In many of the interviews I have conducted over the last few years, contemporary curators often refer to the amnesiac effect of missing literature, and what Brian O'Doherty called 'radical forgetfulness' towards innovative pre-white cube exhibition forms. So the institutionalization of 'the white cube' since the 1950s meant that 'presence before a work of art means that we absent ourselves in favour of the Eye and the Spectator.' (O'Doherty 1976) According to O'Doherty such a disembodied faculty meant that art was essentially seen as autonomous and experienced primarily by formal visual means.

Aside from the series of essays that made up *Inside the White Cube*, first published in *Artforum* in 1976, there had been very little subsequent examinations of display practices of the early twentieth century, less still the notion that contemporary art curation was affected by any lack of contextualizing history. The 1990s could be said to have begun the process of remembering, during a moment of emergency when curatorial programmes had little material to refer to by way of discourse specific to the curatorial field.

It was into this epistemic gap that contemporary curatorial discourse began to take shape in the 1990s, and a generation of curators emerged during what Michael Brenson called 'the curator's moment' (Brenson 1998). I would argue that the prioritization of all things contemporary within recent curatorial projects, alongside the concentration on an individualization of the curatorial gesture has created a particular strand of discourse that is hermetic at times. At the same time it is self-referential, curator-centred and, most evidently, in a constant state of flux: curatorial knowledge is now becoming a mode of discourse with unstable historical foundations.

From surveying the key debates within publications dedicated to contemporary curatorial practice, it is apparent that curatorial discourse is in the midst of its own production. Curating is 'becoming discourse' where curators are willing themselves to be the key subject and producer of this discourse. So far, for those unwilling to accept the provision made for the figure of the curator within the reconfigured cultural field of production, critical response has been maintained at the level of an over-simplified antagonism, where the practice(s) of artist and curator are separated out. If it is to continue, the gap between curatorial criticism and curator-led discourse will only widen further.

References

Adorno, Theodor W. and Max Horkheimer, 'The Culture Industry: Enlightenment as Mass deception' in *Dialectics of Enlightenment,* (Verso Classics, London & New York, 1997), trans. John Cummings, [first published as *Dialektik der Aufklarung* in 1944, first English translation in 1972].

Althshuler, B., *The Avant-Garde in Exhibition: New Art in the 20th Century*, New York, Harry N. Abrams, 1994.

Bauman, Z., 'On Art, Death and Postmodernity – And what they do to each other' in Hannula, M. (ed.) *Stopping the Process: Contemporary Views on Art and Exhibitions* (Helsinki, NIFCA, 1998).

Bos, S. and Gillick, L., 'Towards a Scenario: Debate with Liam Gillick' in *De Appel Reader No. 1: Modernity Today: Contributions to a Topical Artistic Discourse* (Amsterdam: De Appel, 2005).

Bourdieu, P., *The Field of Cultural Production*, New York, Columbia University Press, 1993.

Bradley, J., 'International Exhibitions: A Distribution System for a New Art World Order' in Townsend, M. (ed.) *Beyond the Box: Diverging Curatorial Practices* (Banff, Canada: Banff Centre Press, 2003).

Brenson, M., 'The Curator's Moment – Trends in the Field of International Contemporary Art Exhibitions' in *Art Journal* (winter, 1998).

Bryan-Wilson, J., 'A curriculum for institutional Critique, or the Professionalisation of Conceptual Art,' in Ekeberg, J. (ed.) *New Institutionalism, Verksted No.1* (Oslo, Office for Contemporary Art Norway, 2003).

Buchloh, B., 'Since Realism there was...' in *L'Exposition Imaginaire: The Art of Exhibiting in the Eighties* ('s-Gravenhage, SDU uitgeverij, 's-Gravenhage: Rijksdienst Beeldende Kunst, 1989), pp. 96–121.

Buren, D., 'Where are the Artists?' in Hoffmann, J. (ed.) *The Next Documenta Should Be Curated by an Artist* (Frankfurt: Revolver, 2004).

Esche, C., 'Debate: Biennials' in *frieze 92* (2005), p. 105.

Ferguson, B. W., Greenberg, R. and Nairne, S. (eds.), *Thinking About Exhibitions*, London & New York, Routledge, 1996.

Foucault, M., *The Archeology of Knowledge*, London and New York: Routledge, 2003.

Farquharson, A., 'I curate, you curate, we curate' in *Art Monthly 269* (London, 2003), pp. 7–10.

Ferguson, Bruce W., 'Exhibition Rhetorics,' in Greenberg, Reeesa, Bruce Ferguson and Sandy Nairne (eds.) *Thinking About Exhibitions*, (London & New York: Routledge, 1996), p. 178.

Ferguson, B. W., Greenberg, R. and Nairne, S., 'Mapping International Exhibitions' in Greenberg, Reeesa, Bruce Ferguson and Sandy Nairne, (eds.) *Thinking About Exhibitions*, (London & New York: Routledge, 1996).

Filipovic, E. and Vanderlinden, B. (eds.), *The Manifesta Decade: Debates on Contemporary Art Exhibitions and Biennials in Post-Wall Europe* (Cambridge, Massachusetts, MIT Press, 2005), pp. 47–57.

Filipovic, E., 'The Global White Cube' in Filipovic, E. and Vanderlinden, B. (eds.) *The Manifesta Decade: Debates on Contemporary Art Exhibitions and Biennials in Post-Wall Europe* (Cambridge, Massachusetts, MIT Press, 2005).

Filipovic, E. and Vanderlinden, B. (eds.), *The Manifesta Decade: Debates on Contemporary Art Exhibitions and Biennials in Post-Wall Europe*, Cambridge, Massachusetts, MIT Press, 2005.

Lind, M., 'Stopping my Process: A statement' in Hannula, M. (ed.) *Stopping the Process: Contemporary Views on Art and Exhibitions* (Helsinki: NIFCA, 1998).

McEvilley, T., 'Foreward' in O'Doherty, B. *Inside the White Cube: The Ideology of the Gallery Space* (Berkeley, Los Angeles, London: University of California Press, 1999).

Mesquita, I., 'Biennials, biennials, biennials...' in Townsend, M. (ed.) *Beyond the Box: Diverging Curatorial Practices* (Banff, Canada: Banff Centre Press, 2003).

Miller, J., 'The Show you love to hate: A psychology of the mega-exhibition' in Ferguson, B. W., Greenberg, R. and Nairne, S. eds. *Thinking About Exhibitions* (London & New York, Routledge, 1996).

Miller, J., 'Arbeit Macht Spass?' in Hoffmann, J. (ed.) *The Next Documenta Should Be Curated by an Artist* (Frankfurt: Revolver, 2004).

Obrist, H. U., and Tawadros, G., 'in Conversation' in Hiller, S. and Martin, S. (eds.) *The Producers: Contemporary Curators in Conversation (2)* (Newcastle: Baltic & University of Newcastle, 2001).

Obrist, H. U. et al., 'Panel Statement and Discussion' in Marincola, P. (ed.) *Curating Now: Imaginative Practice? Public Responsibility* (Philadelphia: Philadelphia Exhibitions Initiative, 2001).

O'Doherty, B., *Inside the White Cube: The Ideology of the Gallery Space*, 4th edition, Berkeley and Los Angeles, University of California Press, 1999.

O'Neill, P. and Siegelaub, S., 'Action Man: Paul O'Neill interviews Seth Siegelaub', *The Internationaler*, issue 1 (Sheffield, August 2006).

O'Neill, P., 'The Co-dependent Curator' in *Art Monthly 291* (2005).

Peterson, M., 'Open Forum' in Hoffman, J. (ed.) *The Next Documenta Should Be Curated by an Artist* (Frankfurt: Revolver, 2004).

Richter, D., 'Curating Degree Zero' in Drabble, B. and Richter, D. (eds.) *Curating Degree Zero, An International Curating Symposium* (Nuremburg, Verlag für Moderne Kunst, 1999).

Rugoff, R., 'Rules of the Game' in *frieze 44* (1999).

Sandqvist, G., 'Context, Construction, Criticism' in Drabble, B. and Richter, D. (eds.) *Curating Degree Zero, An International Curating Symposium* (Nuremburg, Verlag für Moderne Kunst, 1999).

Schade, S., 'Preface' in Drabble, B. and Richter, D. (eds.) *Curating Degree Zero, An International Curating Symposium* (Nuremburg, Verlag für Moderne Kunst, 1999).

Staniszewski, M. A., *The Power of Display: A History of Exhibition Installations at the Museum of Modern Art* (Cambridge, Mass., MIT Press, 1998).

Stevens, I., 'IT'S SO TWO YEARS AGO' in *Contemporary 21*, issue 77 (2005).

Storr, R., 'Reading Circle' in *frieze 93* (2005).

von Bismarck, B., 'Curating' in Tannert, C., Tischler, U. (eds.) *MIB – Men in Black: Handbook of Curatorial Practice* (Berlin & Frankfurt am Main, Künstlerhaus Bethanien & Revolver, 2004).

Watkins, J., 'The Curator as Artist' in *Art Monthly 111* (London, 1987).

Wilson, Mick, 'Curatorial Moments and Discursive Turns', in O'Neill, P. (ed.) *Curating Subjects* (Amsterdam & London, de Appel & Open Editions, 2007).

Curatorial Strategy as Critical Intervention: The Genesis of *Facing East*

Liz Wells

Exhibition involves imposition of order on objects, brought into a particular space and a specific set of relations with one another. The ordering may be in accord with established classifications and habits of display or may challenge conventions; but is necessarily rhetorical in calling attention to artefacts brought together to be subjected to visual scrutiny. Exhibition commands visual attentiveness. This is taken for granted in museum and gallery studies.

The creative role of the curator is perhaps less well understood. The figure of the contemporary art curator is a relatively new feature of the world of the art museum (*MJ* 2004). I remember a photography conference at the Victoria & Albert Museum, London, some years ago, when curators were referred to as 'the new carpetbaggers' of Europe. It is obvious why (insensitive) curators might acquire such a reputation, especially as curators work very closely with artists during periods of project development and, then, once an exhibition is over, from the artist's point of view, may seem to lose interest in their work. But the role of the curator is not well understood. Not long ago, a faculty Associate Dean, responsible for research in a post-92 British university (happily not the one where I work) commented to me that surely curating was 'just organizing'. My response was a little sharp! Someone else once remarked to me that he always thought of curators in terms of facilitation for artists, meaning that it hadn't previously occurred to him that curators might initiate an exhibition concept, seek out artists and research contexts, negotiate with galleries and publishers (for catalogues), in effect, shaping creatively in their own right. Indeed, some comments on the role of the curator do leave one wondering how exactly people think exhibitions come about!

Curating as research process

I curate exhibitions of landscape photography, which may include video and installation. Landscape can be defined as the cultural representation of space as place (Massey 2005). Site and space, political and spiritual identity, are complexly inter-woven. Landscape may affirm or extend our view of our relation with land, challenging dominant aesthetics and subject matter, bringing image and ideology into question. This chapter focuses on the genesis of a particular exhibition, *Facing East: contemporary landscape photography from Baltic areas*, in order to explore something about the making and workings of exhibitions. My central purpose is to argue for an understanding of curating as a research process which, as with any such process, involves investigation, discovery and critical reflection, central to which is the definition and refining of key research questions. I want also to indicate some of the ways in which an exhibition may stand as critical intervention.

How did this particular exhibition come about and what makes exhibitions substantial, let alone radical? It came about, as so often, through a form of serendipity. I had been working on British and American landscape photography, and I was considering broadening the horizons as I am researching a book on contemporary photographic landscape practices. Sian Bonnell, Director of Trace Gallery in Weymouth, who was involved in initial proposals for a photography festival in Bournemouth, approached me for an exhibition proposal and introduced me to those who run the gallery at the Arts Institute in Bournemouth, on the south coast of England, without whose support the project would not have happened. 'Text plus work' is their central gallery emphasis, and they wanted to commission a new show as their festival contribution. They were also interested in touring the exhibition for two years subsequent to the festival. In the event, the festival did not develop as originally envisaged, but the tour for this exhibition surpassed all expectations and was subsequently extended for a further year, having been booked for its sixth and seventh venues, a degree of circulation which is more or less unprecedented in contemporary photography in the United Kingdom.

When I was first approached, in 2002, I realized that the festival as planned would coincide with the enlargement of the European Union in May 2004, so it seemed obvious to look at a region within which there was a strong interest in landscape, and also a changing set of social and political relations. From a research point of view, the fundamental purpose of the project was critical evaluation of photographic work from Scandinavian and Baltic areas which takes land, landscape, identity and environment as thematic focus. My concern was with the relation between aesthetic strategies and ideological issues.[1] I applied to the Arts and Humanities Research Board (now Council) for funding, identifying key research questions as follows:

- Does contemporary landscape photography in Scandinavia and the Baltic States offer a challenge to more established aesthetics and concerns?
- If this is the case, in what respects is this challenge evident?

- What trajectories and differences can be discerned within and between the various nations, in terms of themes and aesthetics?
- How is landscape as a historical genre perceived by contemporary photographers?
- Is landscape photography in this region viewed in terms of the relation between land, landscape and identity – and how is this manifest?
- How does this relate to recent political histories, in particular the dominance of Soviet Russia in the east of the region for much of the twentieth century – affecting Finland as well as the Baltic States?

Of course, there are no comprehensive or conclusive answers – but these questions oriented the research and, thus, the final selection of work for the exhibition. I should add that, courtesy of the AHRC, I was able to travel extensively in the Baltic region, visiting archives and meeting with artists, curators and arts administrators, all of whom offered positive support for the project.[2]

It goes without saying that, in researching towards exhibitions, I read widely in terms of social and historical context as well as aesthetics and art history. I particularly explored previous exhibition catalogues, if they appear to have some bearing on my research questions. As with all research, it is difficult to identify the precise effects of preliminary research or to explicitly link initial processes of exploration with final exhibition outcomes. Arguably, the connection resides in the confidence with which it becomes possible to view, appraise and critically situate bodies of work, having previously informed oneself as fully as possible and stimulated visual appetite. Research comes to underpin curatorial 'voice'. Curatorial voice operates through initial definition of field and identification of key research questions, through selection of work, through the 'theatre' of exhibition which is fundamental to rhetorical affects, and through ways in which the project and the work of individual artists is contextualized in accompanying materials. Exhibitions wherein a curator has determined a theme or proposition, or used the work of others merely to illustrate it and produce writing geared towards anchoring and constraining interpretative potential, rarely hold interest for very long. But where an exhibition has been carefully thought through, substantially contributing to knowledge within a particular field, 'voice' operates complexly, in effect, setting up some sort of dialogue between works included, as well as between the curator and the works. The multiple discourses through which this dialogue resonates contribute to quality of audience engagement.

Facing East

Audience is a problematic notion. We can engage psychoanalytically and deconstructively with spectatorship processes, or we can follow Bourdieu into sociological analysis, but neither tells us much about what actually happens as individuals explore and respond to an exhibition (Bourdieu 1994; Bourdieu & Boltanski 1990). In many respects, viewers lie beyond curatorial control. In producing catalogue essays or exhibition statements, we assume that viewers have interests coinciding with that of the curator, in my case, combining the academic, the socio-political and the aesthetic. Of course, they may not. At the initial opening of *Facing East*, I was approached by a Russian woman, now living in the south of England, who had come to see the work because it was from Baltic areas; she was thrilled to find the region where she was born depicted in the further reaches of one picture. There is no way I could have anticipated this. Likewise, at a previous exhibition, on women and landscape, which included work based in the Egyptian desert, an elderly man took little notice of the exhibition concept or the work but started recounting his wartime memories of crossing the desert.[3] Such anecdotes remind us that 'audience' is essentially unknowable. Spectators forge an independent sense of an exhibition; they bring their own subjectivity, desires, history and cultural experiences into play.

Facing East includes fifteen bodies of work by sixteen artists (two work in collaboration) and encompasses a range of aesthetic strategies and thematic concerns. The artists included are based in Norway, Sweden, Finland, Estonia, Latvia, Lithuania and Denmark (Russia, Poland and Germany also have Baltic coasts, but their cultural centres lie elsewhere – Moscow, Berlin, Warsaw/Krakow). Given that little work from this region has been previously shown in Britain, I wanted to offer a fairly broad-based overview, indicating a range of photo-methods, issues and resonances. Indeed, if an exhibition is to offer some form of critical intervention, rhetorical tactics have to be carefully considered. The complexities of artists' intentions, concerns, working methods and contexts of production, aesthetic strategies and effects play a crucial role. From a curator's point of view, selection of work is central to critical strategy. Where possible I meet with artists since discussion about the genesis of specific projects and images and their critical reflections on their own work helps me to situate their work conceptually within an overall project as well as respecting their intentions, perceptions and preferences.

The title of the exhibition is deliberately enigmatic, which I hope attracts interest or speculation. There is some explanation in the booklet which accompanies the show: 'As borderline states between Soviet Russia and Western Europe, the Nordic countries and the smaller Baltic states have had to "face east". With the break-up of the former USSR, and the easing of travel restrictions across the Baltic Sea, they now face west. But, we "face east" to them. As the European Union enlarges, our curiosity about cultural difference extends.' In the text which accompanies the show, I added that 'To face east is to face the dawn, to witness new possibilities'. This chapter is to some extent based on the introductory text. The exhibition explores some of these new possibilities: changes and modes through which tensions between continuities and change are being explored.

The exhibition does not include older work; but historical research was essential in order to comprehend what might be under challenge. For instance, 'Explosion No. 1' by Petter Magnusson (Figure 1), a young Swedish photographer who spent some years studying in Norway, in effect challenges the Norwegian cultural icon of the mountain, which, as I found, was central to the photographic archive. The wooden house at the

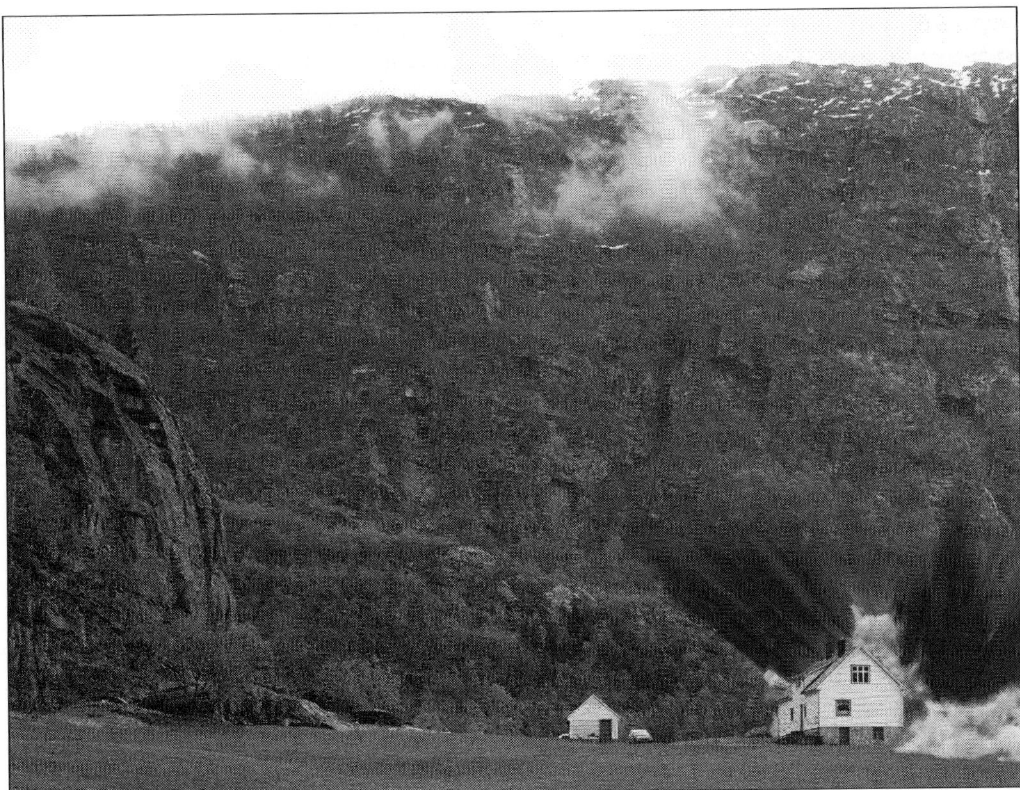

Figure 1. Petter Magnussen, 'Explosion No. 1', 2002, original in colour.

foot of the mountain by a fjord, offering solitude away from city crowds, remains part of the Norwegian dream. This digital assemblage explodes the rural idyll, bringing together the house, the mountain and the drama of the clouds. Scale, composition and heavy framing parody the pictorialist. The explosion may reference mining that, with fisheries and North Sea oil, centrally supports the Norwegian economy. But meaning is to some extent open. Magnussen remarks,

> It could be a disturbance or mining in a classic romantic landscape, with a possible ecological comment, or it could be war in the peaceful north, or an absurd attempt at terrorism outside of NY; or it could be some more mystical force in action, or the dream of an explosion, or an experiment in putting sublime forces/images up against each other in an investigation into an updated romanticism, a natural disaster, or even, as someone guessed, the peasant's home brewery exploding...[4]

Although certain openness of interpretation is integral to the picture, the mountainscape idyll is definitely in question. Likewise, as Norwegian photographer and archivist Per Olav Torgnesskar, in *Prospects*, 2002, reminds us through his series of 'postcard' images, rural and small town scenes may be dull and journeys remarkably banal. This body of work was in two parts. First, fifteen images from an extensive series in which he used postcard size and format to make images of ordinary places. The pictures were based both upon actual images available to him as then an archivist in the Royal National Library, Oslo, and upon his memories of the endlessness of journeys with his parents as a child stuck in the back seat of a car with little of note to view. We also included video *Norwegian Scenarios*, 2000, constructed from television news footage which, again, testifies to the ordinariness of the everyday. Both photographers thus challenge the dominant iconography of the Norwegian landscape as snowy, mountainous sublime.

Exhibition installation enhances critical effect. Also concerned with contemporary Norway, Ane Hjort Guttu (like Torgnesskar, based in Oslo) links the effects of natural light with the modernistic, reflecting cultural change. Each picture in her series, *Modernistic Journey*, 2002, is intended as a separate image, but in the show we effectively constructed a diptych through juxtaposing a picture in which sunlight animates the upper edge of a mountain annexed with one in which sun falls across a modern apartment block; parallel geometries drawing attention to this paradoxical similarity of effect. Although each was made as a separate piece, through pairing two pictures I was able to suggest interrogation of the nature/culture binary. A further picture captures the reflection of a white block of flats in the lake landscaped into the foreground. The observer is not conceptualized as modernist in the sense of extolling modernity, so much as postmodern in observing ways in which culture incorporates nature. Landscape, however abstract and symbolic, is always at one level about place and human intervention. Layers of historical development are marked in Herkki-Erich Merila's series *Lunatica*, 1999, connoting moonlight and, of course, lunacy. Estonian rural scenes are viewed by night; the presence of roads and factories is marked. Fields have been harvested, but the hay now sits in the shadow of agri-industry. Car headlights – the ultimate symbol of everyday modernity – rather than moonlight, illuminate the harvest stacks and distant industrial plant. This is, of course, *somewhere*, but it also stands for *everywhere*. This series articulates tensions – nature/culture, tradition/modernity – within each image.

Critique is not always obviously integral to the image, especially cross-culturally. There is a well-worn joke about survival under the Soviets – you could become a communist, an alcoholic or a photographer. Photographers claimed to observe, and tell things as they appeared; it was difficult to condemn someone for documenting something. Gestures of resistance and renewal may be expressed through form. For many in the former Soviet states, landscape offered a relatively unconstrained field of practice; aside from restrictions on photographing in certain military areas, landscape photographers *could* experiment pictorially. Latvian photographer Mara Brasmane (Figure 2) worked in street documentary from the 1960s on; but she also explored the changing Daugava estuary from Riga to the Baltic coast, observing shapes made by plants within the flow of water or held within the illusory solidity of ice. Graphic surface, timelessness, repetition and cyclical renewal speak through this extensive series of work; light is part

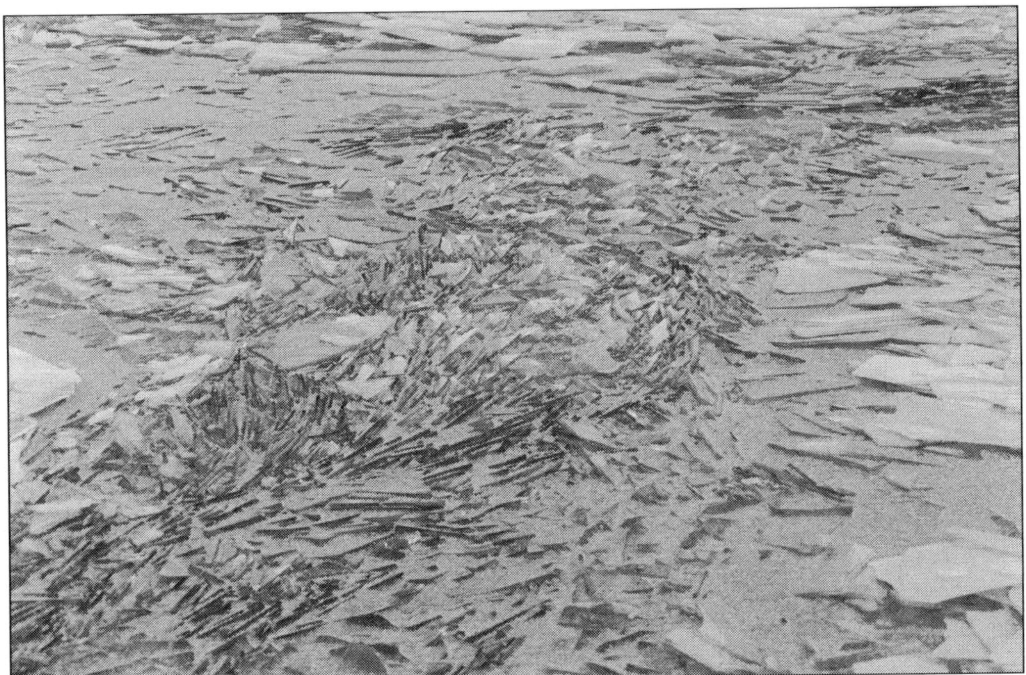

Figure 2. Mara Brasmane, from *Waters*, 1999–2001, original in colour.

of the 'moment' of the image, and nature seems transcendent. This appears traditional and, indeed, it is. But the work refuses the imperatives of socialist realism, in effect offering a mini-challenge within the particular historical context (although this work was not much exhibited in the Soviet era). Viewed in Britain it does beg explanation; my reasons for including it are not at first apparent.

Pictures by Lithuanian Remigijus Treigys, likewise untypical of the Soviet era, depict rural or coastal scenes from the Baltic coastal region where he lives. His *Distressed Landscapes*, 1999–2003, are dark and mysterious; shadows predominate and detail is obscure. Significantly, an essay on his work is titled 'The Invisible Side of the Void' (Naru 2004). Surface intrigues; he not only retains 'blemishes' but also touches the paper-enhancing marks of making; each image is, thus, unique. Treigys is one of a number of Baltic artists in the 1980s associated with what some critics defined as 'distressed aesthetics', involving emphasis on the pictorial and an eschewing of documentary idiom which together indicated refusal of the heroic norms of socialist realism. Again, in a British context, this is not immediately evident. Taken away from the Soviet context, the work resonates through complex layering of observation, association, perceptions of time and space, nostalgia, tone and mood and the geometry of the image. The exhibition text on which this essay draws comes into its own in indicating effects of such very different contexts and strategies relating to production. That said, neither

Brasmane nor Treigys were motivated in terms of resistance; their concerns are much more existential.

Use of colour is relatively recent in all three Baltic states; equipment is limited and materials are expensive. Thus, there has been a direct leap from the authoritative rhetoric of black and white to the fluidity of the digital. This is not uncontroversial. Andrejs Grants, who has been influential since the 1980s for naturalistic documentary and who seems to have taught every young photographer in Latvia, resists what he sees as the undermining of 'authority of record'.[5] Some of his comments did seem to echo debates in Britain in the 1980s. But nothing directly replicates. Grants told me that he values 'mystery' in the picture; different layers, something spiritual. In a post-Soviet context emphasis on the existential also implies anti-materialism (in the Marxist sense), again, perhaps, passive resistance. Gatis Rozenfelds, who was taught by Grants, takes a different line on the advent of colour and the digital: he wants to challenge what he terms 'beauty landscape', to find something 'more truthful'.[6] His series, *Weekends*, 2002, concerns the shaping of new suburban landscapes, but also explores colour as a means of speaking about land. The images note everyday scenes and, to British eyes, may appear relatively ordinary photographically. (British debates of the 1980s about colour and documentary seem outdated now!) In the Baltic region his work is seen as very original; it was included in the third Baltic triennial.[7] I included it for two reasons: first, to balance the more abstract aesthetics seen in some of the Baltic work thus contributing to demonstrating to a British audience something of the range of contemporary interests and practices, and second, in terms of subject-matter, to indicate everyday ordinariness. It is quite difficult to place in relation to other work in the exhibition, as here it does not seem particularly radical, nor does it startle or entice. Interesting ontological points relating to digital colour as opposed to, what is clearly seen by some as, a more considered aesthetic of hand-printed monochrome, do not come across.

Considerations

Exhibition themes emerge as works are juxtaposed with one another. Exhibition space facilitates or constrains what can be achieved as both conceptual and aesthetic considerations are taken in to account in the hanging, along with basic practical issues such as where will larger work fit, which walls can take the weight of heavily framed pictures, what will be the effect of the movement of daylight near gallery windows, what space needs to be left clear around fire exits and so on. When I was first asked to talk about my experience as curator for the show, *Facing East* had been to two venues with rather different set-ups and audiences.[8] The primary audience at the Arts Institute at Bournemouth is students and staff, although the gallery is also open to the public. By contrast, Impressions Gallery in York was a specialist photography gallery; the majority of visitors will have gone there intentionally and the exhibition attracted an apparently unprecedented level of interest for the time of year (4,708 visitors). Both these galleries differ from the three following venues, two of which are arts/media centres and the third of which is also the local library. In such cases, installation decisions have to take into account attracting the attention of visitors whose reason for being there was, for instance, to go to the cinema. In such instances, questions of which work to hang opposite a cinema entrance, near a café, or down a corridor, become especially salient.

The Arts Institute at Bournemouth has two galleries across a corridor. Both galleries have large French windows and, in April/May, natural light was dramatic as it moved and changed the feel of the space over the course of each day. A short stroll allowed for most of the work to be scanned. What came to matter was that each body of work could hold its own within the space and that pictures were complemented and enhanced through juxtapositions. This meant paying attention to obvious issues such as being careful where smaller work, or work within which colour is less vibrant, were placed in relation to other works which threatened to dominate. The corridor came into its own as a space for the series of Norwegian 'postcards' and the effects of daylight in the galleries were utilized to emphasize Nordic qualities of light. Hanging decisions also entailed some thematic connections. For instance, colour documentary photographs from the woodlands of middle Sweden were hung facing colour imagery of wildlife in rural Finland. At Plymouth Arts Centre there are three galleries, only one of which has natural light, a factor which became crucial in determining which bodies of work were hung in that relatively small room. In York the gallery was radically different. Impressions Gallery – which closed in 2006 pending a move to Bradford, Yorkshire – was a converted house with five rooms on two floors and a hallway with stairs. Work by various artists had to be grouped in twos and threes, which made questions of aesthetic strategies and thematic links much more predominant. This changed the viewing experience as each room acquired a particular emphasis and atmosphere, and it was likely that the audience would view the show room by room.

For instance, in York, one of the upstairs galleries included work from Denmark and Sweden which variously speaks of communications and migrant labour. Denmark apart, the rural population throughout the region is sparse; many live in relative isolation. The climate is unforgiving, distances are extensive and train or road transport may be slow.

Landscape photography from Baltic areas

Winds howl across the flatlands of Denmark between the North Sea and the Baltic. Agriculture is now industrialized, but traditionally Denmark and South Sweden were family farming areas, rural communities, facing each other across the Øredok sound. Joakim Eskildsen's (Figure 3) tribute to his grandmother, is based on a not uncommon early twentieth-century story of sisters sent from the relatively poor south of Sweden to live and work on a farm in more affluent Denmark. This extract from a larger installation includes a portrait of his elderly grandmother and a study of her hand, on which years of manual labour seem etched. The black-and-white pinhole photo-aesthetic lends distance to the rural landscape, but, in fact, this was only three generations ago. We are reminded not only of personal history, but also of the relative speed of change. In Øredok (1998), John S. Webb documents this coastal area in south-west Sweden,

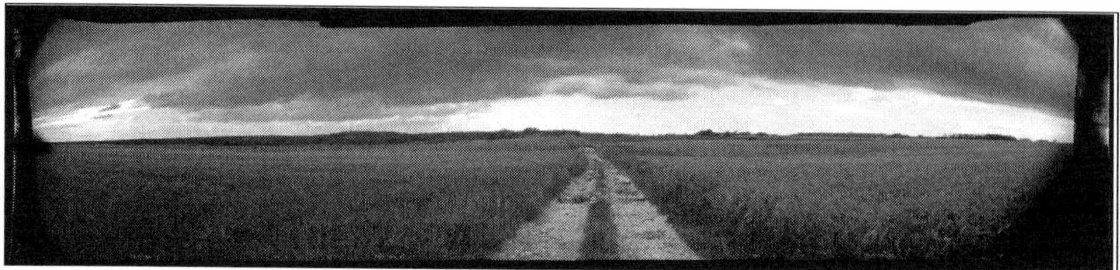

Figure 3. Joakim Eskildsen, from *Requiem*, 2000.

previously something of a nature reserve, now eroded by roads and industrial plants congregated around the motorway bridge which, since 2000, has linked Sweden with Denmark, finally terminating the relative isolation of the north from the rest of Western Europe. The work is in the form of a series of 360-degree panoramas, digitally stitched, and thus disorienting for those with intimate knowledge of the local landscape. The eight panoramas are mounted in two vertical blocks of four, each implied narrative of change underscoring others as we contemplate the changes wrought. In Sweden rural activities, such as berry-picking, formerly associated with family days out or community harvesting, have become organized commercially and, as Swedish artist Margareta Klingberg (Figure 4) notes, offer a source of seasonal employment for 'new Swedes' from eastern Asia and elsewhere and migrant workers from former Soviet areas. Woodlands and closeness to nature may remain a part of Swedish consciousness, but the realities of industry and city culture cut across traditional imagery.

The Finns are proud of their woodlands and lakes, but inland is also boggy and rugged; ice, snow and limited daylight in winter make existence and survival exceptionally difficult. Wild animals, and hunting, carry significance founded in need. The popularity of wildlife photography, involving treks to forest hides, echoes this – the photograph acting as substitute 'trophy'! Juha Suonpää's (Figure 5) humorous, anti-pastoral pictures, mostly from the eastern border forests, formed part of his doctoral study of this masculine pastime. At one level, the work is humorous: a bear, eating convenience food, stands still to be photographed, and a photographer disguises himself behind a tree, wearing antlers, to fool passing wildlife. This image along with Magnussen's explosion were the two pictures favoured by the various galleries for private view invitations and more general PR. Indeed, the (badly) disguised photographer features on the front cover of the Arts Institute booklet accompanying the exhibition. They are striking images, but so are many of the others in the show; I presume it is thought that humour and paradox seduce contemporary audiences. But a number of more symbolic points are encoded: the blues of the sky and the water in which a cow has drowned precisely match that of the Finnish flag, and a distant line where managed forestry gives way to wilderness marks the Russian border. From a Finnish perspective the implications of this are multi-layered, simultaneously reminding us that Russia once ruled Finland, and noting the unruliness of the landscape on the Russian side of the

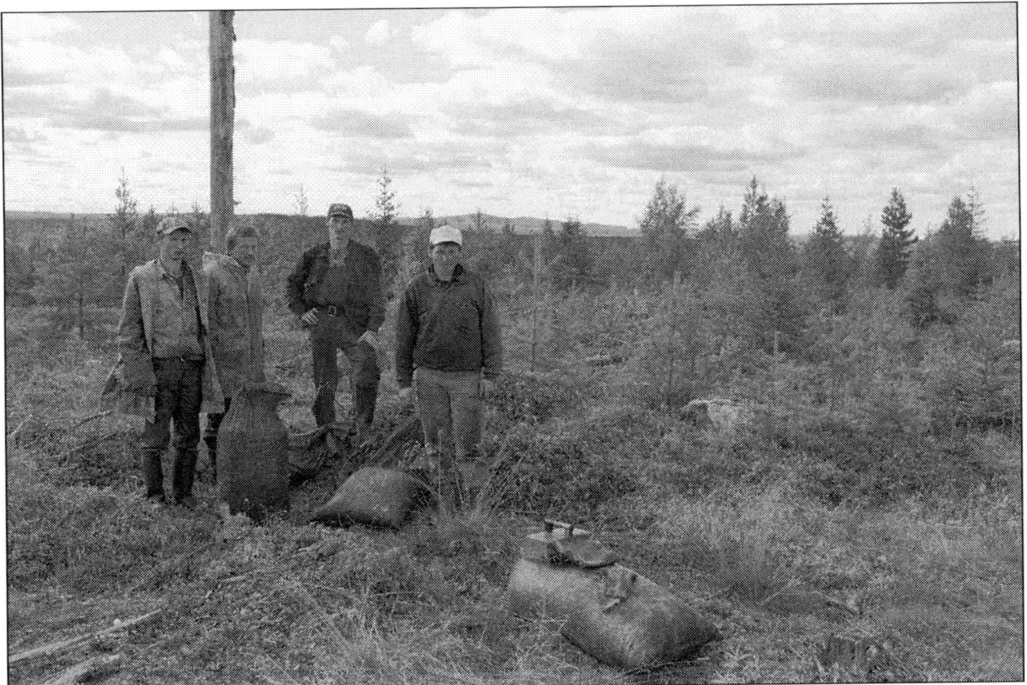

Figure 4. Margaretta Klingberg, from *From Home*, 2001–2002, original in colour.

border whilst, paradoxically, regretting loss of Finnish wilderness as it has given way to managed woodlands. Indeed, forestry is now big business; birch trees, which once grew randomly amongst the lakes, now stand regimented through organized planting. Commercial logging has cleared acres of woodland. In their extensive visual research on change in northern forest areas, Ritva Kovalainen and Sanni Seppo comment on the implications of the loss of what for many is a primary space of contemplation, a part of Finnish identity; a spiritual home. Their starting point for *The End of the Rainbow* was an interest in the spiritual and the shamanistic, although as the visual research developed it became increasingly analytical and political (Kovalainen and Seppo 1997). Their concern is with the disappearance of forest, change in the Finnish woodland landscape and forest identity; for the Finns, forest is crucial space of spiritual replenishment, where human culture remains relatively unmarked. But after 50 years of intensive logging nearly all the natural forests have disappeared. The project is ongoing. *Facing East* includes two long panoramas (2003) portraying individuals in rural spaces clearly in process of change. The artists also interview these local habitants who recount memories of their place within the woods and what the woodlands meant to them (headsets allow visitors to simultaneously listen to the interviews). Indeed, industrial development in Finland only dates from the second half of the twentieth century; nature remains central to Finnish 'soul'; summertime in the lakes or gathering wild berries and mushrooms in autumn is still common. The sauna cabin by the cold

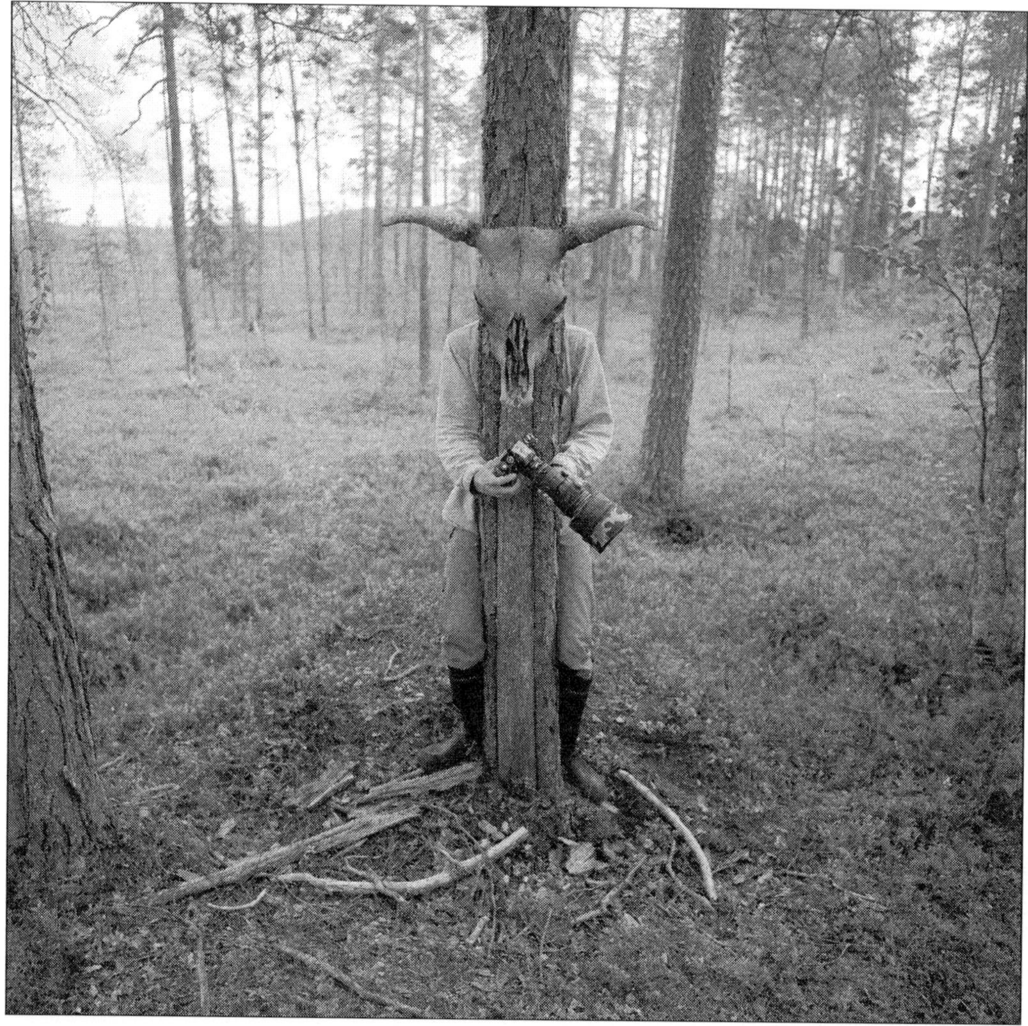

Figure 5. Juha Suonpää, from *Wilderness*, 1990s, original in colour.

lake offers an elemental spiritual experience, transcending simple cleansing and health. Just *being* is important; in *Like a Breath in Light* (ongoing) Marja Pirelä's breathing is marked in a series of images taken at different times of year, always from the same position, sitting with a pinhole camera on her knee, facing north across the lake, open to the effects of elemental light and colour. The ensuing abstract images are suspended behind glass, as a group of floating impressions of light and colour, shifting in intensity in response to movement of light within the gallery.

The University of Industrial Arts in Helsinki, capital of Finland, is a major centre for masters and doctoral level studies in photography. Professor Jorma Puranen's

1990–1991 series on Lapland, language and nomadic Sami peoples are widely known in Britain (Gupta 1993). The critical foundations of his work offer an influential example of the social and philosophic edge that we can expect from contemporary Finnish landscape photography. Jari Silomäki, in his *Weather Diary* (ongoing), points to tension between the global and the local, as place, personal experience and the distant backdrop of world events blend together. To play with words, they are 'con-fused' into a sometimes uneasy relationship which confuses any sense of specificity of individual experience. Every day he takes a photograph, printing in colour and hand-writing some comment on it which relates to that day's experience. The comment may reference the news, or world events, or his own immediate personal situation and experience. That this is amalgamated from his point of view is inscribed through his own handwriting. Depth of colour reflects light and exposure times, maybe linked to events. For instance, on the day on which Silomäki made for 'Turku, the day US bombed Afghanistan', he was expecting the news. He had his camera set up on a tripod, ready for exposure for the length of the news item; hence, the purple intensity of the sky. Several of his daily photographs are shot in northern Nordic nightlight, where the sun never quite sets, reminding us of extraordinary qualities of the landscape there. Riitta Päiväläinen's

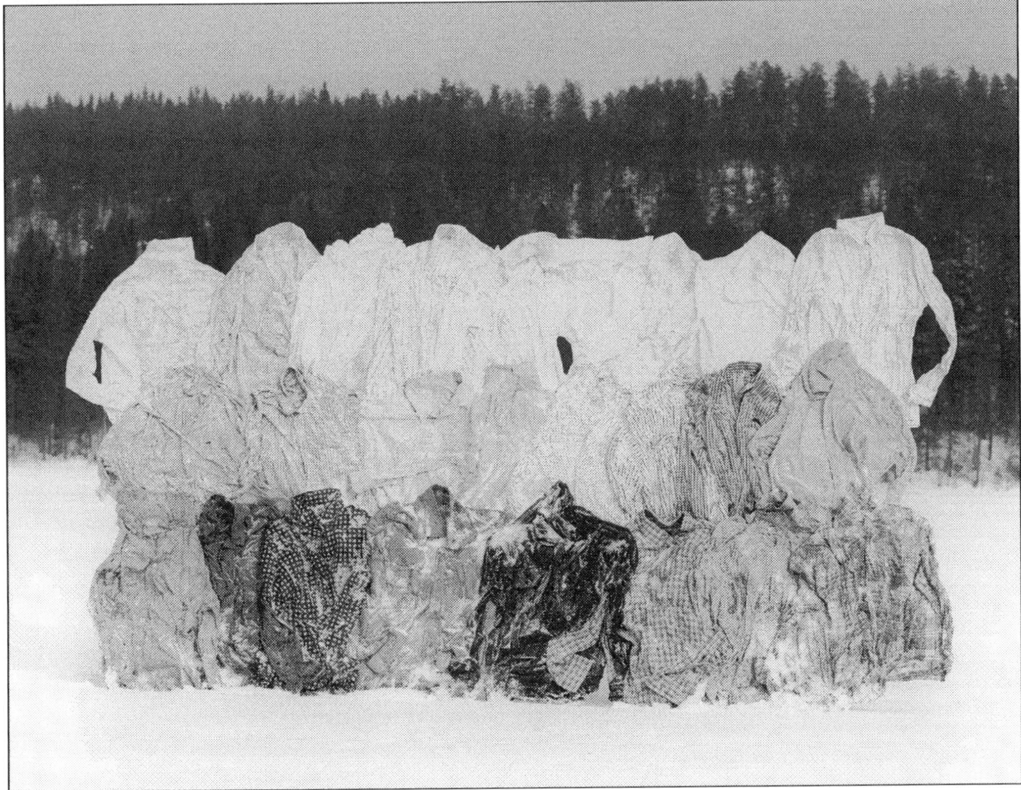

Figure 6. Riitta Päiväläinen's, 'Portrait', 2001, from *Vestige* – ice series, original in colour.

(Figure 6) evocative photographs of clothing, standing upright, frozen in the icy landscape, eerily devoid of the people who might have once worn the garments, imply human transience and vulnerability relative to continuity or change in land and landscape.

Conclusion

If exhibition articulates curatorial 'voice' through research parameters and through selection of work to be included, then installation operates as evocation. As I have indicated, gallery space influences ways of working. For instance, the more narrative series about work and transport links, Eskildson's grandmother, Klingberg's foreign workers and Webb's new roadways were grouped together. The frozen shirts, the pinholes of the lake and the daily diary formed a further, more philosophical, grouping. At Impressions Gallery they shared one of the upstairs galleries, creating an intensity of reference to sky and snow in what the Programme Manager nicknamed the 'ice' room.

In summary, we can conceptualize curatorial voice and strategy in terms of a number of inter-related levels of evocation. Artists 'speak', more or less assertively, through their work. To some extent, work is appropriated to the interests and vision of the curator, although, in my experience work refuses subjugation. Artistic affects are contained by, or rupture, the authority of the curator. Viewers engage with photographs as art objects, as representations, as symbolic instigators – of memory, fantasy and reverie – and, as I have already remarked, respond for themselves. Comments and feedback often surprise me. This encounter is ordered through the selection and juxtaposition of imagery within the specific gallery space which, in effect, results from dialogue between the curator and the works. It is also inflected through interpretative indicators in accompanying labels or catalogue essays. Indeed, it is through installation, and through written contextualization (or gallery talks), that the critical intentions of the curator may become most evident. Curatorial strategy becomes most effective as critical intervention when it is intended not to close down exploration but, rather, to invoke a range of issues and emotions, representations and debates, in order

Notes

1. Research for the exhibition also underpins a chapter on landscape photography and national identity in my forthcoming book, *Land Matters* (working title), in which I take Scandinavian and Baltic work as a case study.
2. I should like to acknowledge the support of AHRC, and also of FRAME the Finnish fund for art exchange for funding transport of Finnish works to the UK.
3. Liz Wells' (curator) *Viewfindings: women photographers, 'landscape' and environment* opened at Newlyn Art Gallery in 1994 (subsequent tour to Watershed, Bristol; NMPFT, Bradford; Zone Gallery, Newcastle). I overheard this conversation when I happened to be in the gallery.
4. E-mail from artist, 23rd February 2004.
5. Andrejs Grants, discussion with author, Riga, August 2003.
6. Discussion with artist Riga, August 2003.

7. *What is Important?* 3rd Ars Baltica Triennial of Photographic Art, tour, Baltic region 2003–2005.
8. The exhibition opened at the Arts Institute at Bournemouth in April 2004, then toured to Impressions Gallery, York (20 November 2004–22 January 2005). By the time of finalizing this paper for publication it had also shown at Plymouth Arts Centre (spring 2005), Lighthouse Media Centre, Wolverhampton (May 2005) and the Dick Institute, Kilmarnock (autumn 2005). Further bookings include Tulley House and Gallery, Carlisle (autumn 2006) and The Yard Gallery, Nottingham (spring 2007).

References

Bourdieu, P., *Distinction: a social critique of the judgement of taste*, London, Routledge, Kegan and Paul, 1994.

Bourdieu, P. with Boltanski, L., *Photography: a middle-brow art*, Cambridge, Polity Press, 1990.

Gupta, S. ed., *Disrupted Border*, London, Rivers Oram Press, 1993, pp. 96–103.

Kovalainen, R. and Seppo, S., *Puiden Kansa*, Helsinki, Pohjoinen Gallery, 1997. (www.puidenkansa.net/EENGLANTI%20BOOK/Englanti%20Book.html).

MJ, Manifesta Journal, no. 4, Amsterdam, November 2004. Abstract used for PR.

Massey, D., *For Space*, London, Sage, 2005.

Naru, A., 'The Invisible Side of the Void', 2004, translation supplied by the artist.

Wells, L., *Facing East, Contemporary Landscape Photography from Baltic Areas*, Bournemouth: the Arts Institute, 2004.

No Place Like Home: Europa

Sophia Phoca

'The curator, like the artist, must aid art's renewal through its own works.'
(Millar 2000)

I come from a small village called Phocata on the island of Cephalonia in the Ionian Sea. When I was a child I used to spend long summers there, at my grandfather's house who lived near an old woman called Kiría Európé (Mrs Europe). Amongst all the other aging villagers she stands out in my memory because of her extraordinary name. In Greek villages the ritual of greeting neighbours is performed on all possible occasions and as this usually happens several times a day, I had habitually uttered her name, again and again, every day, each summer, year after year.

This peasant woman from the village of Phocata had carried the spirit of Levantine admiration for Europe, throughout the twentieth century. I, for the latter part of it, had irritably repeated that name, each time unknowingly affirming our shared history: that utopian desire she embodied, of being other than Ottoman.

In the late 1990s while Kiría Európé lay dying on the island that the Italians had dubbed 'Cephalonia-melancholia' during the war, Deimantas Narkeviãius was making a film with a 1970s Soviet camera, recording his attempt to locate the geo-centre of Europe near Vilnius. When he finally reaches it, identified by an unimpressive memorial plaque, it stands like a solitary grave, and from this unremarkable field, he shares with us a lonesome testimony to the death of twentieth-century Europe.

Europa: Film and Video from the Centre of Europe
Deimantas Narkeviãius' 9-minute, 16mm film, *Europa 54° 54'–25° 19'* (1997), informed the title and the conceptual framework of an exhibition I co-curated at Tate Modern in

2004. *Europa: Film and Video from the Centre of Europe* put to question the idea of a geographic centrality, much like the film's 'unsettling revelation that the centre of Europe is empty' (Verwoert 2003a: 77), and in doing so, suggests a contingent collapse of ideological certainties based on assumptions of centrality and marginality.

Modernist counter-cultural discourse has been associated with utopian ideas, established in opposition to notions of centrality. In film and video, ideas of centrality have been highly contested, traditionally situated in relation to oppositional politics, as in experimental versus mainstream. The collapse of a foundational 'centre', as suggested in the film, has allowed for discourses and identities to emerge beyond binary identification. This condition saw the development of what has been referred to as 'psychogeography', where inner personal spaces are brought to bear on exterior locations. Theories of 'no-place' situate new utopias in the space between the internalized fantasy and the external world; while 'non-places' are now referring to globalism and supermodernity which has re-placed notions of 'centrality' in relation to developing technologies. It is in this context that new ideologies of technology are emerging. *Europa: Film and Video from the Centre of Europe* looked at how these ideologies continued to explore and destabilize the 'centralizing' effects of a technological supermodernity in a newly emerging Europe.

In the first part of this chapter, I will focus on the issues raised by co-curatorial praxis and discuss the meanings and values generated by different approaches: the artist-curator, the performative-curator, curatorial post-production, self-reflexive curation and co-dependent curatorship. I will explore how we, in curating *Europa: Film and Video from the Centre of Europe*, negotiated these roles as a team and the authorial ideologies inscribed in these forms of curatorial practice.

In the second half I will briefly outline the conceptual curatorial framework relating to notions of place and placelessness which informed the film and video work finally selected for exhibition. Because a very wide range of time-based work was shown (fifty-nine films and videos in total), it will be impossible to address the full extent of the meanings produced, or the interrelationships generated by the curatorial debates that emerged from them, except in a generic context with regard to the extended and multi-faced collaborative nature of this project.

Finally, I will look at the discourses which developed with regard to the reception of this exhibition and how it produced a new and thought provoking debate on the ideology of technology with regard to concepts of place.

Co-curatorial praxis

When I initiated the collaboration with Tate Modern, it was in response to a trend for international museums to develop alliances with educational institutions. Such collaborations are usually motivated by a need to generate match funding from the educational establishments as well as to challenge the perception of staleness pervading museum exhibitions. I approached Dominic Willsdon (then curator of Public Events at Tate Modern) and put forward a proposal to stage a series of screenings and talks at Tate Modern. The cultural authority of Tate Modern meant that our shared curatorial values would be given extensive exposure.

We gathered a collaborative team together made up of myself, Dominic Willsdon and Stuart Comer (curator of Film and Video) from Tate Modern; curator Martin Clark and film-maker and artist Andrew Kötting. Martin Clark's curatorial background and interests played a significant role in the shaping and development of this project. For example, in 2004 he curated *Candyland Zoo* where he conjured up the zoo as a poetic conceit for utopianism. Clark's approach was to create complex relationships and intertextual readings in the selection and positioning of individual works, making connections and juxtapositions between them. His interest in the relationship between institutional spaces and curatorial practices had also informed my own practice.

We considered the issue of the curators' 'authorial voice': how could such an 'authorial' voice be produced through a series of dialogues, collaborations and relationships that transcends the blandness of 'programming by committee'? Who would be speaking and on behalf of whom? What kinds of curatorial practice would we be advocating? 'Curating is a job that brings together a lot of different people. No one pretends that the idea is dreamt up in isolation' (Burnett 2005: 4). Yet when speaking with a unified voice on behalf of an institution it is important to keep vigilant about what that voice is saying and how discourses are being circulated. In this context what discourses would be articulated, what modes of curatorial practice would be advocated, what ideologies and values would be promoted? How would we avoid the risk that individual or unorthodox voices would become homogenized and diluted under a proposed unified institutional perspective? Would our roles be designated to those of 'behind the scenes' managers, organizers or match-funding facilitators without any artistic or conceptual input?

According to Foucault, ultimately authorship rests with the founders of discursivity rather than individuals or texts. Self-reflexive anxieties with regard to the authorial role of the co-dependent curator have been written about extensively, but as JJ Charlesworth suggests, such reflexivity can become the 'narcissistic display of an uncertain me, me, me.'(Charlesworth 2006: 4). It is the polemic rather than the author that needs to be foregrounded. So the issue at stake is not so much authorial as ideological. If, as Roland Barthes has argued, the author has been replaced by the text, would the curatorial modes of practice upheld by us survive under the constraints imposed by such a major institution?

While we clearly were determined to have a significant input on that polemic, it soon became evident that the Tate curators would be making the decisions on the theme as well as what would and would not be shown. The 'authorial gate-keeping' would remain firmly in their control: they would be making the rules. It was up to us to either negotiate and input into this process or see the dissolution of the collaboration. The rules were as follows: all the work would be single screen; the Tate could veto work proposed, the work would be located within a European context while the framework would be that of a single exhibition and advertised as such, the screenings and associated talks would take place as independent events.

One of the first difficulties we encountered from a curatorial point of view was the fact that all the work needed to be single screen. As Alex Farquharson has pointed out: 'When it comes to exhibitions of finished objects (paintings, sculptures, photographs and films, for example) efforts to foreground the curatorial frame often end up being clumsy, interfering and trite.' (Farquharson 2003: 16)

The fact that any installation or performative work could not be included would by definition limit the scope of performative curating. However, we agreed on a series of single-screen programmes followed by seminars and discussions hoping that the seminars and talks may allow for meanings and values to be disseminated in a less predetermined way.

Instead of contesting the constraints imposed by the hegemonic nature of our co-curatorial relationship with the Tate, we started to focus on and mediate our shared cultural and critical values and most significantly how the unity of the work could be defined through subsequent discourse and, therefore, possibly allow for elements of conceptual 'post-production' to emerge in the collation of work. We agreed to do this in two ways. One was to develop a conceptual framework and the other was to begin to identify work we wanted show. The way we would do this was by breaking down in two working parties. I volunteered to set up the discursive framework, and Clark, Kötting and I formed a working party where we brought together work which we wanted to include and from that developed a shortlist which we then took to the Tate team. We wanted the two to inform each other.

Place and placelessness
With regard to the conceptual framework, the theme of 'Place and Placelessness' was agreed on. This trope was partly responding to the concerns of the team as well as contemporary visual theories and curatorial practices stemming from the 2003 Venice Biennale *Utopia Station* curated by Molly Nesbit, Hans-Ulrich Obrist and Rirkrit Tiravanija, which had located the concept of utopia firmly in the contemporary cultural zeitgeist.

The notion of place has traditionally been understood 'externally' as a geographic, anthropologic, economic, or political site, as opposed to 'internally' as a disembodied space in terms of psychoanalysis, memory or philosophy. With the collapse of foundational certainties, the concept of place has become destabilized as seen in the emergence of 'psychogeographic' configurations. Psychogeography was articulated by

Iain Sinclair as a form of flâneurie, here referring to the way with which the representation and understanding of the external world expresses the internal psyche.

Ideas of utopia, or non-place, have been taken up to articulate the boundary between the internalized, space and its projection onto the external world. Whilst modernist utopias were associated with countercultural idealism, new formations of utopia have become conceptualized as non-places: places that do not and cannot exist beyond desire. Significantly, new digital technologies and 'time-space compression' have created a globalizing sense of place. Postmodern notions of spectacle have colonized and transformed all aspects of contemporary culture, most notably contemporary representations of conflict and the body. Non-places, it can be argued, emerge as a consequence of globalism and supermodernity, and is associated to 'screen' space, airports, supermarkets and motorways – places where organic social interaction is impossible. Global displacement through migration and exile has meant that the notion of homeland is no longer perceived as stable. Cultural identity and the body (national, religious, sexual etc.) are again no longer assumed to be firmly located in a specific place, within fixed cohesive identities. Consequently, we have seen a zealous return to a desire for certainties with newly emerging religious and national fundamentalisms. Associated to this we have seen the return to essentialist identity politics.

We decided to concentrate on film and video originating from the margins with an emphasis on places undergoing political, cultural and economic change due to these global reconfigurations. Closer to 'home', the collapse of the former Soviet bloc in eastern Europe and the emergence of a new extended European Union now resonated as a significant shift in our cultural and political imaginations relating to ideas of 'non-place' and new utopias.

While avant-garde and experimental Anglo-American film and video have been extensively researched, written about and showcased, there has been very limited debate on film and video practices emerging from outside this context. The objective of this exhibition was to explore how European film and video artists were responding to these transitions and configurations of place or placelessness.

But how do these concerns relating to notions of 'place' refer to time-based work? What emerged is not simply an understanding of the moving image as used to portray 'place' in its various manifestations (a geographically located notion or a disembodied concept) but a sense that notions of non-place and utopia are represented by the medium itself. That is an engagement with how contemporary practices are exploring new technological ideologies.

Ideologies of technology
Although concerns about form and process are still forgrounded in contemporary praxis, how are these configured when they are no longer bound up in utopian countercultural canons? If modernist experimental film and video saw itself existing as

an oppositional ideological form – that is, other to mainstream forms – how do contemporary practices see themselves operating outside this binary framework? Some key areas and themes of interest emerged, relating to documentary, documentation and subjectivity as well as 'performance', 'sound' and 'non-linearity'. Chris Marker's films have been associated to a return to modernist theories of distantiation linked to the essayist tradition of film-making. In his work, formal concerns regarding time, space and framing, as well as ideas relating to the indexical role of the document and memory are foregrounded. These are associated to philosophical theories with regard to the act of 'recording' in relation to truth and the real, where notions of fiction and subjectivity are seen as being inherently inscribed in the documentary process.

The ubiquitous role of the camcorder in contemporary practices with its potential to continuously 'document' has meant that the role of the document has foregrounded issues relating to the value placed on such 'documentation'. Questions are raised regarding which forms of such 'documentation' are culturally privileged over others. This has generated a post-observational documentary body of work, which emphasizes the unmediated low-tech technologies of digital recording. Bill Nichols has noted:

> 'Observational documentary (Leacock-Pennebaker, Frederic Wiseman) arose from the availability of more mobile, synchronous recording equipment and dissatisfaction with the moralising quality of expository documentary.' (Nichols 1991: 33)

Like observational documentary, these new practices have developed with the availability of new, cheaper and more mobile technologies, however, unlike observational modes; the concern of these practices is not established according to their predecessors' desire to critique expository forms. Whilst modernist ideologies of technology sought to use new advancements in order to generate new meanings, the artists we were interested in were rejecting such a utopian vision. Instead these works' reflexivity draw attention to the absence of readily available sleek effects such as replay, non-linear time, clean/glossy imaging, special effects and multi-screens. The new easy-access software programmes which produce such effects were being rejected by the artists who instead are using the process of 'recording' as a way of exploring notions of 'subjectivity, 'fiction', 'truth' and the 'real' associated with Marker's concerns with time and memory as well as in relation to the neo-utopian, self-reflexive struggle to represent.

The autobiographical impulse and performance art of the 1970s and their continued impact on contemporary practices are linked to ideas of documentation. Elizabeth Cowie argues that these practices have their origins in conceptual art, where the body becomes the 'material' object rather than the idea.

> 'If for conceptual art, it is the idea that is the material, yet it is only apprehended through a performance which thereby produces a domain of the sensual in which the idea emerges through form, becoming realised in the conjunction of a

materiality, a physical presence (thus, not expressed by such a form, but produced by the formal play).' (Cowie 2005)

Video art's continued engagement with notions of evidencing through the document has been reconfigured by the ubiquitous recording of easy access video camera/editing. In this context the 'performative' element is re-presented over and over again 'like language itself, the video or film record makes present what is absent, and past.' (Ibid.)

The use of sound has also changed significantly in contemporary practice. A key feature is the influence of MTV culture, where image tracks are being cut to sound. Also the increased visibility of soundtracks in digital editing has contributed to sound now being approached as a key aspect of time-based media, rather than just a post-production tool. Or when it is used as a post-production tool this is done reflexively to emphasize the discrepancy between sound and image. Another factor is that all time-based practices are now defined by a broader matrix of video technologies including professional and non-professional uses (television, advertising, home movies, cyber space), as well as traditional moving image (fiction, documentary, experimental). With regard to issues concerning narrative, the use of non-linear time and space is now a dominant trope in both narrative and non-narrative forms.

It was these ideas that contributed to the bringing together of the work selected.

The work
We were keen to include work from eastern Europe into the exhibition as a lot of this work would be difficult to source and access on an individual basis. We agreed on a unique programme of Polish women's performance video art. Many of the films shown where screened for the first time since their staging twenty or thirty years ago. The screening was followed by a conversation between Ron Lukasz Ronduda, the Media Curator at the Centre for Documentation and Research, Centre for Contemporary Art, Warsaw; the artist Marysia Lewandowska and Elizabeth Cowie. Ronduda and Lewandowska contextualized the archival process undertaken to collect the work and discussed it in relation to its geo-historical context and art practices.

During the discussion, Cowie pointed out that these performances existed in a 'contingent moment' and were presented as 'provocative interventions in specific historical spaces and times'. Whilst film had enabled them to become 'preserved', they were no longer the 'same' work. Cowie commented on the remarkable openness of Poland during the Cold War for allowing representation of such radical aesthetics in relation to gender and sexuality. With reference to Zofia Kulik's work where the actress Ewa Lemanska's is 'marked, bound, displayed, revealed, distorted, penetrated', Cowie suggests that she acts like a

'Possible metaphor for Poland and the Modernist project of twentieth century socialisms – all those various ideological positions which have played upon the people and the body politic of Poland.' (Cowie 2005)

Zygmunt Bauman's thesis that the holocaust was a consequence of modernist ideals of progress resonates here, as the twentieth century has seen some of the worst atrocities in the name of utopian modernism and, of course, while the bearers (rather than perpetrators) of that horror have often primarily been women.

German film-maker Ulrilke Ottinger explores ideas of `normative' and `perverse' sexualities in her work. Again the notion of 'place' is sited on the body, but here the body is other and 'deregulated'. Eve Kosofsky Sedgwick refutes the notion of biologism or 'natural' gender or sexuality. For her, gender is determined by the binary framework of masculinity and femininity. Sexuality, on the other hand, is determined by its slippage from semantic meaning, traversing both sides of the sex/gender dyad, but also exceeding them.

The trans-gender/sexual characters in Ottinger's films inhabit such projected spaces, where subjects exist beyond difference and 'otherness'. In *Johanna D'Arc of Mongolia* (1989), Ottinger explores ideas of lesbian love and difference through women who meet on the Trans-Siberian Express where they are kidnapped by a nomadic Mongolian princess. In this film Mongolia becomes the exotic allegorical place where same-sex relationships are explored. *Freak Orlando* (1981) is made up of five parts; these are extended narrative fragments which subvert notions of myth, history and psychiatry, through the trans-gendered character of Orlando, who exists in a carnivalesque world of 'freaks'. Ottinger's work was selected as she proposes the notion of place allegorically, a space where 'queer' identities are celebrated outside a binary sexual framework.

Constatine Giannaris' road movies *Hostage* (2005) and *North of Vortex* (1991) were also screened. Both films explore sexuality and identity through the landscape in relation to the cultural signifiers these places represent. While *North of Vortex* is inspired by the poetics of the beat generation, the North American road movie *Hostage* (which was premiered at the Tate) draws on the road movie as the site of contemporary urban migration. The now familiar sight of armies of displaced economic migrants walking across Europe was last seen after the end of World War 2. In this film, Giannaris takes the story of an Albanian migrant in Greece who, in 1999, seized a public bus in Greater Salonica and took its passengers hostage. This event was televised live as the bus crosses Northern Greece into Albania, where the chaotic negotiations with Greek police and media dramatically cease as the hostage taker is shot.

Giannaris' film focuses on the alleged rape of the Albanian by the Greek customs officers as the catalyst for the crisis. *Hostage* takes these events and constructs a meta-narrative where the 'rape/revenge' theme and the politics of power are played out on the male body. The film suggests that identity, be it gendered, national or religious is finally always sited on the body and its contingent sexualities and desires. The Albanian immigrant, (despite being male) is raped for violating the power structures of patriarchal Greek society; that is, he had sex with the wife of a customs officer. Through the act of sodomy, the Greek men reclaim their cultural authority. The film's outcome suggests that while on the one hand the Albanian young man is unable to articulate this unspeakable act, instead 'acting out' its consequences by taking the bus hostage, the Albanian authorities, on the other, silence him altogether rather than acknowledge the ideological implications of male rape and more significantly the metaphorical 'rape' of Albania by the West.

In the post-screening discussion, Mark Nash argued that while *Hostage* has been seen as Giannaris' least overtly 'queer' identified film, it is deeply and subtly rooted in the politics of difference, which for Giannaris extend beyond a binary framework of gay versus straight. Instead notions of difference are, as Foucault has stated, always sited on the body and always inscribed in a discourse of power. So the economic and power dynamics between eastern and western Europe will be necessary played out in relation to sexuality and the body.

The exhibition included a unique collection of contemporary video work from eastern Europe and what emerged conceptually from this vast collection of work was the preoccupation with negotiating and exploring the new transitions in relation to technological, cultural, political and sexual identities. For example, Sislej Xhafa's *Stock Exchange* (2000), where he performs the language of a market trader against a Ljubljana train station, reflects on Kosovo's capitalist aspirations for a stock market. In Bosnia, notions of conflict are played out and explored time and again in different forms (scratch, documentary, performance) but the most iconic is *Run Rabbit Run* (2002) by Pavle Vuckovic of an anthropomorphic white rabbit being chased and killed in a snow-laden landscape, seen as a metaphor for Serbia's bloody revolution. Most poignantly Adrian Paci's allegory of Albania's death seen is as a reconstruction of the artist's folkloric funeral.

Yet it is Deimantas Narkeviãius' work and in particular *Europa 54° 54'–25° 19'* that most informed the formal and aesthetic concerns of *Europa: Film and Video from the Centre of Europe*. In this film he uses the lexicon of old-fashioned Eastern bloc newsreels. During the fall of Ceausescu in 1989 Romania, I was struck by the hand-held anarchic shots on the news, which in western reportage signified the urgency of unmediated testimony. Instead, Narkeviãius refers to this aesthetic being the norm in Soviet Lithuania. In his work he returns to this form, often using voice-over, much like the commentaries used in such footage. In *Europa 54° 54'–25° 19'* the disembodied film-maker's voice-over recalls memories of travelling which is unrelated to the image, recording the view from a car window. This disjunction between sound and image draws attention to the discrepancy between the personal and the collective. It is a formal device used repeatedly by Narkeviãius.

The disjunctive montage of image and commentary affects a number of significant displacements in the interpretation of the film. First of all, you are made aware of the way in which your attention constantly shifts from audio to the visual. After the film you realise gaps have appeared in your memory of the film precisely in those moments when you focused on the commentary following the images, or vice versa when the visual fascination of the images distracted you from reflections in the voice-over. (Verwoert 2003b)

While Narkeviãius is seemingly addressing the task at hand, finding the centre of Europe, he is also reminding us of the constraints on travel imposed by the Soviet occupation. The disjunctive sound and image invite us to consider the role of memory in constructing meanings and question the role of reportage and documentary forms in their claims to represent reality.

A new emerging Europe
When in April 2006 I was invited to visit Budapest's School of Visual Communication, MOHOLY-NAGY University of Arts and Design, to give a presentation of my work, I spoke about the exhibition and showed *Europa 54° 54′ – 25° 19°*. The low-tech emphasis of the work initiated a vigorous debate on the ideology of technology. After six years of fetishizing high-tech, in a culture that had been deprived of it for so long, the implied cultural critique inscribed in returning to the aesthetics of the Soviet low-tech hegemony was challenging to my hosts. While the high-tech seductive effects of late capitalist iconography were finally on offer, artists like Narkeviãius had chosen to forgo these and in doing so he had reneged on both the promise of the new technologically 'supermodern' eastern Europe as well as the oppressive regime it had emerged from. At the end of the talk, course leader Erika Katalina Pasztor explained that she had found the discussions 'inspirational' and would be curating a show on 'low-tech' video in Budapest that year.

A discourse on the ideology of technology, generated from the edges of Europe was being circulated in our new emerging Europe.

References
Augé, M., *Non Places, An Introduction to an Anthropology of Supermodernity*, New York, Verso, 1992.
Barthes, R., 'The Death of the Author', *Image, Music, Text*, Flamingo, 1984.
Baudelaire, C., *The Arcades Project*, Belknap Press, 1999.
Bauman, Z., *Modernity and the Holocaust*, Polity Press, Cambridge, 1991.
Burnett, C., 'The invisible curator', *Art Monthly*, no. 291 November 2005.
Charlesworth, JJ, 'Curating Doubt', *Art Monthly*, no. 294, March 2006.
'Clark, M., Deimantas Narkeviãius and Martin Clark in Conversation, Starr Auditorium, Tate Modern, 24th October 2004' in *Deimantas Narkeviãius, Once in the XX Century*, published by Arnolfini, distributed by Cornerhouse Publications 2006.

Cowie, E., 'Performance art by Polish women in the 70s and 80s. Paper given at the symposium, *Europa: Film and Video from the Centre of Europe*, Starr Auditorium, Tate Modern, 7th November, 2004.

Farquharson, A., *Curator and Artist, Art Monthly*, no. 270, October 2003.

Foucault, M., 'What is an Author?' in Rabinow, P. (ed.) *The Foucault Reader*, London, Penguin, 1984.

Gange, J. & Hand, J., Montage & Mimesis in Central Station in Panting L. & Tallant, S. (eds.), *Central Station, London, Milch Gallery Catalogue*, 2000.

Gange, J., 'Viral Infection – a semiology of the post-viral' in *Besides it's Always Others who Die, Post Viral*, Phoca, S. (ed.), 201 Gallery, Catalogue, 2001.

Millar J., Something Between the Two, in *Curating in the 21st Century*, Wade, G. (ed.), University of Wolverhampton, 2000.

Morgan, F., 'Besides it's Always Others who Die', *Dazed and Confused*, no. 74, February 2001.

Nichols, B., *Representing Reality*, Indiana University Press, 1991.

Phoca, S., 'Candyland Zoo', *Contemporary*, issue 61, 2004.

Sedgwick, E. K., *Epistemology of the Closet*, University of California Press, 1990.

Verwoert, J., 'Home Truths', in *frieze*, issue 72, January/February, 2003.

Verwoert, J., 'The Role of a Lifetime, in *The Role of a Lifetime*, a film by Deimantas Narkeviãius in Barratt, P., and Gleadowe, T,. (eds.), *Art and Sacred Places*, 2003.

Selected Video/Filmography

Acostioaei, Dan, *Essential Current Affairs*, Romania (2002); Bajevic, Maja, *Double Bubble*, Bosnia (1999); Becirovic, Alma, *Survived 'N' Lived Another Day*, Bosnia (2001); Braila, Pavel, *Shoes for Europe*, Moldova (2002); Cantor, Mircea, *Double-Headed Matches*, Romania (2002); Felipov, Oana, *Banana*, Romania (2002); Floricic, Alen, *Untitled*, Croatia (1999); Galeria, Mala, *An 'action' documentation, Self-identification*, Warszawa, Poland (1980); Johannson, Tiia, *Namebook*, Estonia (1996); Kaljo, Kai, *Domestic Violence*, Estonia (2000); Kaljo, Kai, *Love Letter to Myself*, Estonia (1999); Konopka, *Barbara, Interferences*, Poland (1985); Kulik, Sofia, *Open Form*, Poland (1971); Kutera, Anna, *Presentation*, Poland (1974); Leko, Kristina, *In Her 25,802nd Day*, Croatia (2000).

Lemke Konart, Iwona, *The Limits of Human Possibilities*, Poland (1984); L. L., Natalia, *Consumptive Art*, Poland (1973); Marcolla, Jolanta, *The Kiss*, Poland (1975); Mihaltianu, Dan, *La Revolution Dans Le Boudoir*, Romania (1999); Narkeviãius Deimantas, *Once in the XX Century*, Lithuania (2004);

Nemeth, Hajnal, *Strip tease or Not*, (2001).

PART 2: CURATING AND THE INTERDISCIPLINARY: ENCOUNTER, CONTEXT, EXPERIENCE

CRITICAL SPATIAL PRACTICE: CURATING, EDITING, WRITING

Jane Rendell

With a background in architectural design, followed by doctoral research in architectural history, and then a period teaching public art and writing art criticism, my work has focused on interdisciplinary meeting points between different disciplines – between feminist theory and architectural history, conceptual art practice and architectural design, art criticism and autobiographical writing. Through collaborative and individual research, both books and exhibitions, this chapter looks at a number of curatorial and editorial projects I have been involved in from the late 1990s and how these relate to my work as a sole author of architectural history and art criticism.

In exploring issues of method or process that discussions of interdisciplinarity inevitably bring to the fore, Julia Kristeva has argued for the construction of 'a diagonal axis':

> Interdisciplinarity is always a site where expressions of resistance are latent. Many academics are locked within the specificity of their field: that is a fact...the first obstacle is often linked to individual competence, coupled with a tendency to jealously protect one's own domain. Specialists are often too protective of their own prerogatives, do not actually work with other colleagues, and therefore do not teach their students to construct a diagonal axis in their methodology.[1]

Engaging with this diagonal axis demands that we call into question what we normally take for granted, that we question our methodologies, the ways we do things, and our terminologies, what we call what we do. The construction of 'a diagonal axis' is necessarily a difficult business. Kristeva's phrase 'expressions of resistance' suggests that the problem encountered when disciplinary procedures are questioned is related to identification, a key term in psychoanalytic theory.[2] And in using the term 'ambivalent' to describe the encounter between disciplines – an 'ambivalent movement between pedagogical and performative address' – Homi Bhabha also points to the unconscious qualities at work in interdisciplinary practice.[3] It is precisely for this reason that I am a passionate advocate for interdisciplinarity; such work is not only critical and intellectual, but also emotional and political. In demanding that we exchange what we know for what we don't know, and give up the safety of competence for the dangers of potential incompetence, the transformational experience of interdisciplinary work produces a potentially destabilizing engagement with dominant power structures allowing the emergence of new and often uncertain forms of knowledge.

Strangely Familiar

Strangely Familiar: Narratives of Architecture in the City – an exhibition, symposium and catalogue, whose working group included architects, graphic designers, film-makers, multimedia artists – was produced as a response to an invitation to curate and design an architectural exhibition. The curatorial and editorial team, comprising Iain Borden, Joe Kerr, Alicia Pivaro and myself, chose to critique the notion of architectural history written only by architectural historians, consisting of boards on walls describing the work of famous architects.[4] Instead we invited academics from disciplines outside as well as inside architecture, such as cultural studies and geography, to provide a narrative

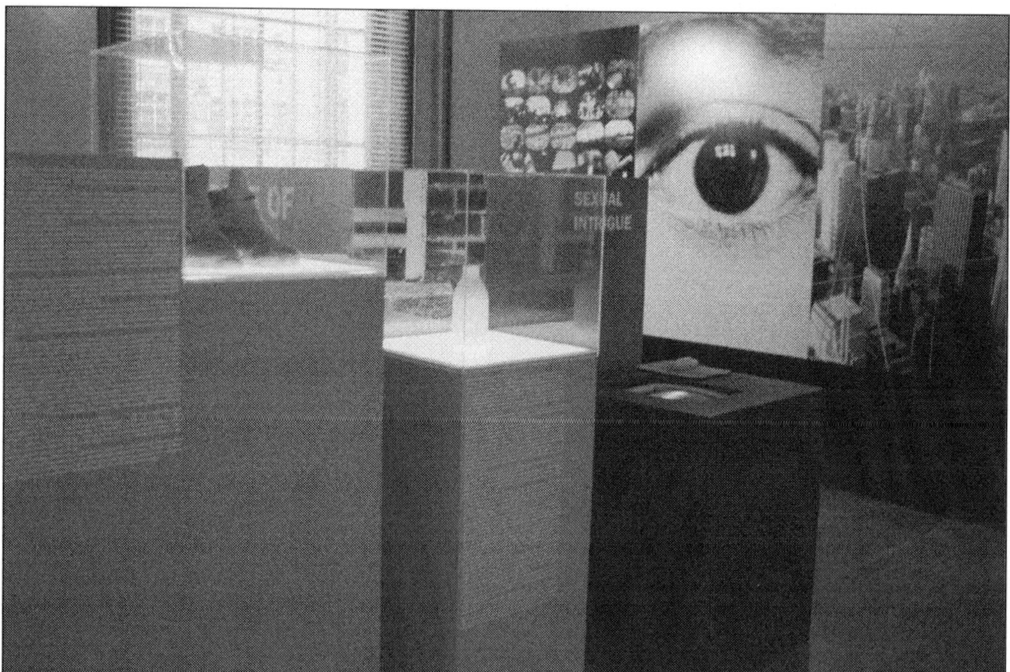

Figure 1. *Strangely Familiar*, The Royal Institute of British Architects' Gallery, London, 1995. Photograph: Iain Borden.

(a thousand-word text), several images and an object related to a specific site in a city. The catalogue comprised an edited collection of these visual narratives, while the exhibition took the form of a mini 'Manhattan' built of coloured plinths, one for each contributor including their narrative and related object.

Each interpretative stance revealed a place that was 'strangely familiar', familiar because certain aspects were already known, strange because they were revealed in new ways. The contributions investigated a diverse range of subjects and adopted a variety of interpretive and analytical procedures. From these, *Strangely Familiar* identified three editorial and curatorial themes for engaging with public space: memory and remembering; domination, resistance and appropriation; experience and identity. We adopted these themes as organizational strategies that worked to give the catalogue a conceptual clarity and the exhibition an aesthetic coherence using different colours to indicate one of the conceptual themes. Yet in hindsight the strong visual identity of both catalogue and exhibition made it difficult for the more complex, subtle and often unrecognizable tactics of urban resistance to emerge.[5] In order to develop further the dialogue between design intention and user occupation, for *The Unknown City*, the book that followed *Strangely Familiar*, we extended our editorial invitation to contribute essays to practitioners as well as theorists, asking artists, writers, film-makers and architects to comment on how they understood the relationship between the production and experience of the city.[6]

Intersections

In my view, the edited book is an invaluable site for developing both multi- and inter-disciplinary debates. The editorial process has, for me, often involved identifying a new area of study, one located at the meeting point between previously distinct and separate areas of thought. This was the case for *Gender, Space, Architecture: An Interdisciplinary Introduction*, where we, myself along with co-editors Iain Borden and Barbara Penner, brought together over 30 seminal texts relevant to studying the relationship between feminist theory and architectural space. We organized the book into three sections, the first and the third parts both followed a historical trajectory which explored the development of feminist theory over the past 30 years, through gender and women's studies in the former and architectural design, history and theory in the later. In the middle section we adopted a spatial rather than temporal attitude to our editorial role, and selected essays drawn from a number of related fields, from anthropology to philosophy, to indicate the broad range of disciplinary procedures pertinent to the study of gender and space. For *InterSections: Architectural Histories and Critical Theories*, a set of specially commissioned essays, which I co-edited with Iain Borden, we took a different approach to our editorial role and approached architectural historians and theorists, asking each author to address the relationship between critical theory and architectural history in their own work and to develop an essay which explored their own research processes and the development of their conceptual thinking as integral to the subject matter of the chapter.[7]

At the same time as working on these edited volumes in my own individual research, I was investigating the interdisciplinary meeting point between feminist theory and architectural history, specifically examining the ways in which feminist theory questions the methods of architectural historical enquiry, the subjects and objects we choose to study and the ways in which we study them. For *The Pursuit of Pleasure*, I was seduced by two texts, one a feminist polemic, the other an urban narrative.[8] These two texts created places of methodological struggle – dialectical sites where questions of spatial and historical knowledge were raised – where I was located between theory and history. It was the intellectual labour involved in sketching out this theoretical context for conducting feminist architectural history in my individual research that enabled me to locate the key works on gender, space and architecture in numerous disciplines and realize that there was a need to bring them together in one edited volume.

A Place Between

It is also possible for individual research and collaborative research to work the other way around, for an edited project to establish themes, which can then be explored further through an authored book. When I was invited to guest edit an issue of *The Public Art Journal*, I asked a number of theorists and practitioners to reflect on my proposition: in what ways could public art be thought of *as* social space. I was interested in how various forms of 'spatial practice' carried out by public artists engaged with the kind of issues developed through 'spatial theory', in the writings of cultural geographers and critical theorists. The various artists and writers who contributed to the volume each addressed public art as 'a place between', from art and architecture collaborative muf, who discussed their work in terms of a place between people, as 'what it takes to make a relationship to make a thing', through to cultural geographer Steve Pile's essay on the city as a place between what is 'real' and what is dreamed.[9]

For several years after the publication of the journal, I continued to position myself in 'a place between' art and architecture, theory and practice, exploring the patterning of intersections between this pair of two-way relationships. In *Art and Architecture: A Place Between* I traced the multiple dynamics of this investigation and, in so doing, drew on a range of theoretical ideas from a number of disciplines to examine artworks and architectural projects. At its core, *Art and Architecture: A Place Between* is concerned with a specific kind of practice, one that is both critical and spatial, and that I call 'critical spatial practice'. In art such work has been variously described as contextual practice, site-specific art and public art; in architecture it has been described as conceptual design and urban intervention. To encounter such modes of practice, I visit works produced by galleries that operate 'outside' their physical limits, commissioning agencies and independent curators who support and develop 'site-specific' work and artists, architects and collaborative groups that produce various kinds of critical projects from performance art to urban design.[10] Although described as an authored book, this project could also be thought of in a curatorial sense, as the selection and arrangement of a number of artworks and architecture projects.

It is perhaps through distinct forms of selection and arrangement that the difference between editorial and curatorial practice is defined in my work. Both roles, curator and editor, work by continually developing and clarifying the relation between the establishment of a theme at an initial and general level, followed by the selection of works that indicate the range and scope of possibility inherent within a theme, concluding with particular manifestations of that theme through the specific contributions. The degree to which the editor/curator imposes and follows through the potential offered by an initial conceptual framework varies, from those projects where the individual works, often artefacts that have already been produced (as in *Gender, Space, Architecture*), realize a pre-existing thematic, to those where the production of new works generates the final composition both materially and conceptually, often involving a critique of the initial editorial/curatorial proposal. However, the activities of editor and curator differ according to the qualities, codes and processes associated with the contexts in which they operate, while texts and books traditionally prioritize sequence, where arrangements tend to be structured according to the 'before' and the 'after', objects and sites allow for more spatial possibilities in arrangement, allowing multidirectional aspects of production and reception to come to the fore particularly through simultaneity and juxtaposition.

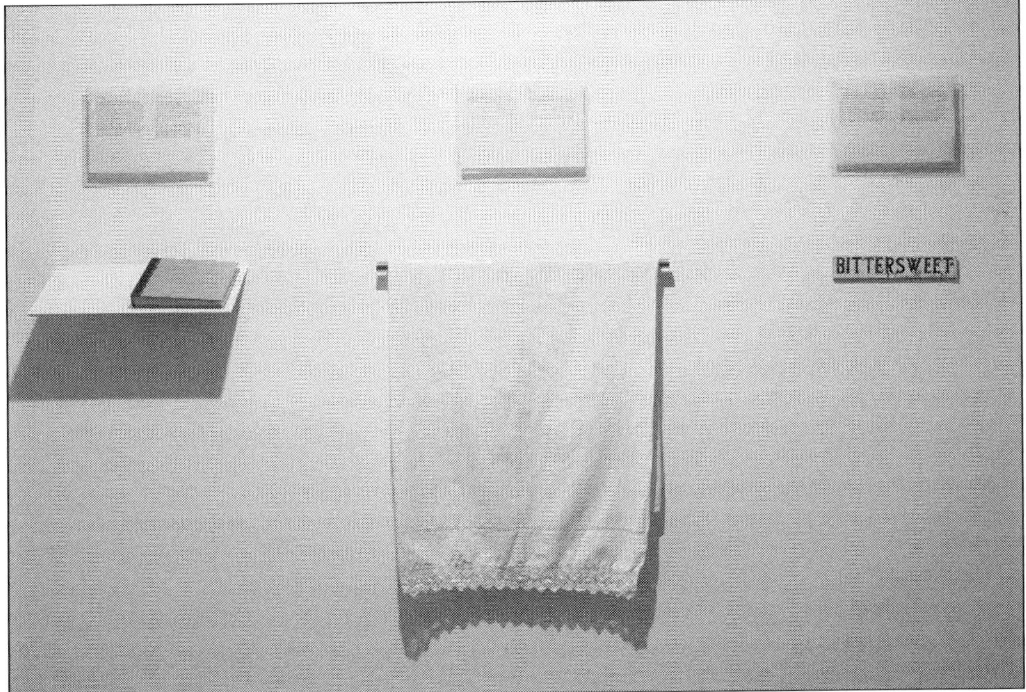

Figure 2. Jane Rendell, 'Les Mots and Les Choses', 2002, *Material Intelligence*, Entwistle Gallery, London. Photograph: Entwistle Gallery 2002.

Material Intelligence

In 2003, I became involved in curating an architectural exhibition, but in an informal capacity through conversations with Bobbie Entwistle who approached staff and students at the Bartlett School of Architecture to contribute to an exhibition at the Entwistle Gallery, which became called *Material Intelligence*. The works she selected for the exhibition constituted artefacts that had been produced as part of an architectural design process; for example, drawings, photographs, models and other types of object. An important discussion focused on whether the exhibits required any written or spoken explanation, for example, in the form of accompanying statements drafted by the curator or narratives written by the architects. We both agreed that the exhibition was stronger visually without texts placed on the gallery walls. But in retrospect, in my opinion, this decision produced a problem. An art gallery setting expects and effects specific conditions, positioning all objects within its physical parameters as 'artworks' *Material Intelligence* was no exception. As a result, the artefacts exhibited were viewed as artworks not as part of architectural design process. This resulted in a tendency to consider them as isolated objects when they had been fabricated not as solo entities but with an imagined other in mind – an architectural design, in some cases an intended 'building'. An accompanying narrative might then have worked, not to explain the artefacts on display, but to situate them in relation to the objects to which they implicitly referred, and to architectural design discourse as well as fine art.

Spatial Imagination in Design

During 2005, as director of a research cluster, 'Spatial Imagination in Design', funded by the EPSRC and AHRC as part of *Designing for the 21st Century*, I had the opportunity to work with colleagues Peg Rawes and Penelope Haralambidou in an editorial and curatorial capacity, and much of the project description that follows is drawn from as well as developed out of the editorial introduction to the project co-authored with Rawes.[11] Our cluster was composed of fifteen members, drawn from architecture, exhibition, product and interactive design; fine and public art; psychotherapy, history, economics and philosophy; structural engineering and construction management, with project partners Kate Trant of CABE (Commission for Architecture and the Built Environment) and Greg Cowan of the RIBA (Royal Institute of British Architecture). Through a series of three workshops, each one devised and led by different cluster members, we explored the spatial imagination as a mode of perception and tool of production in the experience and design of space, through particular design processes of 'modeling', 'writing' and 'drawing'.[12]

From the outset it was the group's intention to develop their understandings of the spatial imagination through the production of artefacts. The site chosen for the exhibition of these works, The Domo Baal Gallery, housed in an eighteenth-century house in Clerkenwell, London, provided an important context for the development of the research – this was a location that provoked the spatial imagination of all members of the cluster, both through the architectural features of the original design, but also through patterns of historical and contemporary occupation.

Designed between 1730 and 1750, the textured edge and central rose of the white ceiling in the main first-floor room of the gallery were the most evocative manifestations of the delicacy of spatial imagination in the rococo, an architectural style connected with this historical period. The initial occupation of the building as a family home and a solicitor's office had left traces, for example, in the form of a double door, hinting at the complex negotiations between domestic and institutional space which continue in the building today, where the everyday and private life of a family coincide closely with the ongoing and public activities of an art gallery.

This space provided an opportunity for each cluster member to make a new work which drew on collective understandings gained from previous conversations, visits and walks, yet informed by each individual's own particular interest in the spatial imagination. The final works exhibited as *Spatial Imagination* took the form of proposals and exhibits – including sound pieces, texts, drawings and models – that operated across the disciplines of art, design and architecture and communicated the spatial imagination through a configuration of material designs.

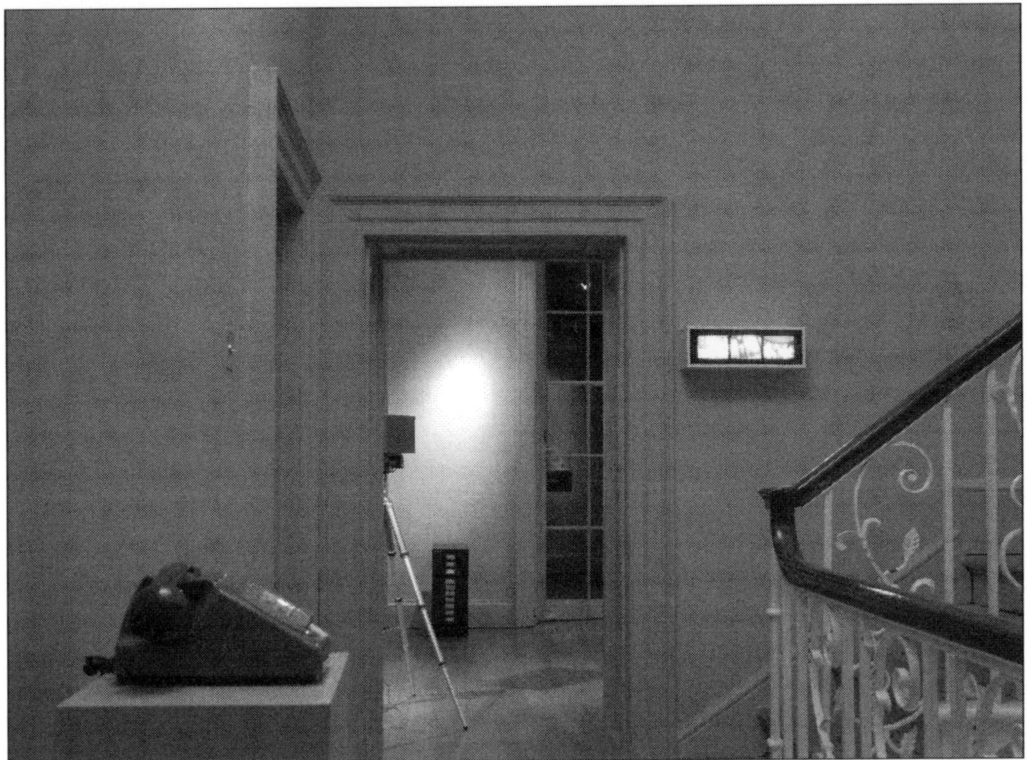

Figure 3. The work of Peg Rawes (foreground), Katja Grillner (mid-ground), Nat Chard (background), Rory Hamilton (far wall), *Spatial Imagination*, The Domo Baal Gallery, London, 2005. Photograph: David Cross of Cornford & Cross.

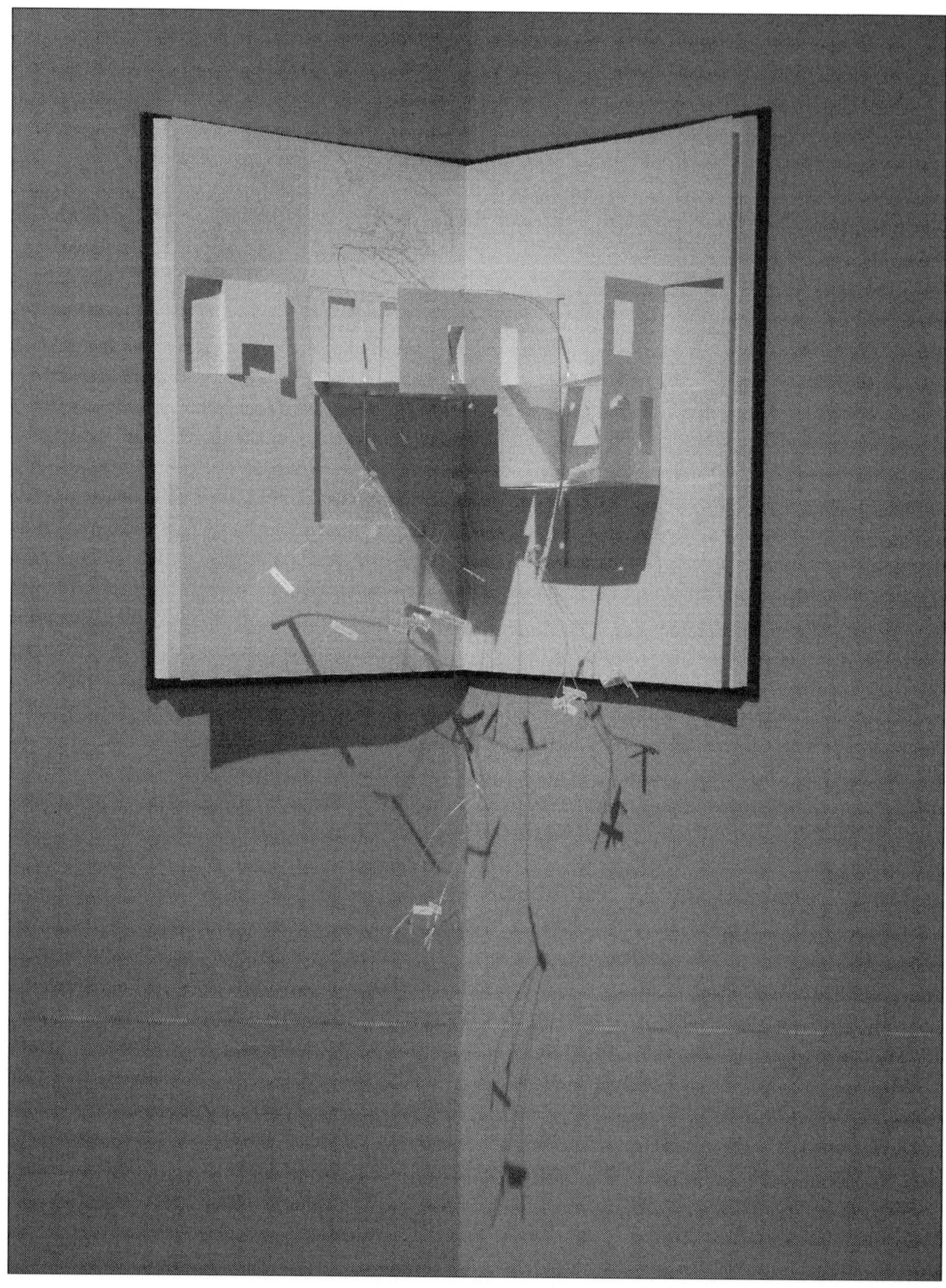

Figure 4. Penelope Haralambidou, '3 John Street: 1: 50', *Spatial Imagination*, The Domo Baal Gallery, London, 2005. Photograph: David Cross of Cornford & Cross.

Out of the production of these art and design works, three key preoccupations emerged: first, an interest in the use of the imagination in the operation of political power – both as a tool of oppression and of resistance; second, an understanding of imagination as a space of ambiguity between designer and user; and third, a desire to combine the traditionally separated design processes of drawing, writing and modelling in new hybrid forms of art, design and architectural practice. For example, artist Brigid McLeer's 'writing-as-drawing', located in the gap between the double doors, in re-writing Alain Robbe-Grillet's novel *La Jalousie* (1957), which explored how the emotion of jealousy heightens the perception of space between individuals. In placing the architectural model she produced as a design tool for curating the exhibition in the corner of the gallery, architect Penelope Haralambidou's 'drawing-as-model' demonstrated the extent to which the imagination produces multiple space-times, producing a *mis-en-abyme* or a space within a space. In repeatedly writing the word 'purdah' (a word which refers to a screen or architectural element as well as a veil or item of clothing), my own work transformed the first-floor window to the street – an architectural site of visual connection – into a screen – one of separation. Where the definition of purdah in certain versions of the Koran demands covering as a response

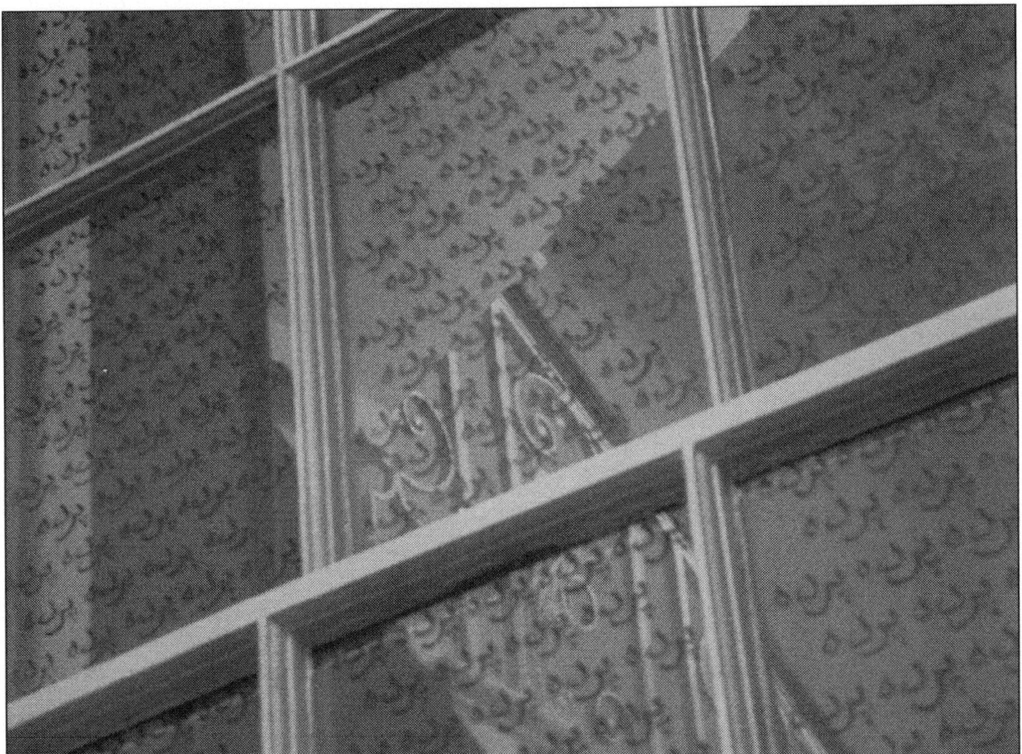

Figure 5. Jane Rendell, 'An Embellishment: Purdah', *'Spatial Imagination'*, The Domo Baal Gallery, London, 2005. Photograph: David Cross of Cornford & Cross.

to female embellishment, 'An Embellishment: Purdah' suggested that artifice structures rather than decorates divisions in the gendering of space.

Each piece was an example of the materialization of the spatial imagination in action, drawing attention to the important role practice-led research plays in critiquing the traditional methods of academic research as well as the conventions of architectural design. As physical statements, the exhibits did not seek to be understood as demonstrations or applications of pre-existing theoretical ideas, but rather as provisional works, which registered the importance of discovery in the process of art, design and architecture. The accompanying catalogue played a key role in providing a view of the works in progress. In the editorial we offered a framework for thinking about the ways in which the cluster's research interests ran through the different practices, methods and works in the exhibition. And through image and text, each cluster member contributed their own perspective on the various ways in which the spatial imagination is both a tool for investigation and proposition in the design of objects and spaces.

Critical Architecture

Over the past two years, I have also been working on another collaborative project, *Critical Architecture*, with Mark Dorrian, Murray Fraser and Jonathan Hill, this time a conference, a special issue of *The Journal of Architecture* and a co-edited book. *Critical Architecture* brings together essays and projects that examine the relationship between criticism and critical practice in architecture, exploring architectural criticism as a form of practice and considering the different modes of critical practice that comprise architectural design – buildings, drawings and texts – as forms of criticism. The division of criticism and design in architecture hinders the production of innovative work, and so we decided to locate the themes of *Critical Architecture* at four different intersections between architectural criticism and architectural design: 'Criticism/Negation/ Action' (Mark Dorrian), 'The Cultural Context of Critical Architecture' (Murray Fraser), 'Criticism by Design' (Jonathan Hill) and 'Architecture-Writing' (Jane Rendell). These conceptual strands structured the conference and the special issue of *The Journal of Architecture* and will be used to frame the debates in the co-edited book. The themes reflect issues of concern to practitioners and theorists alike, and allow the relation between criticism and design to be negotiated by contributors in varying ways.

'Architecture-Writing', my own particular theme, explores the new ways of writing architectural criticism produced when criticism is considered a form of critical practice. Discussions in art criticism concerning art-writing have begun to introduce questions of subjectivity, positionality, textuality and materiality in new critical writing practices and re-think the relationship between criticism and critical practice in the visual and performing arts.[13] I am interested in how the issues this debate raises might allow us to speculate upon the relation of creative practice in architectural and spatial criticism.

Recently in my own writing as an art and architectural critic I have explored the position of the author, not only in relation to theoretical ideas, art objects and architectural spaces but also to the site of writing itself. This interest has evolved into a number of 'site-writings' that investigate the limits of criticism and ask what it is possible for a critic to say about an artist, an architect, a work, the site of a work and the critic herself and for the writing to still 'count' as criticism. Elsewhere I have outlined in more detail the conceptual framing of this project;[14] here I will briefly summarize these concerns before ending this chapter by presenting a piece of 'site-writing'.

Site-writing

Feminists in visual and spatial culture have drawn extensively on psychoanalytic theory to further understandings of subjectivity in relation to positionality, making connections between the spatial politics of internal psychical figures and external cultural geographies.[15] I am interested in how art criticism can engage with this work in order to investigate the spatial and often changing positions we occupy as critics materially, conceptually, emotionally and ideologically.[16] Such a project involves rethinking the terms of criticism, specifically judgment, discrimination and critical distance.[17] 'Site-writing' takes up this challenge and by repositioning the artwork as a site, starts to investigate the spatiality of the critic's relation to a work, adopting and adapting both Howard Caygill's notion of strategic critique,[18] as well as Mieke Bal's exploration of the critic's 'engagement' with art.[19] Current discussions concerning relational aesthetics[20] and dialogic practice[21] continue to position the critic 'outside' the artwork; I suggest instead that the position the critic occupies needs to be made explicit through the process of writing criticism. Rather than write *about* the artwork, I am interested in how the critic constructs his or her writing in relation *to* and in dialogue *with* the artwork. The focus on the preposition here allows a direct connection to be made between the positional *and* the relational.[22]

Theoretical explorations in literary criticism of the author's different subject positions in relation to the text, as multiple 'I's' as well as 'you' and 's/he' are of relevance here,[23] as are the writings of post-colonial critics who have woven the autobiographical into the critical in their texts, combining poetic practice with theoretical analysis to articulate hybrid voices.[24] To consider questions of voice in criticism, in connection to relation, dialogue and encounter, involves objective and subjective, as well as distant and intimate positions. From the close-up to the glance, from the caress to the accidental brush, such an approach can draw on spaces as they are remembered, dreamed and imagined, as well as observed, in order to position and re-position critic and reader in relation to a work and challenge criticism as a form of knowledge with a singular and static point of view located in the here and now.

'Site-writing' is what happens then, when discussions concerning site-specificity extend to involve art criticism, and the spatial qualities of the writing become as important in conveying meaning as the content of the criticism.[25] My suggestion is that this kind of criticism or critical spatial writing, in operating as mode of a practice in its own right, questions the terms of reference that relate the critic to the artwork positioned 'under' critique. This is an active writing that constructs as well as traces the sites between critic and writer, artist and artwork, viewer and reader.

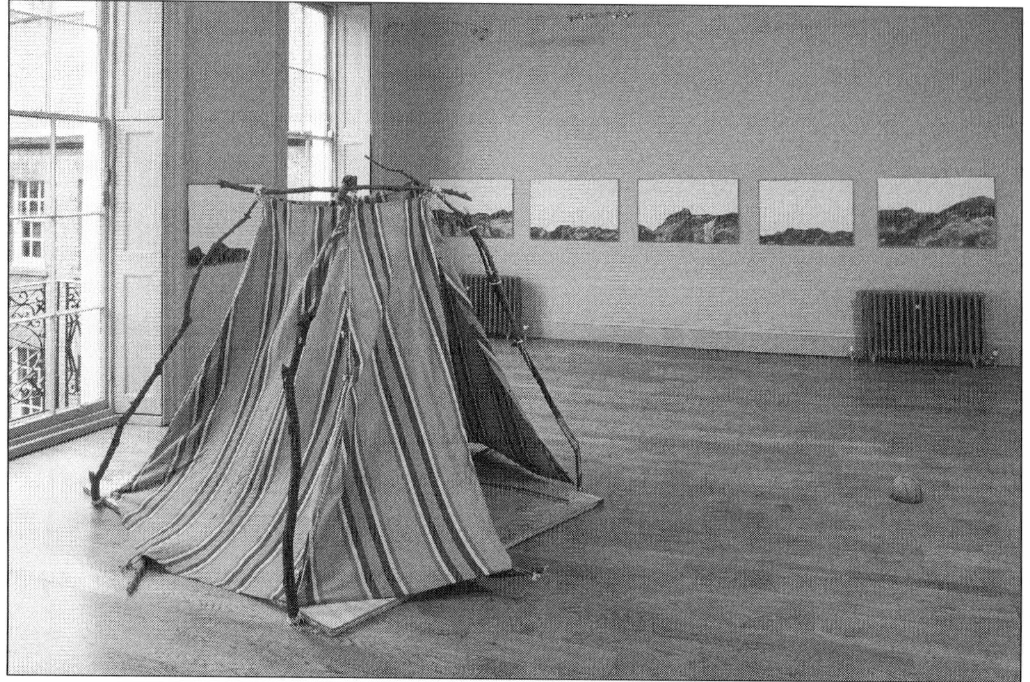

Figure 6. The work of Jan Peters (foreground) and Martina Schmid (far wall), *Ausland*, The Domo Baal Gallery, London, 2003. Photograph: The Domo Baal Gallery.

An imagined place as the site of critical writing was something I had theorized but not fully engaged with until I wrote 'Everywhere Else'.[26] This catalogue essay written for the group show *Ausland* develops my interest in imagining the spatial memories of others. Each of the three artists included in the exhibition engages with forms of architectural and spatial representation –Martina Schmid produces foreboding mountainous landscapes on folded paper from doodles scribbled while daydreaming, Silke Schatz draws large-scale architectural perspectives of places she remembers in fine-coloured pencil, while Jan Peters works in video presenting narratives of his experiences in labyrinthine buildings. I describe the sites materially present and those places I imagine the artists might have encountered and remembered in producing their work. The text is written as a detailed empirical account, moving between the artworks and the sites they refer to, as well as the location of the gallery itself.

Everywhere else

The cat's paw is large enough to cover the mountain crest; his tail is as long as the sunlit gully. But look more closely you can see that the mountain top is the edge of a dense cluster of loops drawn on a sheet of cartridge paper, folded many times. And the cat, having walked across the mountain range, has been sent on his way, relieved that his paw did not leave a mark on the paper.

Three figures sit cross-legged on the floor in a room whose function is unclear. Two windows frame views onto a London street and the door in the wall opposite opens onto a kitchen that stretches the width of the house. At the kitchen table a girl sits, her sulky head is bent over a book. Mounted on the wall behind her is a piece of cartridge paper, folded many times, covered in hundreds, thousands of tiny little loops, drawn in ink. Beside the drawing, on the mantelpiece is another drawing, smaller, this time perched rather than hung. This one is made of tiny lines drawn in pencil over a painted surface. A horizon line splits the canvas, creating on the mantelpiece, in the foreground, a smoother profile, more hilly than the rugged mountain range that lurks behind in the alcove.

As she draws, she daydreams, different voices weave in and out, stories on the television, conversations in the room. She is in a state of almost mindless concentration, at any moment her attention can wander. She slips to a summer meadow high up in the German countryside. Sitting there in the afternoon sunlight, just before the shadows of the surrounding mountain peaks fall across her lap. She wonders how she can feel a stranger in her own country. When the room comes into focus again, she is in another place. The paper on her lap is covered in many patches of tiny loops. How will they ever meet? When the joins are invisible, you can lose yourself in the middle; when the upper edge is neat, you can journey along the horizon.

The walls in this room look like they are covered in loops too – but up close it is possible to see that these are figures, lots and lots of small numbers. These are financial indices, specific quantities with particular functions, which appear here as surface ornament. In the opposite corner, two sofas are placed at right angles to one another. On the floor between them sit three women, a cat and one half of a pair of shoes. On one sofa art catalogues and CVs spill across the cushions. Behind the other sofa is a long box containing a large drawing, rolled up. This is a drawing of another room, by another hand, drawn from memory.

This is a room that matters, but that she was never quite part of. It was his room really, a room that he lived in before she entered his life, a room in which he may have loved others. To draw it is to conjure it into existence, to try to hold it down, to remember it as it was for her. The lines she draws are clear-headed and precise. She draws in a light, hard pencil, sometimes in graphite, sometimes in colour. She draws in perspective with the certainty of an architect. But the point of convergence never holds still. From where she is looking, the room shifts in her memory, her focus changes. Looking back into the past, there are many places where eyes might meet.

Between the two sofas, a second door leads out into the hallway, where an elegant staircase winds its way upstairs, to a room overlooking the garden. This room will soon contain one of her large perspective drawings. There is talk of a tent filled with her cushions to be placed in the centre of the room, where you can lie back and watch him talk of his journey.

He travels hard, day after day, moving through corridor after corridor, to try and understand the geometry of the place. But no one on the inside will tell him where he is. If he doesn't know where he is, how will he know who he is? So he draws himself a map on the palm of his hand to remind him of where he has been, to remind him that 'he is in the house'.

She too has been on many journeys, back from where she has come. Sometimes she uses the folded paper as a diary, one square per day. To remember days and places, she makes marks, one after another, slowly filling up the paper. Sometimes she records a now distant journey, marking all the squares at once, with no sense of sequence. If you fold and unfold the paper you can read one place next to, rather than before or after, another. In the patches of light and shadow she has made over time you can see the horizon of a mountain which you might have visited last summer.

In Hanover, this time, not London, three figures face a mirror. A man with wet hair is seated in the foreground bending his head downwards, only half his face is visible in the mirror. Behind him a woman leans forward with a pair of open scissors in her hand. She is cutting his hair. (Years down the line, cross-legged in the room full of numerical figures, we will see her profile again.) There is a third person, the face obscured by a camera, two hands adjust the lens; a photograph is taken. The photograph shows three artists, who today live somewhere else.

The light from the window hits her face in profile. She sits next to me on the floor, cross-legged. A third woman sits opposite, her back to a sofa. We talk of where we have come from. She was born in Russia, or was it Poland, or perhaps she said Australia? It is hard for me to remember her story, but it was also hard for her to tell. She comes from somewhere between fact and fiction. I tell them I was born in Dubai, but have moved from place to place so many times that London is my home, simply because it is not everywhere else.

My critical intention here has been to question the constitution of a legitimate subject or object for art criticism, and to expand the possibilities of criticism by suggesting that the critic can move beyond the works themselves to discuss the places imagined or remembered by the artists as well as the gallery or site of their economic exchange. The building in which the Domo Baal Gallery is located, a Georgian terraced house in Bloomsbury, London, is also the curator's home. As a critic you have access to the administration spaces or rooms 'supporting' the gallery and also to the private and domestic rooms of the house. Artworks can therefore be found in a number of different settings, exhibited in the gallery, stored under sofas, propped up on the kitchen mantelpiece, suggesting that as a critical spatial practice criticism needs to expand its si(gh)tes.

Notes

1. Julia Kristeva, 'Institutional Interdisciplinarity in Theory and Practice: an interview', Alex Coles and Alexia Defert, eds., *The Anxiety of Interdisciplinarity, De-, Dis-, Ex-*, v. 2, London: Black Dog Publishing, 1997, pp. 3–21.
2. See, for example, Jessica Benjamin, *Shadow of the Other: Intersubjectivity and Gender in Psychoanalysis*, London: Routledge, 1998, p. 25 and Diane Fuss, *Identification Papers*, London: Routledge, 1995, pp. 2–3.
3. Homi K. Bhabha, *The Location of Culture*, London: Routledge, 1994, pp. 163.
4. Iain Borden, Joe Kerr, Alicia Pivaro, Jane Rendell eds., *Strangely Familiar, Narratives of Architecture in the City*, London: Routledge, 1996.
5. In Michel de Certeau's discussion of practices, he uses the terms tactic and strategy. For de Certeau, strategies seek to create places that conform to abstract models; tactics do not obey the laws of places. See Michael de Certeau, *The Practice of Everyday Life*, Berkeley: University of California Press, 1988, p. 29. For Henri Lefebvre, spatial practices, along with representations of space and spaces of representation, form a trialectical model where space is produced through three inter-related modes. See Henri Lefebvre, *The Production of Space*, Oxford: Basil Blackwell, 1991. It is possible to draw connections between de Certeau's strategies and Lefebvre's representations of space on the one hand, and de Certeau's tactics and Lefebvres's spaces of representation on the other and suggest a distinction between those practices (strategies) that operate to maintain and reinforce existing social and spatial orders, and those practices (tactics) that seek to critique and question them. I favour such a distinction and call the latter critical spatial practices, a term which serves to describe both everyday activities and art practices which seek to resist the dominant social order to global corporate capitalism.
6. Iain Borden, Jane Rendell, Joe Kerr with Alicia Pivaro eds., *The Unknown City: Contesting Architecture and Social Space*, Cambridge, Mass.: The MIT Press, 2001.
7. Jane Rendell, Barbara Penner and Iain Borden eds., *Gender, Space, Architecture: An Interdisciplinary Introduction*, London: Routledge, 1999 and Iain Borden and Jane Rendell, eds., *InterSections: Architectural History and Critical Theory*, London: Routledge, 2000.
8. The feminist text was Luce Irigaray, 'Women on the Market', *This Sex Which Is Not One*, (1977), (trans. Catherine Porter with Carolyn Burke), Ithaca: Cornell, 1985, pp. 170–91 and the urban narrative, Pierce Egan, *Life in London; or, the day and night scenes of Jerry Hawthorn, Esq, and his elegant friend Corinthian Tom, accompanied by Bob Logic, the Oxonian, in their Rambles and Sprees through the Metropolis*, London: Sherwood, Neely and Jones, 1820–1. See Jane Rendell, *The Pursuit of Pleasure: Gender, Space and Architecture in Regency London*, London and New Brunswick: The Athlone Press, Continuum and Rutgers University Press, 2002.
9. See Katherine Clarke of muf, 'How to: a description of what it takes to make a relationship to make a thing', in Jane Rendell ed., *'A Place Between'*, special issue of *The Public Art Journal*, issue 2, (October 1999), pp. 42–3 and Steve Pile, 'Between city and dream', in Jane Rendell (ed.) *'A Place Between'*, special issue of *The Public Art Journal*, issue 2, (October 1999), pp. 10–11.
10. Jane Rendell, *Art and Architecture: A Place Between*, London: I.B. Tauris, 2006.

11. See Peg Rawes and Jane Rendell eds., *Spatial Imagination*, London: The Bartlett School of Architecture, UCL, 2005. See also spatialimagination.org.uk.

12. The conference was held in November 2005 at The Bartlett School of Architecture, University College London, organized by Jane Rendell and Jonathan Hill of the Bartlett, in association with AHRA (Architectural Humanities Research Association) represented by Murray Fraser of the University of Westminster and Mark Dorrian of the University of Edinburgh. The conference was part funded by the British Academy and part funded by The Bartlett School of Architecture. See Jane Rendell ed., 'Critical Architecture', special issue of *The Journal of Architecture*, (June 2005), v. 10. n. 3 and Jane Rendell, Jonathan Hill, Murray Fraser and Mark Dorrian eds., *Critical Architecture*, London: Routledge, forthcoming 2007.

13. See, for example, Alex Coles, 'The Bathroom Critic', *Art Monthly*, 263 (February 2003), pp. 7–10; Michael Archer, 'Crisis What Crisis?', *Art Monthly*, 264 (March 2003), pp. 1–4; Rasheed Araeen, letter in response to 'Crisis what Crisis', *Art Monthly*, 265 (April 2003), pp. 12–3; Matthew Arnat, 'The Middle Distance', response to Michael Archer, *Art Monthly*, 265 (April 2003), p. 43; Peter Suchin, 'The Critic never Sleeps', *Art Monthly*, 266 (May 2003), p. 41; Michael Archer, 'Critical Task', letter in response to 'The Critic never Sleeps', *Art Monthly*, 267 (June 2003), p. 9; Rasheed Araeen, 'Opportunism', letter in response to 'Critical Task', *Art Monthly*, 268 (Jul-Aug 2003), p. 14; J. J. Charlesworth, 'The Dysfunction of Criticism', *Art Monthly*, 269 (September 2003), pp. 1–4. The debate then turned to the role of the artist/curator, but has recently reverted to discussions of criticism in the form of artist Dave Beech's attack on critic Julian Stalleybrass. See Dave Beech, 'Art's Debunkers', *Art Monthly*, 283 (February 2005), pp. 2–4. See also Jane Rendell, letter, 'Art Writing', *Art Monthly*, 272 (December-January 2003–4), p. 15.

14. See, for example, 'Architecture-Writing', in Jane Rendell ed., *Critical Architecture*, special issue of *The Journal of Architecture*, (June 2005), v. 10. n. 3, pp. 255–64. See also 'Travelling the Distance: Encountering the Other', David Blamey ed., *Here, There, Elsewhere: Dialogues on Location and Mobility*, London: Open Editions, 2002, pp. 43–54; 'Writing in place of speaking', Sharon Kivland and Lesley Sanderson eds., *Transmission: Speaking and Listening*, v. 1, Sheffield Hallam University and the Site Gallery, 2002, pp. 15–28; 'Site-Writing', Sharon Kivland, Jaspar Joseph-Lester and Emma Cocker eds., *Transmission: Speaking and Listening*, v. 4, Sheffield Hallam University and the Site Gallery, 2005, pp. 169–76; 'From Austin, Texas to Santiago Atitlan, and back again', Felipe Hernandez, Mark Millington and Iain Borden eds., *Architecture and Transculturation in Latin America*, Amsterdam and New York, Rodopi Press, 2006, pp. 43–58 and 'From Architectural History to Spatial Writing', in Elvan Altan Ergut, Dana Arnold and Belgin Turan Ozkaya eds., *Rethinking Architectural Historiography*, London: Routledge, 2006.

15. See, for example, Susan Stanford Friedman, *Mappings: Feminism and the Cultural Geographies of Encounter*, Princeton: Princeton University Press, 1998; Diane Fuss, *Identification Papers*, London: Routledge, 1995; Elizabeth Grosz, *Volatile Bodies*, Indianapolis: Indiana University Press, 1994; Irit Rogoff, *Terra Infirma*, London: Routledge, 2000 and Kaja Silverman, *The Threshold of the Visible World*, London: Routledge, 1996.

16. See Jane Flax, *Thinking Fragments: Psychoanalysis, Feminism and Postmodernism in the Contemporary West*, Berkeley, Los Angeles: University of California Press, 1991, p. 232; Donna Haraway. 'Situated Knowledges: the Science Question in Feminism and the Privilege

of Partial Knowledge', *Feminist Studies*, v. 14, n. 3, (fall 1988), pp. 575–603, especially, pp. 583–8 and Elspeth Probyn, 'Travels in the Postmodern: Making Sense of the Local' in Linda Nicholson ed., *Feminism/Postmodernism*, London: Routledge, 1990, pp. 176–89, p. 178. See also Rosi Braidotti, *Nomadic Subjects*, New York: Columbia University Press, 1994 and bell hooks, *Yearnings: Race, Gender, and Cultural Politics*, London: Turnaround Press, 1989.

17. Howard Caygill, *Walter Benjamin: The Colour of Experience*, London: Routledge, 1998, p. 34 and pp. 64 and 79.

18. See Hal Foster's discussion of critical distance and identification, for example, in Hal Foster, *The Return of the Real: The Avant-Garde at the End of the Century*, Cambridge, Mass.: The MIT Press, 2001, pp. 223–6.

19. See Mieke Bal, *Louise Bourgeois' Spider: The Architecture of Art-Writing*, London and Chicago: University of Chicago Press, 2001, p. xi. See also Norman Bryson, 'Introduction: Art and Intersubjectivity', Mieke Bal, *Looking in: The Art of Viewing*, Amsterdam: G+B International, 2001, pp. 1–39.

20. See, for example, Nicholas Bourriaud, *Relational Aesthetics*, (trans. Simon Pleasance and Fronza Woods), Paris: Les Presses du Réel, 2002.

21. See, for example, Grant H. Kester, *Conversation Pieces: Community and Communication in Modern Art*, Berkeley: University of California Press, 2004.

22. The significance Trinh T. Minh-ha assigns to the shift from speaking 'about' to speaking 'to' has been stressed by Irit Rogoff who underscores how, instead of taking power relationships to produce spatial locations, it is possible for a change in position to advance a change in relationship. See Irit Rogoff's discussion of Trinh T. Minh-ha's assertion in Irit Rogoff, 'Studying Visual Culture', in Nicholas Mirzoeff ed., *The Visual Culture Reader*, London: Routledge, 1998, pp. 14–26.

23. See, for example, Italo Calvino, *Literature Machine*, London: Vintage, 1997, p. 15 and Roland Barthes, *The Grain of the Voice: Interviews 1962–80*, (trans. Linda Coverdale), Berkeley and Los Angeles: University of California Press, 1991, pp. 215–6

24. See Gloria Anzaldua, *Borderlands/La Frontera: the New Mestiza*, San Francisco: Lute Books, 1999 and Hélène Cixous. 'Sorties', (trans. Betsy Wing) from Susan Sellers ed., *The Hélène Cixous Reader*, London: Routledge, 1994.

25. On art and site-specificity see, for example, Alex Coles ed., *Site Specificity: The Ethnographic Turn*, London: Black Dog Publishing, 2000; Nick Kaye, *Site-Specific Art: Performance, Place and Documentation*, London: Routledge, 2000; Miwon Kwon, *One Place After Another: Site Specific Art and Locational Identity*, Cambridge, Mass.: The MIT Press, 2002.

26. Jane Rendell, 'Everywhere Else', *Ausland*, comprising artists Jan Peters, Martina Schmid and Silke Schatz, (London: The Domo Baal Gallery, 2003).

EXHIBITIONS AND THEIR PREREQUISITES

Chris Dorsett

Closed systems

Some influential accounts of audience reception treat the act of interpretation as a closed system constructed entirely within the responsive mechanisms that come into play as, for example, a reader reads a novel or, as this essay will report, exhibited things meet their viewers. If we look hard at exactly what does 'come into play' in these circumstances, we should also note that visiting a gallery or museum can register with an exhibition-goer in a multitude of ways. Contrast the sense of obligation one brings to reading an exhibition label with the excitement of standing near a famous painting in a crowded public gallery. Are these reactions within or without the mechanisms in question? For an artist-curator like me it is difficult to know where to draw the line. Nevertheless, if interpretation is a closed, self-organizing system, all sorts of metaphorical descriptions help us conjure the creative work of an exhibition audience. One pictures a whirlpool of responses spontaneously forming with nothing more than the flow of everyday experience to explain its presence.

But, as we shall see, the point of likening interpretation to a closed system is to allow no rupture through which artistic or curatorial ambition can enter in a determining role. On this account the artist working single-mindedly in a studio and the curator writing a proposal to a museum are retroactive constructs, 'prerequisites' (to introduce

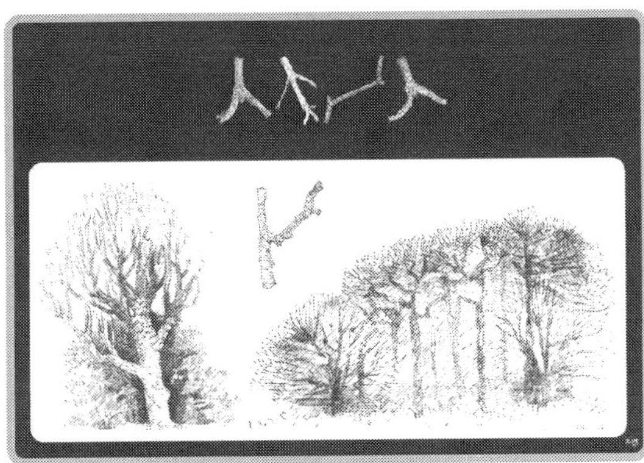

Figure 1. Signage for Kew Gardens, 2004.

a convenient shorthand) generated as by-products of the appreciative and critical consumption of artworks. In terms of cause and effect this may seem back to front but as a hypothesis about audience practices we are celebrating the creativity of exhibition-goers not just in the arts but also throughout the museum world and, as this chapter shows with an example from Kew Gardens, an artist-curator can respond to the closed system of 'exhibitions and their prerequisites' in any number of contexts.

A story

As a starting point, I give a short description of visiting a gallery. It was 1984, a curious year that had been assigned (certainly, for as long as I can remember) to our most alarming fears for the future. Afterwards this calendar date became just another year and the source of the dystopian heat, George Orwell's celebrated novel, was returned to the shelf with a different role in the literary canon. This background detail strikes me as important because the twelve months of that year were lived in something like a semiotic fissure as bit by bit, with the passage of time, many much-loved idioms ('big brother', 'newspeak', 'doublethink') were separated from the temporal location to which they had been so convincingly attached.

My story concerns the semiotic fissures that open up within the process of interpretation. In November of that year I visited a large Victorian museum in the Midlands to see a survey of contemporary art assembled by a team of curators. The show was extremely well attended and both people and artworks, in my initial perambulations, surrounded me with densely populated vistas that were not that different to those outside as I walked from the station to the gallery. As with the street, so too with the many sub-territorial worlds of a mixed exhibition: as I began to pace out my presence across the expanse of museum floor, there was everywhere around me the kind of communal behaviour, a subtle employment of manners and tact, that maintains successful 'passing-by' in public situations.

This fluid state continued until, here and there, particular artworks held me in place for long enough to turn my perambulatory viewing into an arrested point of view. Once this happened things were different: other visitors now took evasive action to pass me. And the vistas disappeared. One kind of perceptual experience (the equivalent of, say, sightseeing) was replaced by a form of rapt attention in which I was consciously standing back to encounter a spectator's object. In other words, by coming to a standstill I had given myself certain powers as a viewer. I was now in a position to scrutinize the qualities I found encoded before me and, as a result, award or withdraw my approval.

So far in this story I have described gallery-going within, on the one hand, the multiple vistas generated by walking through a public space and, on the other, the breaking up of those experiences as they are channelled into states of attentiveness during interpretatively minded viewing. Both are surely very familiar. They make up the moments before we start thinking about the contents of artworks. And yet within my description, even though we fall short of actually interpreting 'meanings', we can still entertain a sort of phenomenology of exhibition-going. If one wanted to incorporate these fuzzy peripheral responses into a closed interpretative system, then a phenomenological investigation, one that brackets our assumptions about what counts as an exhibition experience, is probably a good way of acknowledging all that is wayward alongside all that is said to be to the point in gallery-going.

On the occasion I am reporting a third type of encounter extended my response. In a second-story gallery the passage of exhibition-goers across an aging wooden floor disturbed the delicate balance of a small abstract sculpture. This diminutive object, poetically vulnerable in appearance, was suddenly lying in pieces before me. Indeed it may have been my approach that made the sculpture finally succumb to actual vulnerability. Having watched the exhibit collapse, a state of interpretative blankness took over. Thinking back, this experience was like being given a cup of coffee when you thought you were getting tea. When an expectation is unfulfilled we do not know what we have experienced. For a short time the taste is not tea, nor is it coffee. Poised before the broken sculpture, my ability to adjust from one interpretation to another was similarly frustrated. I was trying to negotiate an exhibition experience that involved neither a beckoning vista nor (sadly) a spectator's object and the result was an absence of receptive response.

Interpretative communities

With this description we have an account of an exhibition experience that loses touch with the possibility of interpretative sense-making. Even though the disruption was short-lived, the situation was so unsettling that, as I recall, I could not easily slip back into my previous modes of engagement. I now neither passed by nor stood still but hung around reassessing and reorganizing my understanding of what had happened. In a perverse way, I felt energized by this state of affairs. Over the years, in one kind of exhibition or another, various types of mechanical breakdown have had a similar effect. Each time I found it invigorating to move out of reach of the customary procedures by which meaning is constructed. With this kind of experience in mind, perhaps the zero-point receptive process, we can now turn to the theorist most responsible for promoting the process of reception as a mechanism built entirely of the assumptions and beliefs of the audience.

With essays such as *Interpreting the 'Variorum'* (1988), the literary critic Stanley Fish made a celebrated contribution to Milton studies and became, by the mid-1970s, the leading exponent of reader-response theory. He tells us that the procedures of interpretation alone account for the authorial content of poetic works. This is how the idea works. The lines of Milton's poems generate a pressure for judgment and then fail (and this is the key concept), through semantic slide and conceptual slippage, to deliver a stable conclusion. What happens in the act of reading really depends on:

'...a moment of hesitation or syntactic slide, when the reader is invited to make a certain kind of sense only to discover (at the beginning of the next line) that the sense he has made is either incomplete or simply wrong.' (Fish 1988: 311)

As a result, the reader 'comes away from the poem not with a statement but with a responsibility' (Fish 1988: 314). This means that, in the final analysis, interpreters have to manage by themselves because the real goal of the interpretative process is not a hidden meaning awaiting recovery but an action of the mind in which interpretative closure is continually, to use Fish's favoured term, 'hazarded' (Fish 1988: 320–323).

For the various ways in which we keep hazarding conclusions Fish invented a new category of autonomous audience action: the interpretative strategy. From the well-positioned viewpoint of an attentive reader, certain references are selected and revisited for the *contradictory* movements of the mind they entail. Similarly equipped receptors tend to make similar choices and, as a result, parallel strategies of selection eventually cohere as a collective entity that Fish calls an interpretative community. Within these communities some members, following their strategic inclinations, specialize in initiating codes of instruction to achieve the desired conflictive effect. These codes circulate within a community in the same way that an unfinished musical score might get passed around a group of like-minded musicians. As usage grows, communal acceptance generates the formal object we call a new poem (Fish 1988: 321). For all those involved, the persona of the poet is a strategic construct, an interpretative instruction designed to trigger certain kinds of response. Thus, for the reader-response theorist, whilst there was most certainly a historical person called John Milton, 'Milton the poet' is the creature of a highly creative strategy for the on-going process of interpretative sense-making (Fish 1988: 326–325).

A contemporary artist-curator can surely live with this description. The School of Fine Art in which I undertake research, to take an exemplary manifestation of an interpretative community, is full of students seeking viable artistic personas in relation to the receptive (and not so receptive) responses of the staff. Few art school people would deny the emphasis Fish places on audience power. The idea that the intentional agent we call an 'author' as a construct is long familiar from Barthes and Foucault and to judge by the key texts that turn up in research proposals, fashionable curators such as Nicolas Bourriaud still find it useful, as Fish did 30 years ago, to treat audience reception as a performative response to a code by comparing artworks to musical scores and exhibition-goers to interpretative performers.

Musical analogies

Indeed, analogies with musical practices are a good way of drawing out what Fish means by a code of instruction. In *For Whom the Bell Tolls: Reading and Hearing Busnoy's 'Anthoni Usque Limina'*, the musicologist R. C. Wegman (1997) borrowed the concept of an interpretative community to describe how personal, communal and spiritual identities were brought into imaginative interaction through the performance of motets in medieval church services. The vocal ensemble achieved by each member of a congregation and by the congregation in relation to (or so they believed) the angelic choir congregated above, transformed the act of worship into something very like an interpretative strategy aimed at incorporating an attentive heavenly audience into the earthly process of praising God. When motets such as Busnoy's *Anthoni Usque Limina* are performed in a concert hall today and enjoyed by an audience of secular music lovers it is clear that liaisons with angels are not part of the score (even for those who like early music authenticity). As a contemporary interpretative community we have our own communal agreement about what counts as musical sense and, on these terms alone, a composer called Busnoy survives. 'His' score continues to be performed.

Thus, interpretations are always fresh and liable to go off as fashions change. However, it is the strategy rather than the codification that is historically dynamic. A recent book by Myles Weber shows that J. D. Salinger's failure to publish novels after his 1960s bestseller *Catcher in the Rye* has not inhibited 40 years of critical enthusiasm. Commentary has been sustained by what Weber calls 'volumes of silence', non-physical codes of instruction that can be interpreted like an authorial text. An interpretative community, it seems, can summon up strategy-affirming interpretations even in the absence of material support. Fish would certainly agree. There is nothing foundational about a text in the interpretative process. The object we call a poem or a novel is only relevant to the degree that it provokes disagreement. What really counts is the scope that an interpretative strategy has to preserve opposing positions. Books, concerts and exhibitions have a role to play but, as Weber shows us, they are only one technique for keeping contradictory turns of mind turning.

Thus, a community continues to interpret, not because there is an archive of published works that embodies and encodes authorial meaning, but because there is 'just enough stability for interpretative battles to go on, and just enough shift and slippage to assure that they will never be settled' (Fish 1988: 328). An interpretative community is, Fish tells us, a self-generating and temporal entity, a spontaneous collective that achieves and maintains equilibrium. When it eventually declines, it does so through its own capacity to dissipate. Here another analogy comes into view: that of the interpretative community as biological species or environmental ecosystem.

Closed systems again

It is time to acknowledge that Fish makes reader-response theory sound like a naturalistic model of cultural agency of the kind developed within cognitive psychology by writers such

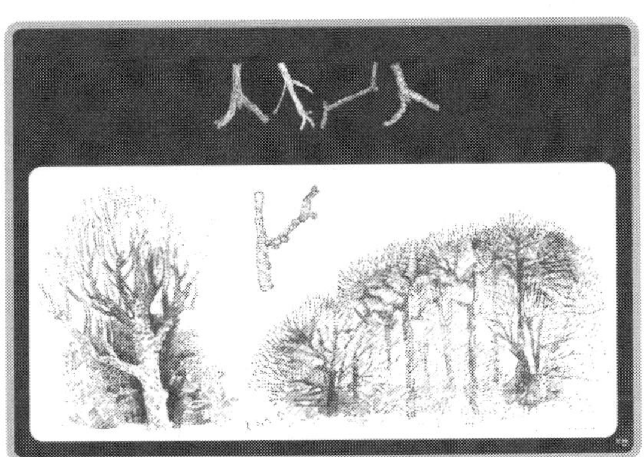

Figure 2. Signage for Kew Gardens, 2004.

as the anthropologist Dan Sperber. There is not room here to consider how far one could, or should, take this correspondence. I do not want to debate the idea that interpretative agreement is like, say, gas particles combining into the systems and arrangements that make up our physical environment. However, I will allow myself just enough semantic slippage to recast Fish's concepts within a naturalistic frame that evokes the sort of biological mechanism that scientists boil down to simple on/off actions. To this end I am interested in the work of a pioneer of neo-Darwinist materialism, Daniel C. Dennett.

In *Consciousness Explained* (Dennett 1993), the philosophical problem of the self-reflective ghost in the human machine is demystified using the kind of rhetorical device Dennett calls an intuition pump. This device is an everyday anecdote refashioned as a thinking tool to assist the reader's comprehension of a complicated or abstract argument. Dennett's 'pump' is a game in which a group of party-goers challenge one of their members, a 'dupe', to guess the contents of a narrative based on a recent dream experience. Whilst the dupe waits outside, the group ignores the idea of the dream and agrees to a systematic mode of response. They will answer all the dupe's enquiries in the follow way:

> [I]f the last letter of the last word of the question is in the first half of the alphabet, the question is to be answered in the affirmative, and all other questions are to be answered in the negative, with one proviso: a non-contradiction override rule to the effect that later questions are not to be given answers that contradict earlier answers. (Dennett 1993: 11)

As a result, the group provides the dupe with opportunities to create his own story using three simple responses: they sometimes say yes, they sometimes say no, and they never contradict themselves. Given time, an apparently consistent, yet entirely accidental, storyline will emerge.

This gives us a very clear picture of a closed system at work. All the engineering is 'in play' and there are no parts external to the process. In these terms Dennett introduces a materialist account of how physical bodies in the physical world can produce the apparently non-physical conscious mind. His explanation needs no recourse to ghosts, or the presence of internal homunculi, or any preliminary creative work held up as prior cause. Like Fish, Dennett describes a 'process of narrative production, of detail accumulation, with no authorial intentions or plans at all' (Dennett 1993: 11). His model counts on the audience (the expectation-driven dupe at the party) to provide the content (Dennett 1993: 14). In other words, as long as there is an interpretative community, the author need be no more than a mechanical system programmed to say either yes or no to expectant enquiries. Thus, a closed system is 'stupid' but still manages to provide 'clever' interpretations. This last characteristic has been endlessly reinforced over the years by computer programmes that approximate living states. For example, the animation software known as *Boids* (created by Craig Reynolds) and *The*

Game of Life (invented by John Conway) both operate, despite the rich variety of effects they create, on a set of rules that can be counted on one hand.

All this makes an absurd and unconvincing caricature of the authors, poets and artists-curators we meet at book launches and exhibition openings, and I am sure that Stanley Fish would distance himself from the idea that his theory has such reductive force. However, the expository power summoned by Dennett's intuition pump does make vivid the difficulty Fish gets into when, having told us that authorial intention is not prior to the reader's act of discovery, he goes on to describe an author anticipating 'the moves he would make if confronted by the sounds or marks he is uttering or setting down' (Fish 1988: 329). Fish seems to be fudging questions about chickens and eggs. In contrast, Dennett makes everything clear: we have an audience operating self-sufficiently and the artistic 'uttering or setting down' realized automatically within the audience's process of interpretation.

Musical analogies again

In order to push this idea forward, I am going to turn once more to the performance practices of musicians. In his essay *The Collective Memory of Musicians* (1978), the French sociologist Maurice Halbwachs (1877–1945) described orchestral performers and their audience members as a single 'system or colony' of interpreters. Within this physical and social unit a polarization occurs between interpreters who use musical scores to remember long sequences of sounds and interpreters who use the production of sounds to remember extended sequences of non-musical experience.

Halbwachs was a perceptive thinker and I can only schematize his ideas here. The musicians he has in mind are technical specialists who try to imagine as little as possible as they engage with the perpetually present-tense business of performing a score whereas his audiences are reverie-oriented dreamers who frequently forget the actual processes at work around them. In this model of an interpretative community we have complementary types of interpreters: those who calculate the moves they would make if confronted (in an audience situation) by their own codes of instruction and those who make decisions about the actions of performers in order to embark on personal, open-ended journeys of interpretative discovery.

At this point we have a much clearer version of the simultaneity implied by Fish. There are two kinds of interpreter either 'calculating' or 'forgetting' in relation to each other. With Dennett's intuition pump it is not difficult to imagine how both sides function together. However, things get cloudy again if you think, like Fish, that calculators and forgetters treat each other in the same strategic way. For a better description of the complementary operations of an interpretative community we need Michel de Certeau's celebrated book: *The Practice of Everyday Life* (1984). In a wonderfully provocative reading of Clausewitz and Kant, de Certeau tells us that where we have a strategy we must also have tactics. When a military strategist gains an overview of the field of battle the ability to see into the distance brings with it the power to prepare future expansions. But achieving a 'mastery of places through sight' offers alternative opportunities to make 'use of the cracks that particular conjunctions open up in the surveillance of the proprietary powers' (de Certeau 1984: 36–37). These cracks are opportunities for the responsive creativity of the tactician. De Certeau provides 'everyday' examples that include the conversational improvisations of the humorist and the treacherous opportunism of the trickster. His examples represent a triumph of time over space (de Certeau 1984: xvi-xxiv & 34–39). At a more physical level, tactical achievements can be observed in the urban walker moving around busy city streets and, in a beautiful image derived from Kant, the maintenance of bodily poise in a high-wire act:

> Dancing on a tightrope requires that one maintain an equilibrium from one moment to the next by recreating it at every step by means of new adjustments: it requires one to maintain a balance that is never permanently acquired; constant readjustment renews the balance while giving the impression of 'keeping' it. (de Certeau 1984: 73).

With this example of tactical skill 'the practitioner himself is part of the equilibrium'. The body continuously re-creates its position from scratch in a form of ceaseless creativity that de Certeau likens to artistic production. Thus, to return to the interpretative community pictured by Halbwachs, the orchestra readjusts from one moment to the next to make the present situation more advantageous and the audience 'run[s] ahead of time by reading space' (de Certeau 1984: 36) to escape (forget) the physical limitations of the present-moment experience.

Back to the story
And so it was within a predominately strategic space that, back in 1984, I made my visit to a municipal museum in the Midlands. As a result, my imagination was duly set free to muse across a wide range of ideas. It was common at the time to treat the environmental circumstances of an artwork as synonymous with its artistic content. Later De Oliveira, Oxley & Petry (1994) were to define installation art in exactly this fashion, as the ultimate activator of museum space. Thus, I was strategically primed to make the perambulatory and attentive routines of the museum an important part of the content of my experience. However, this 'content' constantly led me to consider, not the space in which I was standing, but another location that, spectre-like, kept appearing in the role of prerequisite condition. This was the studio, the site of production of each exhibit that the glossy exhibition catalogue documented with numerous photogenic reminders. When the sculpture collapsed, and a gap opened in the flow of interpretative reveries, the obstinate material resistance of the de-assembled object threw me back on those moments in the process of production where the possibility of nothing is calculated as part of the possibility of something. This was what I found exhilarating. It was, to use de Certeau's terminology, a tactical rather than a strategic triumph that fused the gallery with the workplace in which one teeters on a knife-edge in relation to creative success or failure.

And so, an exhibition accident impeded my interpretative strategies and afforded certain tactical opportunities. This experience was, in effect, a mechanical breakdown within the closed system that generates audience reception. A key component was my bodily 'poise'. I could neither pass by nor stand still. Instead I hovered around reorganizing my understanding of what had happened. Hard up against the materiality of the collapsed sculpture, an interpretative fissure interrupted my creative operations as an exhibition visitor. In such gaps an entirely different way of participating in an interpretative community comes into its own. One adopts the creative readiness of the studio practitioner, the poised tactician who wrestles with uncertainty in workspaces that never correspond to the fantasy studios documented in catalogue photographs. Whilst the latter are prerequisites of our gallery-going strategies, the former are the test sites in which we experiment with our ability to maintain poise in situations dominated by interpretative reverie.

And 'poise' has great phenomenological leverage. It is an idea that has been explored at length by the American philosopher Samuel Todes within his revision of the work of Merleau-Ponty. *Body and World* (Todes 2001) is a phenomenology of the percipient body within its experience of physical extension, resistance and support. The ongoing capacity of the body to cope with the fundamental circumstances of 'being in the world' is for Todes a poised management of the things and persons around us. During my visit to the exhibition my bodily poise continually provided me with 'sensuous proof that the perceptual experience of our immediate future conforms to that of our immediate past' (Todes 2001: 79). Without this conformity I could not make my perceptual experiences 'habit-able' (Todes 2001: 52). This is what disappeared when the sculpture collapsed and then reappeared when the situation corrected itself as an unexpected sense of studio-oriented exhilaration.

Trees walking

In my project *Trees Walking* I deliberately set myself up to lose and regain my poise as an artist-curator. Our culture of arts-science initiatives provides a great deal of scope to experiment in this way. By commuting from one interpretative community to another one can work tactically within the disseminating spaces of other disciplines and other forms of knowledge. At the Royal Botanic Gardens, Kew, visitors construct their own equivalent of a prerequisite site of production using botanical and environmental research. For an artist these locations are certain to be 'uninhabitable', places where only tactics will re-establish the appropriate 'habits' of interpretation. And so, with

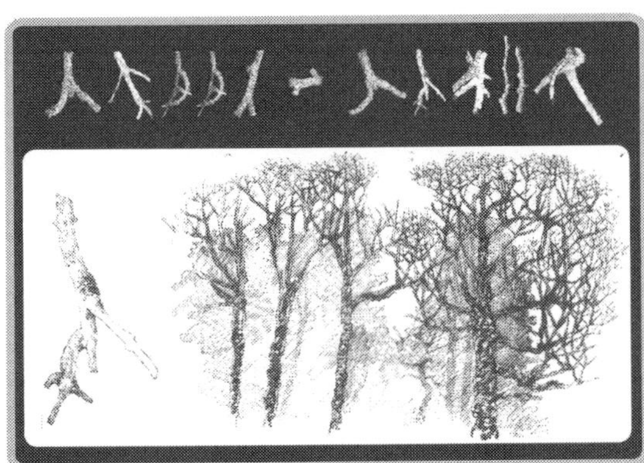

Figure 3. Signage for Kew Gardens, 2004.

funding from the Arts and Humanities Research Council, I joined botanists undertaking field research north of Manaus at the Reserva Ducke in the Amazon rainforest.

During this residency I met Mike Hopkins and his team of postgraduate students who were, in the summer of 2002, busy developing new taxonomic methods for a forest field guide. The external features of trees have determined their identity since the days of Linnaeus (who delineated plant species using peripheral organs) but, as I understood it, the convergence of evolutionary mechanisms in the Amazon has created forest environments that have a broad distribution and frequency of species but look, despite the diversity, more or less uniform. As a result, Hopkins' collected conventional diagnostic specimens such as twigs, flowers and seeds in order to check these visual signs against alternative indicators such as the taste and smell of sap. In this manner his team made intimate sensory contact with large numbers of trees across broad swathes of dense forest. We did a lot of strenuous walking and a great deal of slipping about in wet jungle mud. Every time I moved, I embodied physical and perceptual ineptitude. With each stumble, before I was able to catch myself, my movements shrank to a single instinctive attempt to regain my balance in a terrain that afforded no open views, or potential for forward movement, in any direction. My faltering progress through the thorn-bearing undergrowth required tactical, not strategic, skills. In this distant place I began to plan my work as an artist-curator at Kew by writing down codes of instruction for future promenades on macadamed pathways and broad grassy vistas. From the middle of the jungle, the faraway Gardens seemed an entirely promiscuous space, not just in the context of my own mobility (so curtailed by the forest terrain), but also in relation to the forest trees whose growth in Amazonia is entirely determined by the narrow 'ecological chimneys' that open up in the tightly packed canopy of their collective habitat.

I calculated how the freedom of Kew's audience would, as de Certeau has it, 'run ahead of time by reading space' and, in anticipation, set down my walking instructions using a mock notation constructed from the materials that came to hand: that is, the discarded twigs that lay around me at the end of a hard day's research in the forest. Later, when my 'score' had been elaborated as signage for the *New Views of Kew* festival in 2004, some botanists were quick to tell me that unreadable signs are pointless (Figures 1–3). But interpretative tacticians manage meanings where interpretative strategists fail to make sense. As I walked about Kew Gardens, with my forest instructions 'signed' around me, fellow visitors either declined to register as they passed by or, if they drew to a halt, seemed to think the 'twig talk' did a job: the trees were definitely trying to tell them something.

References

Bourriaud, N., *Postproduction: Culture as Screenplay: How Art reprograms the World*, New York, Lukas and Stemberg, 2002.

Cappock, M., *Francis Bacon's Studio*, London, Merrel, 2006.

Certeau, M. de, *The Practice of Everyday Life*, Berkeley, University of California Press, 1988.

Daly, G. and Zizek, S., *Conversations with Zizek*, Cambridge, Polity, 2003.

De Oliveira, N. Oxley, N. & Petry, M., *Installation Art*, London, Thames and Hudson, 1994.

Dennett, D. C., *Consciousness Explained*, London, Penguin Books, 1993.

Dorsett, C., *Trees Walking: Why is there a Collection of Walking Sticks at the Royal Botanic Gardens, Kew?* Hexham, Artgoes Imprint, 2004.

Eco, U., *Kant and the Platypus: Essays on Language and Cognition*, London, Vintage, 2000.

Fish, S., 'Interpreting the *Variorum*' in Lodge, D. (ed.) *Modern Criticism and Theory: A Reader*, (New York, Longman Inc., 1988) pp. 310–329.

Halbwachs, M., *The Collective Memory*, New York, Harper Colophon Books, 1978.

Hallé, F. and Oldman, R. A. A., *Tropical Trees and Forests: An Architectural Analysis*, Berlin, Springer-Verlag, 1978.

Newhouse, V., *Art and the Power of Placement*, New York, Monacelli, 2005.

O'Doherty, B., *Inside the White Cube*, Berkeley, University of California Press, 2000.

Rosen, C., *The Frontiers of Meaning: Three Informal Lectures on Music*, London, Kahn & Averill, 1998.

Todes, S., *Body and World*, Cambridge, Mass, MIT Press, 2001.

Sperber, D., *Explaining Culture: A Naturalistic Approach*, Oxford, Blackwell, 1996.

Wegman, R. C., 'For Whom the Bell Tolls: Reading and Hearing: Busnoy's *Anthoni Usque Limina*' in Pesce, D. (ed.) *Hearing the Motet*, New York, Oxford University Press, 1997.

PART 3: The Role of the Curator: Contestation and Consideration

CURATING DOUBT

JJ Charlesworth

If the term 'curator' has been around for as long as there were bodies of objects and bodies of knowledge to preserve and perpetuate, its more active derivative 'curating' is a neologism so recent that dictionaries have not yet caught up. Curators continue to exist and perform the task of curating. Yet judging by the recurring and often circular discussions about the nature of curating, the identity of the 'artist-curator', the role of the independent curator, and the politics of 'self-reflexive' curating, all exist in a state of ongoing perennial uncertainty, in which fundamental, if now familiar, questions are rehearsed. Where does the distinction lie between artist and curator? Can we still distinguish artwork and curatorial production in a meaningful way? How do powerful art institutions police and control what gets seen? And how do artists and curators (independent, 'co-dependent' or otherwise) negotiate the hierarchies and divisions of power implicit in these distinctions or, as some would argue, their elimination?

The appearance of the curator as both an eminently present and authoritative figure in the landscape of contemporary art, and as a category of individual whose function is continuously questioned and revised, has become a ubiquitous feature in the world of contemporary art, leading to symposia on 'Curating Now', to special issues of art magazines devoted to 'Curating Now', whilst courses in curatorial studies are multiplying.[1] That the curator has become one of the most talked about and significant personalities within the cultural and institutional economy of contemporary art is worth reflecting on. It is not just a question of the rise of the celebrity curator, although of course the hyper-attention now devoted to curators turns the spotlight on curators of every rank and disposition, from Okwui Enwezor as director of *Documenta 11*, the appointment of a curator such as Hans-Ulrich Obrist at the Serpentine Gallery in London, or relative youngsters such as Jens Hoffman at the Institute of Contemporary Art. Curators and curatorial practice are now as visible as artists themselves.

This increase in attention is not merely the product of a more acute sensitivity to the appointment of people to powerful positions within art's institutions, although that does have something to do with it, especially with the unprecedented expansion of venues for the presentation of contemporary art that has characterized the last ten years, a trend particularly evident in the growth of international biennial exhibitions. More significant, however, is the attention paid to the character of the curatorial endeavour itself, as something not innocent or neutral, but loaded ideologically, epistemologically and institutionally, and in which a consideration of such implications are explicitly rehearsed by curators themselves. Tyler Stallings, one curator canvassed in the 'Curating Now' special issue of *Art Papers*, speaks for many when he describes the curator 'both as a custodian of artworks and as a cultural producer who facilitates projects. This approach obviously blurs a fine line as the curator also, in a way, becomes an artist.' These two lines make a deft summary of the combination of concerns that now operate as common currency in curatorial activity: an awareness of the traditional, if attenuated legacies of museology (custodianship) in tension with the realization of the active and partisan nature of presentation (producer), the ethical ambiguity of wielding this power (a curator 'facilitates' *as well* as 'produces'), and, finally, the practical and conceptual blurring that occurs because curatorship can also be seen as an authorial act or even – given that the presentation of art can now be understood as the synthesis of institution context and artistic content – the product of an 'artist' rather than a curator.

What these different positions describe is the convergence of a number of distinct critical trajectories and their growing assimilation by an ascendant class of practitioner within the art-world's professional structures, which themselves have been transformed by the experience of institutional expansion over the last decade. These critical trajectories have their various roots in the growing disenchantment with the assumptions that governed the presentation of art that fully emerged in the 1980s. Without pretending to offer a comprehensive summary of these trends, we can note a number of influential developments that contribute to contemporary curatorial consciousness. Amongst these are: the critical weight commanded by those artists whose reputation was established under the rubric of 'Institutional Critique'; the cultural significance of high-profile, large-scale exhibitions that put into question the explicit or implicit authorial role of the curator, such as the Centre Pompidou's *Les Magiciens de la Terre* (1989) and Jean-François Lyotard's curation of *Les Immateriaux* (1985); in the British context the destabilization of institutional certainties brought about by recession and the explosion of artist-run and 'DIY' models for artistic presentation; and the complication of the division of function and production between artist and curator that became the focus for that constellation of artists emerging in the 1990s who have become associated with the term 'Relational Aesthetics', the critical support lent by their association with the writer and curator Nicolas Bourriaud.[2]

These are no longer marginal concerns, but have become the history of the problematization of curatorial activity as it is understood by a more recent generation of curators. It's the kind of history that is a staple for those individuals emerging from the new and not-so-new postgraduate programmes in curation. And for that generation, 'self-reflexivity' has become a common term to describe the continuous questioning of all these traditional demarcations in recent practice. Yet at the same time, given that the assimilation of these various critiques of orthodox curatorial traditions comes at a time when the professional opportunities for independent or semi-independent curating have expanded, the emphasis is not on a radical confrontation with the imposition of curatorial and artistic orthodoxy in terms of the formation of institutional relations, but rather leads to the institutionalization of self-consciousness on the part of those who find themselves in the position 'to curate': for 'self-reflexivity', read 'self-awareness', 'self-doubt'.

The expanding, hyper-atrophied uncertainty that accumulates in current discourse on curating is a phenomenon peculiar to the present moment, in the sense that the constant navel-gazing on the part of curators into the terminological black hole that is 'contemporary curating' tends to produce more discussion about its undecidability and fluidity, rather than precipitating any serious theoretical crisis or professional rupture. As independent curator Paul O'Neill pointedly observed in *Art Monthly* 'we are becoming so self-reflexive that exhibitions often end up as nothing more or less than art exhibitions curated by curators curating curators, curating artists, curating artworks, curating exhibitions.'

What drives the expansion of this self-reflexive anxiety? By its nature, and as O'Neill's endlessly recursive Russian doll of curatorial-artistic repositioning suggests, it is not the preserve of professional or institutional curators as such, but has become a critical reflex among those artists and curators for whom the traditional division of artist and curator seems suspect. Such recursive critical manoeuvres could be found, for example, in an exhibition such as Liam Gillick's *Edgar Schmitz*, at London's Institute of Contemporary Arts, in December 2005. As the exhibition programme explained, the exhibition was conceived by the artist 'in response to an invitation by the Institute of Contemporary Arts to create the display for the exhibition *KIOSK* (a travelling archive of art publishing projects). Gillick extended this invitation in turn by asking London-based German artist Edgar Schmitz to collaborate with him on the creation of this project.' Gillick's recent work is exemplary in its exploration of the demarcation between orthodox definitions of the artist and curator, the work and everything else, as well as the institution's limitations and how this regulates what can be seen. As Gillick put it in 2001 at a debate held at the University of Newcastle, what interested him was the pursuit of a 'sub-curatorial activity' and the moments of 'expansion and compression' between the positions of artists and curator: 'When is the moment curatorial position expands into the broader field and when is the moment that the artistic one expands and vice versa, that is, where do they compress?' (Hiller and Martin 2002).

The interrogation of the lines of demarcation, of professional identity and self-identification and of institutional and critical boundaries, have since become common currency for the 'self-reflexive' in art and curating and bear witness to the influence of the various strands of critical activity noted above. Gillick is, of course, closely associated with Bourriaud and the pervasive profile of *Relational Aesthetics*. Add to this the growing acceptance of socially engaged art, in both its state-sponsored and politically oppositional guises: what emerges is a picture of a wide section of artistic practice whose terms of legitimacy rely on a critical opposition to orthodox formulations of gallery-bound, commercialized and institutionalized forms of artistic production and presentation. The problem with this is that the tendency to declare a critical opposition or circumvention of orthodox positions, given that those individuals who now share these positions now form part of the new class of curators, has itself become a new form of collective orthodoxy.

Similarly, the work of those artists of the 1960s and 1970s grouped under the banner of 'institutional critique' casts a long shadow on today's practitioners. Again, the problem for the self-conscious and self-reflexive curatorial practitioner becomes the very success of such critique in influencing contemporary thinking on practice. In her recent article, 'From the Critique of Institutions to an Institution of Critique', artist Andrea Fraser, stalwart advocate of the lasting critical potential of institutional critique, mounts a defensive response to those critics who charged it with having itself succumbed to 'institutionalization' (Fraser 2005). Inasmuch as institutional critique as an approach stands as an influential antecedent to current discussions on the critically self-reflexive in the presentation of art and the role of its institutions, Fraser's attempt to reassert its still radical potential is interesting. In order to rescue it from accusations of assimilation – the palpable sense that institutional critique is 'dead, a victim of its success or failure, swallowed up by the institution it stood against' – Fraser is at pains to develop the idea that the critique of the institution of art is not merely a matter of certain types of intervention into the physical context of the museum, gallery and artwork. Instead, it is an attack on the internalization of those orthodoxies within the *personnel* that make up the art world as a discursive institution. As Fraser would have it, the institution of art…

> is internalised in the competencies, conceptual models, and modes of perception that allow us to produce, write about, and understand art, or simply to recognize art as art, whether as artists, critics, curators, art historians, dealers, collectors, or museum visitors. (Fraser 2005)

There is, then, no outside to the institution of Fraser's critique. The troubling aspect of this (quite apart from the sense that the experience of artworks is merely the effect of the institution, without unaccountable remainder or any difficult excess) is Fraser's shift in emphasis from the particular critical effects of actual artworks on the ground, towards the notion that the orthodoxy of the institution of art is something we – meaning art world people – carry with us already:

> Every time we speak of the institution as other than 'us', we disavow our role in the creation and perpetuation of its conditions…It's not a question of being against the

institution: We are the institution. It's a question of what kind of institution we are, what kind of values we institutionalize, what forms of practice we reward, and what kinds of rewards we aspire to. (Fraser 2005).

One might be tempted to ask Fraser to speak for herself, and not implicate others in this guilt-ridden 'we'. But quite apart from all the cod-psychoanalysing about the 'internalisation' of institutional orthodoxies, her retrieval of a semblance of criticality for institutional critique by repositioning the 'institution' within the subjectivity of art's personnel has some truth to it; one which has relevance to the continued rehearsal of questions of self-reflexivity more broadly, and the question of who exactly is doing the 'self-reflexing'. In the sense that Fraser makes a claim for criticality as a form of insider self-consciousness about the limitations of art practice, with a strong element of guilt thrown in, her defence of institutional critique reflects a broader state of discontented self-awareness of the limits and potentials of art and its presentation, among those who make up its personnel. Fraser's defence of the legacy of institutional critique against those critics who would signal its failure through its assimilation by the institution is in one sense redundant. Whether one agrees or not that the art of institutional critique (Daniel Buren, Michael Asher, Hans Haacke *et al.*) has become co-opted by the institution, this is not so much the point. More interesting is Fraser's emphasis on the subjective nature of the critique of the institution – that it should be a product of 'internalisation'. The irony of this is that in terms of 'internalisation', the influence of institutional critique amongst curatorial practitioners is hardly negligible, so whilst one may take easy shots at the 'recuperation' of artists like Buren, the *success* of such critique is apparent *precisely* in its assimilation by practitioners who make up the art world's increasingly professionalized curatorial class.

In other words, 'self-reflexive' curating and art-making, that move in and out of visibility as they become interchangeable, are both symptoms of a chronic uncertainty surrounding the function of curating, as expressed by the expanding *cadre* of individuals charged with carrying out the function of curator, which is paradoxically expressed more volubly because of the rudely accruing health of that professional group. Curators may balk at the personalization of this problem and protest that there is more to curating than this. The point, however, is that if we choose to talk about an institution as a discursive field as well as a material system, the reflexivity of curating emerges as the uncertainty of curators regarding the definition of their institutional role. The common ambiguity towards 'authorship' makes sense if we understand it as a contradictory expression of personal freedom, and the intuition that authorship, as it translates into the reality of institutional production, slips readily into the more troubled question of authority and power. The argument regarding curating as art, or the *über*-curator as 'author', stems, therefore, from the lack of definition regarding the limits of curating, and the consequently troubling realization of the potentially unfettered power of the agency of curation. The reverse of this, the artist as curator, similarly emerges from the collapse of any viable distinction between the work of artists and the work of curators, whilst the professional and institutional distinction between them remains and is in the process of being professionalized further.

There is here an echo of a debate which has largely been overlooked in discussions about contemporary curating, that of the recent history of the artist-run exhibition space and curatorial practice. In the British context in particular, the disappearance of the artist-run model of curator-artist practice, epitomized by groups such as BANK in the early 1990s, was matched by an almost synchronous appearance of the independent curator as influential 'go-between'. Those curators relayed to large institutions, both public and private, the disparate developments of a new generation of artists, the lack of channels of communication with that community having hindered institutions' attempts to focus on such new work. The independent curator, foot-loose and untethered to the edifice of the major institution, but not subject to the vulnerability, lack of resources and marginality that characterized the artist-run space, may be seen uncharitably as a usurper of the more radical promise held out by artists running their own institutions of presentation.[3] The potential of the new curators as go-between brokers of cultural capital was noted early on by Simon Ford and Anthony Davies in their attack on the 'culturepreneur', although in their satirical future retrospective fictionalization, set in 2009, the function of 'curator' has been subsumed by their 'culturepreneur'. History is the best critic of science fiction; with two years to go, the curator is more omnipresent than in 1999, though whether he or she is now a 'culturepreneur' is of course the contention of Ford and Davies' argument.

In this sense, the ethical and moral ambiguity that surrounds expressions of the purpose of contemporary curatorial practice, by curators, is marked by the realization that whilst the investigation of the institutional ontology and politics of art's presentation has revealed the real possibility of an integrated practice of art in which producers (artists) might control the institutional context of presentation, this has not been realized in practice. If anything, and during the period in which the self-reflexive discussion on curating has emerged, the power of institutions has grown, both in the upgrading of the international temporary exhibition as final arbiter of the global artistic value, but also as large national institutions have reoriented their mission towards gaining greater audience share, a direction which in Britain has been encouraged by funding policy that has tended to prioritize larger institutions over smaller ones.

On the question of radical artistic self-determination it is clear that innovative curatorial practice remains ambiguous, inasmuch as any claim to a synthesis between artistic and curatorial agency has to be tested against the practical reality of who in reality now controls the output of an institution. Whilst such synthetic practice can be seen to function viably in smaller institutions, such as, for example, the ICA's programme under Jens Hoffman, it is not surprising that the bigger the venue, the stronger the pressure to impose the usual conservative demarcation between artists' practice and the business of curation, even if, as with the project *Utopia Station* at the 2003 Venice Biennale (curated by Hans Ulrich Obrist), the urge to acknowledge the promise of such a synthesis is given at least temporary symbolic realization. (Nor is it surprising that one of Hoffman's projects before his ICA tenure was entitled *The next Documenta should be curated by an artist*.) (http://www.e-flux.com/projects/next_doc/index.html).

The current realization in practice of what appears as 'reflexive' is, then, an effect of a self-conscious realization on the part of individuals of the continued power of curating as an institutional function and professional designation. It is located, in a context where the claims for curatorial cultural authority are no longer clear, and are further framed by a history of attempts to critique such power through an adjustment of the relationship between artist and institution, as much as a revision of the status *qua* cultural producer of both artist and curator. Who claims to curate, on behalf of whom, and on what terms? The heightened preoccupation with the authorial aspect of curating might be seen as a defensive reaction to the disappearance of shared critical and cultural values and criteria through which the institutional power of curating is mediated and legitimated. It is not surprising that the nomadic, culturally foot-loose independent curator should be the main source of expression of an individuated and personalized form of curating.[4]

This, then, is the product of the unfulfilled historical trajectory of a critique that has identified the problem as the division of power within the institutions of art, whilst being unable to resolve that division except in a symbolic form. More broadly, it is the product of a cultural epoch where claims to universal and general value are treated with suspicion, yet in which the institutions that previously staked their authority on such outmoded things as élite culture nevertheless continue to operate, but emptied of their previous *raison d'être*. In O'Neill's bleakly funny scenario – curators curating curators curating – what is not proposed is halting the production of exhibitions altogether, nor the return to traditional forms of curatorial practice, nor the transfer of power over curatorial functions to, for example, artists. In this regard one might point to O'Neill's own activities as an interesting counterpoint: *Mingle Mangled*, part of Cork Caucus, a festival of activity held at Cork, Ireland, in 2005, 'riffed' satirically on the popular notion of 'curator as DJ' by asking curators to make presentations about 'cultural re-mixing', in a nightclub (with both an art and club audience), on the condition that they followed them with an actual DJ set. A project that asserted a sense of lively contradiction, rather than an elision of cultural division lines, did so by confusing the proper function, competence and cultural allegiances of professionals who often declare a sentimental attachment to democratic, non-hierarchical and participatory forms of artwork, yet who pragmatically maintain the professional distinction that allow these moments of transgression to function.

The absent factor in this equation is of course the militant self-organization of artists against institutions. There is nothing new about this possibility: the experience of the Art Workers Coalition's demonstration against the policies of the Museum of Modern Art, New York, in 1969, is a classic, if rare, example of artists challenging the terms of practice maintained by the institutions of presentation. Whatever innovations may have occurred in the intervening 35 years, it still remains the case that artists have little direct influence over curatorial functionaries: that it should sound outlandish and fantastic to imagine a world in which artists might – for argument's sake – sack or appoint the director of the Tate, simply demonstrates how little has changed (Harrison and Wood 1992).[5]

Such contemporary and historical examples go against the tendency of consensus and deferral that underpins the culture of curatorial uncertainty. Curating, however much as curators choose to think critically about the institutional norms of artwork and exhibition, nevertheless still has to function practically, institutionally and bureaucratically, by making choices about what should and should not be shown, what is and is not worth the public's attention, and eventually reasserting the orthodox distinction between curator and artist, between who assesses and who produces, and who is subject to assessment. In short: value judgments articulated through the continued power of the institution. Notably, in our disoriented contemporary political and cultural landscape any discipline or profession can find itself perpetually 'in crisis', and continuously in need of reform, while those involved continue a semblance of 'business as usual'. A similar tension exists in the production of contemporary art, in which a curatorial culture of self-reflexivity and critical interrogation can co-exist more or less comfortably alongside persistent orthodox forms of presentation. This pluralizing cohabitation can be the only outcome of a cultural debate that has long ceased to argue over any certain definition of the function of art's institution, and has given up on the possibility of radical transformation of how things are organized.

As with many questions regarding culture and politics today, ideas that were once on the margins are now orthodoxies. If critical approaches to curating today draw on the radical legacies of the past, legacies that in their day opposed the hegemony of bourgeois cultural elitism and its discursive and institutional orthodoxies, simply do not hold sway today. Recurrent expressions of reflexive speculation about the nature of curating, the artwork and the institution by those who constitute it become ritual observances, not radical contestation, inasmuch as they might, in reality, only signify this: that uncertainty, provisionality, open-endedness and deferral are now the preferred orthodoxies of contemporary culture. While the critical impulse to re-shape art and its presentation is important – there is, of course, no blueprint, orthodox or otherwise, to what art should be – the self-reflexive preoccupation with the identity and status of artist, curator and institution plays on the symbolic negation of these positions, but paradoxically can only do so only by sustaining them in practice.

The dramatization of the self-reflexive defers endlessly critical debate on the actual, cultural potential and quality of definable artwork, and the authority and power of curatorial practice over the public space in which that potential is evaluated, justified and given legitimacy. If curating is to be more than a narcissistic display of an uncertain 'me, me, me', caught between wielding power over the presentation of art and the desire to produce it; between justifying power and abdicating it, a less self-reflexive discussion about institutional power, cultural freedom and artistic value is essential.

Notes

1. 'Curating Now: An international Symposium on Curating Contemporary Art in Public Museums and Galleries', held at the Irish Museum of Modern Art, 10–12 November 2004; and 'Curating Now' in *Art Papers*, Sept/Oct 2005 and Nov/Dec, 2005.

2. For an overview of the grouping of artists associated with *Relational Aesthetics*, see Claire Bishop's critical 'Antagonism and Relational Aesthetics', *October*, no. 110, fall 2004.
3. See 'Art Futures', *Art Monthly*, no. 223 (February 1999), pp. 9–11.
4. On the emergence of the 'authorial' mode of curation, see Nathalie Heinich and Michael Pollak, 'From Museum Curator to Exhibition *Auteu: inventing a singular position'*, in *Thinking about exhibitions*, Reesa Greenberg, Bruce W. Ferguson & Sandy Nairn, eds. Routledge, 1995.
5. See 'Art Workers' Coalition: Statement of Demands', in *Art in Theory 1900–1990*, Harrison & Wood, (eds.) Blackwell, 1992.

References

Bourriaud, N., *Relational Aesthetics*, Les Presses du Réel, Dijon, 2002.

Fraser, A., 'From the Critique of Institutions to an Institution of Critique', *Artforum International* v. 44 no. 1 (September 2005).

Hiller, S. and Martin, S. (eds.), *The Producers: Contemporary Curators in Conversation*, BALTIC, 2002.

A Parallel Universe: The "Women's" Exhibitions at the ICA, 1980, and the UK/Canadian Film and Video Exchange, 1998–2004

Catherine Elwes

'The brilliance of *Women's Images of Men* was that it fused three issues that had been fermenting for some time – the rebirth of figurative art, the use of arts as a vehicle for political comment and the emergence of women artists as an important force in the art world.'

Sarah Kent, 1985

The women's exhibitions

It has been my curatorial lot in life to combat, with varying degrees of success, the condition of relative artistic invisibility, my own and that of those whose concerns and strategies I have shared over the years. Women artists in the 1970s and early 1980s suffered widespread discrimination that resulted in their muted presence in the art world. In 1978, a small group of artist-curators became determined to mitigate that erasure and began research towards a series of major exhibitions of women's art. I will attempt to link that project to the work I have been doing in the last six years on the UK/Canadian Film and Video Exchange, a biennial event that is committed to promoting the work of moving image artists from both sides of the Atlantic.[1]

Of course, there are many contextual differences between the two ventures and the world has changed a good deal between the late 1970s and the new millennium. In the early years, feminist curating and what we used to call woman-identified art formed part

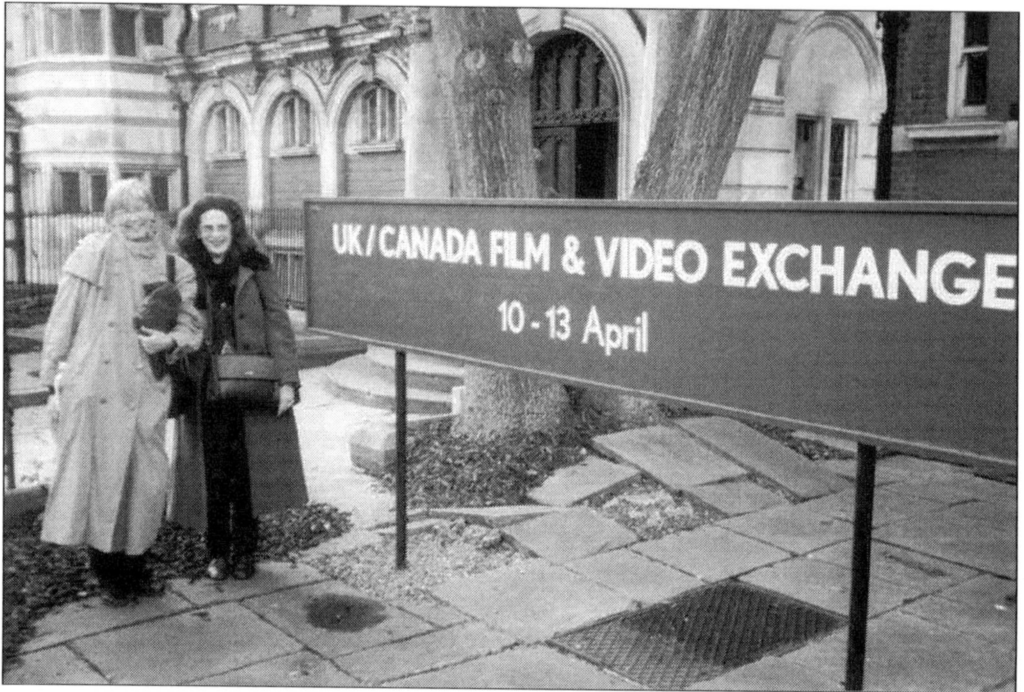

Figure 1. Catherine Elwes with the Canadian artist Val Klassen outside the South London Gallery, 2004. Photo: Uwe Ackerman.

of an organized movement with clear social and political goals. Nowadays, art is only tangentially allied to political activism in spite of the egalitarian pretensions of work inspired by Bourriaud's *Relational Aesthetics*.[2] The various environmental and anti-globalization movements are visible and vociferous but few artists in the new century ally their practice directly to these causes. Although some would hope to raise awareness of today's critical issues, few would claim that their work is likely to bring about change. Sam Taylor-Wood expressed the disaffection with political art that was widespread in the 1990s when she asked, 'Why offer hope when in many instances there isn't any hope. I'm showing things how they are.' (Sam Taylor-Wood in Stallabrass 1999).

In the 1970s, feminist artists still believed that change was achievable. They were determined to overturn the discriminatory practices of curators and art historians that meant they were hidden from history as well as invisible in the cultural landscape of their time. In parallel with the obscurity of women artists, there operated, in the 1970s, the marginalization of figurative art. Painting was dominated by abstraction in its various forms, and the avant-garde, including the feminist avant-garde, favoured crypto-visual installations with an emphasis on theory. As Sarah Kent wrote, figurative pictures were 'held by avant-garde artists and critics to be innately conservative and hopelessly individualistic.' (Kent 1985) Nowhere was it argued that representational work 'could be used to make cogent political comment.' (Kent 1985) As we discovered, it was mainly figuration that provided an outlet for the creative energies of women whose work was unseen and unexhibited. For those working in performance and moving image art, the picture was similar. Although active on the margins of the avant-garde, they were restricted to working in alternative artist-run spaces and at ephemeral international festivals.

Today, few argue that women are debarred from the art world although Tracey Emin has recently bemoaned the disparity between the modest prices fetched at auction for women's art and those of their male counterparts. Figuration is no longer discredited and no one claims that the moving image is peripheral to the mainstream – in fact, video has emerged from its position as a rogue, avant-garde practice to become the default medium of the twenty-first century. However, as is so often the case, the contemporary art world only offers visibility to the few and the practices of three generational groups remain marginal, if not altogether invisible. Many of the first- and most of the second-generation experimental film and video-makers from the late 1960s, 1970s and 1980s and an army of college leavers who have yet to catch the attention of today's curators, occupy a kind of underground or parallel universe to mainstream museum and gallery

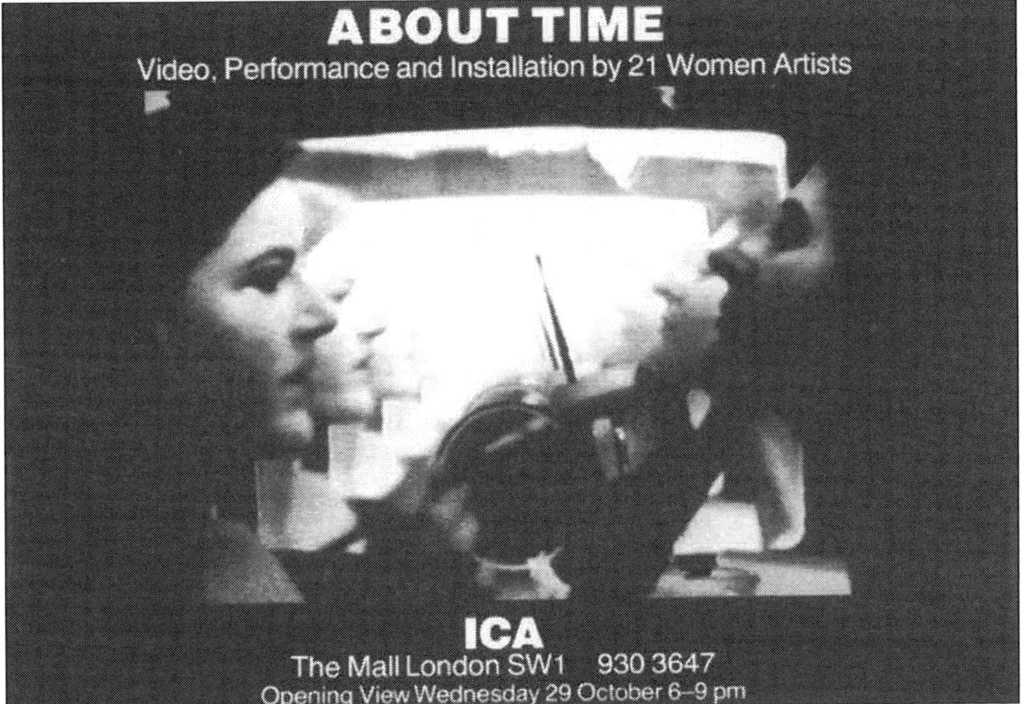

Figure 2. Poster for *About Time*, ICA, London, 1980.

culture. It is these groups that we have been committed to representing in the UK/Canadian Video Exchange.

Many of the curating principles that we apply to the Canadian Exchange were born in the feminist art movement to which I belonged in the late 1970s. In order to illuminate those doctrines, I shall describe in more detail how the *Women's Images of Men, About Time* and *Issue* shows came to the ICA in 1980. Statistics may often be 'damned lies', but they can also be revealing. In the UK, the 1977 Hayward Annual showed 34 men and only 3 women. In the 1978 Hayward Annual, the situation was reversed and 7 men exhibited alongside 16 women. This apparent change of fortune for women was due to the energetic lobbying of feminists who, that year, succeeded in persuading the Hayward to establish a selection panel comprising 5 women. Having 'done' what was considered to be the 'Women's' Hayward Annual, two years later in what was the third Hayward Annual, the Gallery showed 32 men and 2 women. This was the same year that the women's shows took place at the ICA, sparking an explosion of women's exhibitions across London including a show of painting at the ACME Gallery curated by Claire Smith and a *Salon des Refusées* in an independent gallery in South London. By a process of osmosis, an unplanned festival of women's art took place in London in 1980. Just as we were congratulating ourselves that we had turned the tide of fortune

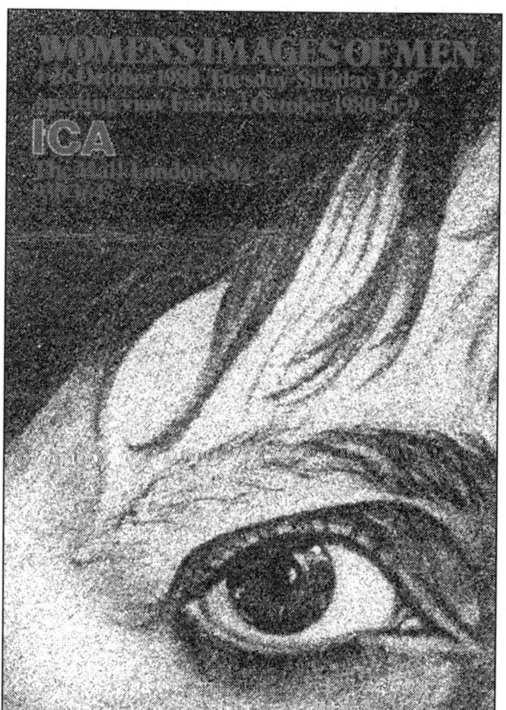

Figure 3. Poster for *Womens' Images of Men*, ICA, London, 1980.

for women artists, the curators of the 1981 *New Spirit in Painting* exhibition at the Royal Academy selected 38 men and no women at all. We appeared to be living in a world of mainstream tokenism and inevitable backlash that followed early feminist activism, in the arts as elsewhere.

It is in the context of this struggle for visibility that, in the late 1970s, a group of women converged on the Women's Arts Alliance, the first and, to my knowledge, the last women's gallery in London. In 1978, just as we were enjoying the supportive experience of a women-only environment, learning drumming and arguing about the feasibility of separatism in the context of giving birth to male children, the ICA distracted us by putting on an exhibition by the sculptor Allen Jones. Jones's well-known equation of the fetishized female body with furniture particularly outraged the artist Nina Jennings who promptly organized a protest outside the ICA. Benefiting greatly from the additional publicity Nina's protest was exciting, Bill McAlister, the incumbent director of the ICA, came out to confront his feminist critics. Nina and her supporters demanded to know why he continued to show such sexist horrors while denying women artists proper representation in his gallery. His exact words are not recorded, but his reply expressed the view that there existed in 1978 no work by women of any value. He then challenged Nina to bring him an exhibition of a quality and ambition to match that of Allen Jones. Then, he declared, he would show it. Nina returned to the Alliance flush with her successful protest at the ICA and put before us the challenge that the director had so confidently thrown down. A committee immediately formed comprising Jacqueline Morreau, Pat Whiteread (mother of Rachel), Joyce Agee and myself.

Our quest was to find works in which women's relationship to men, both as individuals and as a social group, were examined within a figurative tradition, (whilst never compromising that nebulous term 'quality' for the power of the content). For two years we visited women artists in their studios, but more often in their living rooms and kitchens where the vast majority of them produced their work. They generously provided us with slides of their pictures and sculptures, which we then used to support our approaches to galleries. Needless to say, we were turned down by the ICA, then by the Serpentine and various other prominent galleries. However, when Sandy Nairne became curator of exhibitions at the ICA and the critic Sarah Kent and feminist art historian Lisa Tickner took up our cause, we had better luck. The ICA finally agreed to put on two exhibitions, one for painting, sculpture and photography and a second for performance and installation accompanied by a series of film and video screenings. The ICA's one proviso was that *Issue*, the final show in the series, would be curated by the American critic Lucy Lippard.

Women's Images of Men opened in 1980 and was enthusiastically taken up by the mainstream media because of the controversy caused by the substitution of art history's tradition of men looking at women with those same women daring to look back at men. The viewer was now viewed and repositioned as the object of the female gaze. This upset many male

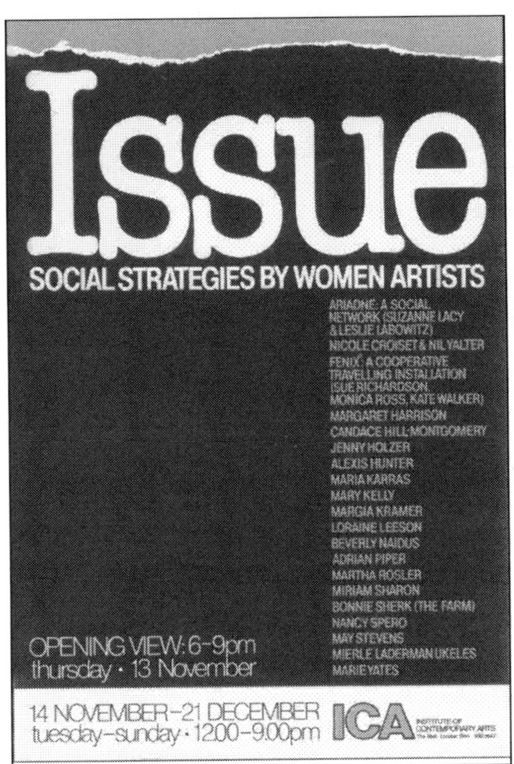

Figure 4. Poster for *Issue*, ICA, London.

critics, particularly Waldemar Januszczak who saw only 'a sea of penises' when he visited the show. Writing in *The Guardian* on 3rd October, Januszczak protested, 'an aura of sensationalism, of penises for penises' sake, underlines the savagery with which some of the exhibitors have entered the arena.' In fact, there was very little genital display among the paintings, sculptures and photographs but enough to precipitate Waldemar's outburst. I could describe at great length the reception of *Women's Images of Men, About Time* and *Issue* in the press and among the general public, but instead I will focus on some less well-publicized curatorial peculiarities of these exhibitions.[3]

The late 1970s was the era of collectives, of non-hierarchical organizations that in the case of women's art groups took a stand against the individualism that underpinned what was perceived to be a male art world.[4] As anyone with a long enough memory will recall, working in a collective is difficult enough, but when an attempt is made to amalgamate a non-hierarchical cluster of individuals with an establishment gallery, further problems can arise. The ICA, probably with the best of intentions, put pressure on us to nominate a 'leader' who would speak for the group particularly when dealing

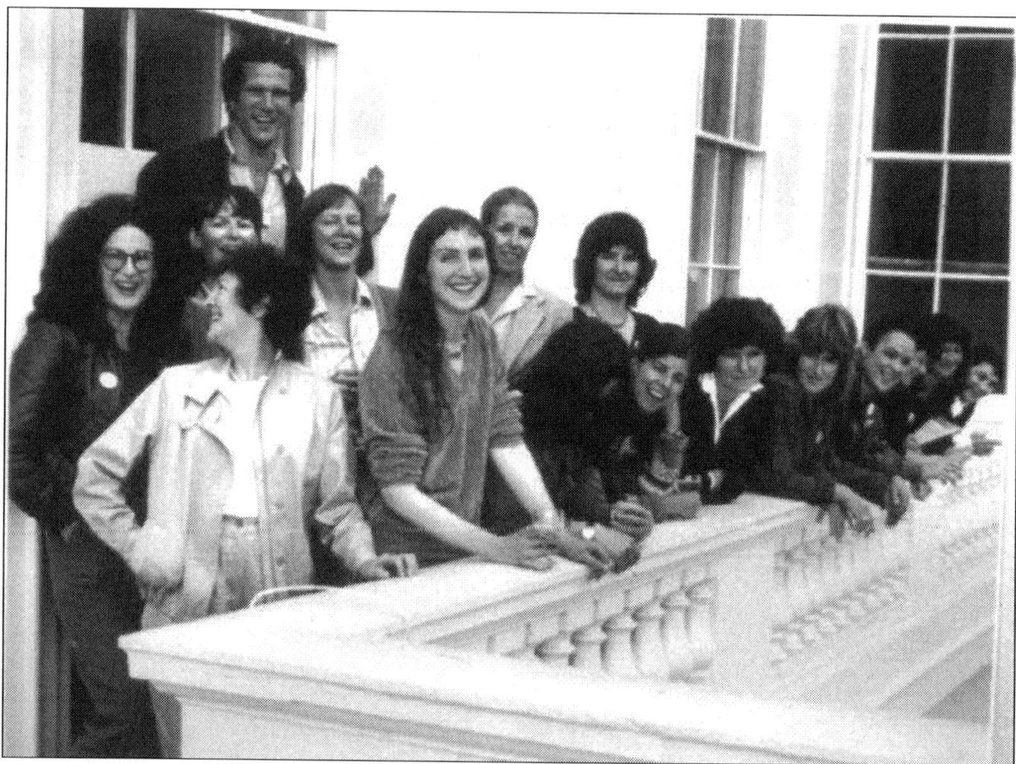

Figure 5. Sandy Nairne with artists from the women's shows including Catherine Elwes, Pat Whiteread, Judith Kazantis, Sarah Kent, Deborah Low, Zoe de Ropp, Margaret Harrison, Alexis Hunter, Lisa Tickner, Jackie Morreau. Photo: Joyce Agee.

with the media. Probably for reasons of my upper middle-class accent, they decided that I would fit the bill. As a hard-line collective, we resolutely resisted this pressure and insisted on executing a quadruple act in any public situation. We certainly made our point about egalitarian principles but in the long term this insistence on collectivism led to historical distortions. Since no single woman came forward to claim curatorial authorship of *Women's Images of Men* and *About Time*, periodically, other women have been credited with the project. The effects that our strategy had on memory was recently demonstrated by Iwona Blazwick (then Sandy Nairne's assistant) when she spoke on Radio 4 about the exhibitions. The only name she could remember from 1978 was Lucy Lippard. On the other hand, Rachel Whiteread never loses the opportunity to publicly pay tribute to her mother's involvement in the struggle for recognition of women's art. The flickering presence of these exhibitions in the canon of art history demonstrates the importance of establishing 'personalities' on which to hang initiatives, a principle that the following generation came to understand so well. Our collective stuck to its egalitarian principles, but paid the price of historical obscurity.

As we all know, in the retrospective eyes of history, an exhibition is consigned to oblivion unless it is supported by reviews, academic endorsements in the form of articles and papers and, nowadays, a conference, a book and several Ph.D.'s must be added to the literature of approval. The work in *About Time* consisted mostly of performance and installation, so unless it was reviewed, nothing would remain other than inadequate photo or video documentation and the scattered memories of audience members who happened to be there on the day. As I have mentioned, *Women's Images of Men* enjoyed enormous critical attention, *About Time* somewhat less, and, interestingly, Lucy Lippard's *Issue* show was barely reviewed in the mass media while attracting serious debate in the art journals. There was no other solution for those of us in the *About Time* show but to review each other's performances, to write our own history. This is how I began writing about art – out of necessity.

The UK/Canadian Film & Video Exchange
Iliyana Nedkova (2002) has discussed exhibitions that are curated by groups of people who relate along what she calls 'friendship lines'. These initiatives are driven, she says, by 'the engine of friendship'. The women's exhibitions at the ICA were driven by the engine of a common subjection to a patriarchal society in general and a male-dominated art world in particular. We were united in adversity. Friendship was something else.

Some twenty years after the women's exhibitions, the UK/Canadian Film & Video Exchange became an enterprise that was undoubtedly driven by a strong element of international friendship if not love, but it was created by another engine, the engine of history. The individual who served as a lynchpin to the project was Stuart Marshall. Stuart was a pioneering UK video artist, influential teacher and theoretician who consolidated one of the first experimental fine art departments at Newcastle Polytechnic in 1973. He was also one of the first UK artists to make work for television and the first individual to devise programmes about the newly discovered illness that came to be known as AIDS. Stuart taught me at the Royal College of Art and included my work in the first Canadian Exchange in 1984. One of the other exhibitors was Maggie Warwick, also originally a student at the RCA. In Canada, Stuart had many friends, among them Lisa Steele, one of the founders of Vtape, Toronto, an artist-run video production and distribution agency that is roughly equivalent to London Video Arts that now forms part of the LUX. It would be fair to say that Stuart Marshall was not only widely respected but also greatly loved by all those who knew him on both sides of the Atlantic. Our connections through Stuart were formalized when Lisa Steele wrote a review of the UK work in the 1984 Exchange in which she was particularly kind about my own tapes (Steele 1984). Twenty years later, Maggie Warwick was appointed Director of Film, Video and Television at the Canadian High Commission in London.

All these threads came together when I visited Toronto in the late 1990s to locate the offices of Vtape and inquire whether Lisa Steele was still employed there. That was ten years ago, and Maggie, Lisa and I have been working on the re-launched UK/Canadian Exchange ever since dedicating our efforts, in part, to the memory of Stuart Marshall who died of AIDS-related complications in 1993.

The contemporary Canadian video scene is somewhat different from the gallery-dominated and ubiquitous video phenomenon we have in the UK. Canada preserves the national network of production and distribution collectives that was more characteristic of the UK in the 1970s and early 1980s. It was easy, therefore, for Maggie and myself to join with Lisa and form another non-hierarchical alliance that periodically called in a number of collaborators from across the Continent who were prepared to slot in with us on equal terms. Over the years, an important characteristic of the curatorial process subtending the Exchange has been the degree of forgiveness that we apply in all our interactions. We allow ourselves to speak out of turn, take risks and when I bungled a somewhat critical aspect of our last UK tour, my colleagues were gracious enough to forgive me. In contrast to my experience of curating the 'women's exhibitions' in 1980, this democratic, 'flat' organization created no institutional problems even when we staged the last Exchange at the South London Gallery in 2003. The only jitter in the proceedings came when the gallery feared Southwark Council might shut us down on account of a homoerotic work by John Greyson that could easily have been condemned as obscene.

Another aspect of Canadian video that contrasts with the UK or the USA is the muted sense of a star system. Although one or two artists like Stan Douglas and Michael Snow have earned international reputations, the vast majority of Canadian video makers are relatively well known in their own country but are only now beginning to find audiences overseas – I like to think, partly through the offices of the Exchange. State sponsorship continues to support local activity and comparatively little commercial money is at stake. In Canadian experimental video, there is also a distinct absence of a generation gap, a gap that is fuelled in this country by commercial galleries who need to market the work of younger video artists on the basis of the exchange-value of newness. This is easier to achieve when the history of the medium remains obscure. In Canada there is less of a premium placed on youth culture inside the world of moving image and most events, screenings and exhibitions include work from established artists as well as mid-career artists and emergent talent. This sense of inclusiveness paralleled our own natural political instincts and we have adopted it as our guiding principle in our curatorial work with the Exchange.

Our curatorial policy has varied across the three Exchanges we have organized to date. However, certain elements remain constant. In common with the ICA shows and the egalitarian principles we adhered to at the time, the curators were paid nothing and all the artists earned the same fee. Although the UK/Canadian Exchange has concentrated on the work of mature but more marginal or emerging artists, we have not deliberately excluded those who have prominent gallery careers. However, many of these have excluded themselves either because their galleries were demanding fees substantially in excess of our flat rate or, as a matter of principle, they do not participate in group shows. However, this was by no means a universal response. Sam Taylor-Wood contributed her piece *Brontosaurus* to the Exchange 2000 and the Chapman brothers showed their tape, *Sacrifice, Mutilation and Death in Modern Art*, a puppet rendition of art disasters up to and including Jackson Pollock's infamous car crash.

The role of the curator
'Curators should understand their position in the food chain.'

James Lingwood (2002)

The Women's shows at the ICA and the Canadian Exchanges were collaborative, non-hierarchical curatorial projects. As a result, all decisions were made by consensus. How well this works as a long-term strategy is debatable. But as a way of bringing to a close my account of curatorial experiences, past and present, I would like to discuss briefly the issue of whether curating constitutes a creative activity on a par with the art itself, as has been frequently suggested in recent years.

Brian Sewell observed that the 2003 Venice Biennale prioritized the ideas of curators over those of artists. 'It was like going to a boxing match', he wrote, one in which 'the managers were in the ring instead of the pugilists' (Sewell 2003). Artists have also trespassed on curatorial territory, adopting a kind of appropriative strategy, collecting existing artworks and influences for their work like postmodern magpies. In his recent ICA exhibition, the artist John Bock used found-footage of films by Kurt Kren and videos by Mike Kelly and Vito Acconci in his adventure playground-style installation. Sarah Pucill has made a film that includes homages to the women artists who have influenced her over the years. Closer to home, I was recently approached by a young American artist who appeared to be collecting feminists for the purpose of legitimizing his singular attitude towards homosexuality. Whether all this appropriative activity constitutes homage or cannibalism is open for debate, but there appears to be taking place a fusion of curatorial and art practices whether carried out by curators or by the artists themselves. Practitioners like Jeremy Deller, Cornford & Cross, Nina Pope and Karen Guthrie hark back to artists such as Christo and consider the planning, negotiation and administration of their projects to be part of the work. Since all the curators in the ICA shows and the Exchanges were artists, that might also be true of my own colleagues, but the business of arts administration, I would suggest, has been part of our lives – not an intrinsic element of our individual practices as artists.[5] As women in the 1980s, we would first have to attain the status of artists before the notion of recasting that profession in some other mould could constitute a secure move. Deller may act as a sort of art events impresario, but this does not in any way undermine his status as an artist.

I for one have always thought of my work as a curator to be separate from my activities as an artist. My colleague Steven Ball has pointed out to me that this assertion denies the importance of the aesthetic and sometimes political choices that are made when programming film and video screenings.[6] The juxtaposition and re-contextualization of individual works can substantially manipulate and alter meanings and the grouping of works into thematic screenings also tends to narrow the attention to particular aspects of a work. A kind of internal dialogue is set up between the works, a dialogue that creates resonances or even dissonances that would not occur under different conditions. My own view is that such internal dynamics are a by-product of the skills that a programmer brings to bear with a certain knowledge of her audience. We are still, at some level, entertainers and might want to avoid boring our audiences as far as possible. Overall, I think of myself as a kind of jobbing curator whose principal role is that of advocate for the ambitions and intentions of the artists. Like a dresser or a make-up artist, I try to show them off to their best advantage by placing them in an appropriate cultural environment. I raise money, write articles about their work for the catalogues, find places for them to stay and organize talks in which they can meet their audiences. In the end, I am in the business of making the artists visible in an often hostile and exclusive art world. None of us makes work to gather dust on a shelf, we all make work to be seen. I do not wish to eclipse the artists we show and I share James Lingwood's view that a little curatorial self-effacement goes a long way. If I have any creative energy left at the end of the day, I channel it into my own practice. And then of course, because I am not absolutely altruistic in my curating activities, I often use the shows I help to create as an opportunity to make visible my own practice.

To conclude...
The strategies we adopted in the late 1970s in the context of a feminist movement in art have continued to serve us well in the 1990s and beyond in our work on the UK/Canadian Exchanges. The practice of non-hierarchical curatorial collaborations allows us to counter the celebrity status of curators and maintain the focus on the work of the artists we wish to bring to a wider audience. The emphasis on overlooked practices and practitioners, both mature and emergent, allows us to make links between generations that do not validate one group at the expense of the other. The equal status

accorded to each artist, both in terms of time-space allocation and payment helps to instigate a sense of community in an art world in which the gap between the stars and the rank and file has grown wider in the years following the demise of what are easily dismissed as idealistic collective exhibition practices in the 1960s and 1970s.

Notes

1. The current Exchange has joined forces with ANALOGUE, a project initiated by myself and Dr Chris Meigh-Andrews. Early video by Canadian, British and Polish artists will be exhibited in December 2006 at Tate Modern, Tate Britain and will tour to FACT, The Norwich Art Gallery and venues in Poland and Canada.
2. See Nicholas Bourriaud, *Relational Aesthetics*, Les presses du réel, 2002. Even the mild-mannered politics of contemporary artists can fluster mainstream critics and it was with relief that Michael Glover, writing in the *Times* on 20th October, 2004, was able to applaud the supposedly political selection of this year's Turner prize. None of them was 'poker-face and humourless' and Yinka Shonibare 'managed to combine cultural and political criticism with a taste for visual extravagance'. Thank goodness.
3. There is a full description of media responses to the women's exhibitions in *Women's Images of Men* (1985).
4. One of the most influential texts in this context was Linda Nochlin's 'Why have there been no great women artists?' in *Art and Sexual Politics*, eds. Thomas B. Hess and Elizabeth C. Baker, Collier Books, 1975.
5. I have to exclude Maggie Warwick from this list. She is indeed an administrator, agent and commissioner, but, like all of us, she trained as an artist.
6. Steven Ball is Senior Research Fellow at the British Artists' Film & Video Study Collection, Central Saint Martins, UAL. His comments were made in conversation with the author.

References

Bourriaud, N., *Relational Aesthetics*, Les presses du réel, 2002.

Cook, S., Graham, B., Martin, S., (eds.) *Curating New Media*, Baltic, 2002.

Elwes, C., *Video Art: a guided tour*, I.B. Tauris, 2005

Elwes, C., *Video Loupe*, KT Press, 2000.

Elwes, C and Morreau, J., 'Lighting a Candle', in *Women's Images of Men*, Kent, S. and Morreau, J., (eds.) Writers & Readers, 1985.

Hess, T. B and Baker, E. C. (eds.), *Art and Sexual Politics*, Collier Books, 1975.

Kent, S and Morreau, J. (eds.), *Women's Images of Men*, Writers and Readers, 1985.

Kent, S., 'Scratching and Biting Savagery' in *Women's Images of Men*, ibid.

Nedkova, I., 'Consolations for Curatorial Inadequacy' in *Curating New Media*, Baltic, 2002.

Steele, L., 'Mythologies and Militarism, just some women trying to change history', *Fuse* magazine, Toronto, 1984.

Sewell, B., *A Venetian bind*, The Evening Standard, September, 2003.

Stallabrass, J., *High Art Lite: British Art in the 1990s*, Verso, 1999.

THOUGHTS ON CURATING

Richard Hylton

Introduction

The invitation to discuss curating seems to me to warrant something more than merely talking about my projects. I would like to view two quite different contexts for my work as a curator. The first will focus on some of my projects at Autograph and the second will focus on an independent project. Prior to discussing some of the projects I have been involved with it might be useful to briefly contextualize my approach to curating, by providing a backdrop to some of its wider issues. Most of my experience has been within the public sector working in municipal, university, or so-called independent spaces, therefore, this is the area I feel most able to comment on. I would like to briefly consider two seemingly unrelated things: firstly, the politics of the professionalized 'curator' and, secondly, the politics of inclusion vis-à-vis public funding. In some ways these two entities seem to typify for me some of the broader problems around the contemporary visual arts terrain.

The curator

My first opportunity to work in the visual arts came in 1990 through an Arts Council Curatorial Traineeship. Established during the 1980s, this programme had been an ongoing strategy to enable art graduates to enter into the visual arts sector. My traineeship took place at the Laing Art Gallery in Newcastle for eighteen months during which time I was encouraged to travel and develop my own major contemporary art project. Around the time I was a trainee, the Arts Council was establishing an MA in Curating at the Royal College of Art (in collaboration with Middlesex University). This course was soon followed by the MA in curating at Goldsmiths College (which was not initiated by the Arts Council). Whilst the growth of the artist-led initiative represents one form of curating, it has been the greater prominence given to curating or to the 'curator' as the instigator of genre exhibitions which has become the source of constant discussion.

One example of this fascination with curating was explored in the project *PILOT: 1 International Art Forum*, London, 16–18 October 2004, which coincided with the *Frieze Art Fair* at the Old Limehouse Town Hall in East London. *PILOT: 1* comprised a number of elements. A group exhibition selected by over 70 artists, curators, writers, collectors and practitioners and featuring artists 'not yet commercially represented' (*International Art Forum*, Introduction, accompanying publication produced as part of the exhibition, DOUBLEPLUSGOOD BOOKS, 2004). The project also included a round-table discussion 'as a way of interrogating the event as well as looking into issues of autonomy economy and notions of democracy' (www.pilotlondon.org/2004/introduction). In the small publication produced to accompany the project, three questions were put to artists and curators alike, including why curating become perceived as an academicized practice and what effects this has had.

In response, the artist and curator Mark Wilsher noted:

> It's just another part of the current over-professionalisation of the art-world, offering a reliable wage and social status to those who like to jump through government funding hoops. (Ibid. 2004)

Whilst Greg Hilty, then Head of Arts Council England's Art and Literature Department, stated:

> Insofar as curating has become an academicised practice, it has heightened awareness of the curator alongside those of the artist and the producer. As the practice of curating becomes more professionalised, these responsibilities will begin to be fulfilled. (Ibid. 2004)

To a degree, I have to agree with Mark Wilsher. The professionalization of curating has prepared vast numbers of curators to deal with the particular requirements of arts-related public funding. However, it also seems to me that rather than creating a broader differentiation of what is good, interesting practice, the ubiquitous 'curator' has merely created a far more consensual and emphatic idea about what the mainstream should be, both commercial and inclusive. Is the function of courses such as Goldsmiths and the Royal College to produce curators to service the agendas of art institutions such as those which overlook the Thames and the Tyne? Despite much discussion about the 'curator' and the 'über-curator', major publicly funded galleries have become more rigid in their programming (and employment) policies – namely, superficially inclusive and exclusively commercial. The art world is part of the context of globalized economies, and the proliferation of curating courses has now, unsurprisingly, taken on an international dimension. The introduction material for the conference, *Curating can be learned, but can it be taught?*, held at the Northern Gallery for Contemporary Art Gallery, Sunderland, reveals that since the establishment of L'Ecole du Magasin in Grenoble in the 1980s, there has been an exponential rise in the number of academic curatorial courses across Europe and the USA, yet this seems to have merely compounded the trend of regulating exhibition programming and curating. The impression exists that no matter which international exhibition or biennale you go to, chances are you will see many of the same participating artists.

Inclusion culture

Since the National Lottery's arrival in the mid-1990s and the Arts 4 Everyone [A4E] scheme in 1994, it was decided that art should be for 'everyone', the idea of an inclusive art world has become increasingly central to the rhetoric of the public arts funding system. Although this scheme was brought in under John Major's Conservative government, the emphasis on 'access' and participation has arguably intensified under New Labour. Publicly funded galleries now appear more than ever to be *seen* to address particular notions of inclusion and central to this strategy has been the promotion of cultural diversity. Public funding for the arts 'cultural diversity' has, from time to time, been used to address anyone who is not white, middle class, able-bodied and heterosexual. (See London Arts, Cultural Diversity Action Plan June 2001.) However, cultural diversity in the visual arts has now undoubtedly become synonymous with that most dubious of constructs: the 'culturally diverse artist'. If the proliferation of the 'curator' has not necessarily guaranteed a more differentiated mainstream, the attempts at making it appear inclusive seems to be ever more fixated with just that, appearance. However, in England, Black and Asian artists remain largely excluded from (or limited by being 'racially' categorized within) the mainstream. Seemingly ever increasing levels of provision provided in the shape of separatist funding and employment opportunities does much to perpetuate rather than challenge the status quo. In terms of employment alone this remains decidedly skewed in favour of white middle-class people who in turn champion a system that ostensibly treats Black and white artists very differently.

Curating at Autograph

I should point out that over the past fifteen years, since leaving art education, I have been relatively fortunate in developing and sustaining not only a curatorial practice, but also employment within the visual arts sector. For a variety of reasons, I do not underestimate this achievement. I should also point out that as a curator, I do not see myself as solely responsible for generating ideas for projects and as such, when running spaces, I have facilitated the work of other curators and artists.

Having completed a curatorial Fellowship at the University of Bradford in 1999, I joined Autograph (The Association of Black Photographers) as a curator. Established in 1988 by photographers Armet Francis, Sunil Gupta and Monica Baker, historically Autograph was an attempt to challenge and confront the exclusion of Black photographers from the mainstream. It 'was launched with the aim to set up a national centre to house the work of photographers of non-European descent in the UK and to initiate a dialogue with photographers worldwide.' (www.autograph-abp.co.uk/events, 2005.) Autograph became a production agency which specialized in developing exhibitions, publications and residencies. It began to provide a profile and visibility for photographers and particular photographic practices that had largely been ignored. From exhibitions such as *Self-Evident* at the Ikon Gallery, Birmingham, UK, 12 August-16 September 1995 and *Africa by Africa: A Photographic View*, Barbican Art Gallery, London, 28 January-29 March 1999 to its production of artists' monographs, Autograph and its collaborating institutions not only supported work which might not have ordinarily been supported, it also afforded some artists the sort of respect and attention rarely offered by the mainstream.

When I joined Autograph in 1999, the idea of photography and the photographer had undergone some significant changes in relation to the visual art sector. Not only was photography being more widely used by artists as well as those who would call themselves photographers, but also, galleries were programming in ways which seemed to increasingly blur traditional boundaries between fine art and photography. Furthermore, from the late 1990s, we had witnessed the demise of galleries such as Camerawork and Cambridge Darkroom and magazines such as *Ten-8* and *Creative Camera*. In tandem with these shifts, the politics of representation had itself undergone some transformation through the 1990s. The old notions of inclusion/exclusion, political certainties of gender, class and race, which had provided the impetus for organizations such as Autograph, had also slowly begun to unravel.

In his essay 'Ethnicity and Internationality: New British Art and Diaspora-Based Blackness' (Mercer 1999–2000), Kobena Mercer expressed the view that artists such as Chris Ofili and Steve McQueen as well as Permindar Kaur and the late Hamad Butt were 'fully congruent with the return of the "crux" of Pop, Minimalism and Conceptualism, their highly individualised projects mark out a strong contrast with the collectivise (sic) ethos of the Eighties.' (Ibid., 1999–2000) He also states that the 'Nineties generation of black British artists were neither invisible nor excluded from the hyper ironic "attitude" in which the yBa was immersed.' (Ibid., 1999–2000) Despite the existence of groups such as Black Audio Film Collective or Sankofa, or art journals such as *Third Text* and *Artrage*, it is arguable whether the 1980s were ever as collective as they may now be read. There are examples in the 1980s when artists were thinking more as individuals than as politically astute collectives. Despite the growing tendency of publicly funded galleries in England to exclude their work, many were content with participating in a wide range of initiatives which not only assisted in further marginalizing their practices, but also justified the tokenism of the visual arts sector.

In placing visual arts within a broader political context, Mercer noted that 'New Labour's project to modernise all aspects of society nonetheless resulted in the retro-centric idiom of Cool Britannia' (ibid., 1999–2000). He also claimed that 'Diversity is now normal, not "special"' and that 'Cultural difference appears more visibly integrated into mainstream markets than even before, but it is accompanied by a privatised ethos in which it is no longer an "issue" for public debate.' (Ibid., 1999–2000) If this was the case, how could Autograph remain relevant to both funding and artistic agendas? The concept of diversity had by the beginning of the twenty-first century (along with the ramifications of the MacPherson Report) begun to affect how the Arts Council saw an organization like Autograph. From years of standstill funding, during the late 1990s, all talk began to focus on funding increases from both the Arts Council and what was then London Arts. There was also the offer of capital expenditure towards buying a building with the Institute of International Visual Arts (inIVA) – Rivington Place is the purpose-built building designed by architect David Adjaye which houses both inIVA and Autograph. Whilst this shift may have, for some, represented years of hard toil and well-earned recognition, it also represented, for me at least, the very problematic nature of an increasingly and overly paternalistic funding system. Between 1999 and 2003, the Arts Council was increasingly promoting its notion of cultural diversity within the arts. Whilst Autograph kept its distance from initiatives such as *decibel*, there was a sense that Autograph was now a 'useful' institution that could by way of increased funding be utilized to alleviate the pressures being exerted on the public arts funding system to become more 'racially' inclusive. For these reasons, it seemed imperative that the programme I would devise should attempt to circumvent the edicts of diversity and inclusion. It is within this context that some of the projects I organized at Autograph can be seen. I felt these projects might not only question the nature and identity of Autograph, but also would attempt to resist, as best they could, speaking for or through the prosaic language of diversity politics. One of the ways I hoped to address this was by curating mixed thematic exhibitions involving Black and white artists – for example, *Landscape Trauma in the age of Scopophilia* (2001) and *The Two of Us* (2001).

Landscape trauma

Featuring the artists Henna Nadeem, Annabel Howland, Camila Sposati, Ingrid Pollard and The Search for Terrestrial Intelligence (STI), a group of artists, scientists and technologists, *Landscape Trauma in the age of Scopophilia*, (Figure 1) used as its starting point the notion of landscape as a political, social or cultural construct. The title comes from Norman Bryson's *The Gaze in the Expanded Field, Vision and Visuality* (Bryson 1998), which scrutinizes the Cartesian model for looking, in which 'the subject conceives of itself as universal centre, surrounded by the stable plenitude of an object world'. (Ibid., 1998). The idea of trauma reflected things happening at the time, from national rail disruption and agricultural crises to farmland disputes in Zimbabwe.

Taking as its starting point Norman Bryson's essay in which the act of viewing is imbued with what Bryson referred to as a politics of vision, the exhibition, *Landscape Trauma in the Age of Scopophilia* considered a terrain vacated by the figurative subject. In the exhibition's catalogue, I described the exhibition as being:

> ...obsessed with images which are both extraordinary and relentlessly engaging. Perhaps this is the perversity and ambiguity of the show. For can one really deny the sheer pleasure and authority afforded by the spectacle of looking? (Hylton 2001)

In the exhibition, Henna Nadeem (Figure 2) and Annabel Howland (Figure 3) literally took a knife to the sanctity of the photograph, which in their own ways questioned the nature of both representation and landscape. Camila Sposati's video installation

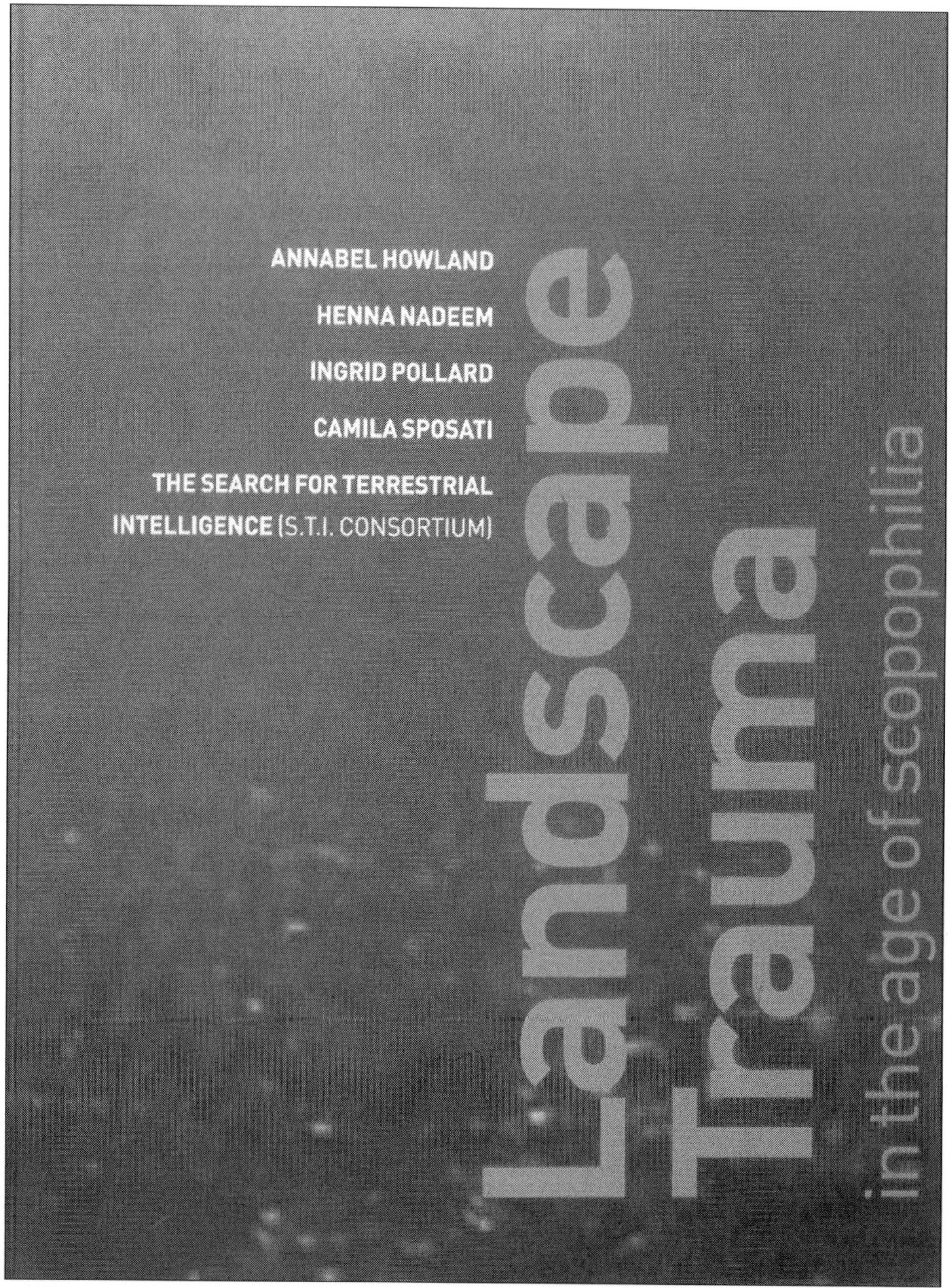

Figure 1. Landscape Trauma exhibition catalogue cover (background image Camila Sposati, *Talk to Me*, 2000 video installation).

Talk to Me was a visual-cum-aural conundrum in which an intimate but disjointed conversation between a man and woman is juxtaposed with a spectacle of a city from nightfall to daybreak or vice versa. Ingrid Pollard's photographs of rock formations (Figure 4), represented for her something of a departure from the use of the figure, through a process of enlargement they appear to portray an imaginary-like terrain. STI produced a pseudo-scientific experiment using the National Remote Sensing Centre in Leicester (Figure 5). Satellites that commonly observe space were turned towards Earth, specifically Plymouth, where some of the group were based at the University. The project explored the subjective, rather than the more familiar objective, persona of scientific exploration. STI referred to the infamous example of this, in the case of the Viking Orbiter space probe which in 1976 relayed images of Mars to Earth and which, after a process of digital imaging, appeared to portray a human face.

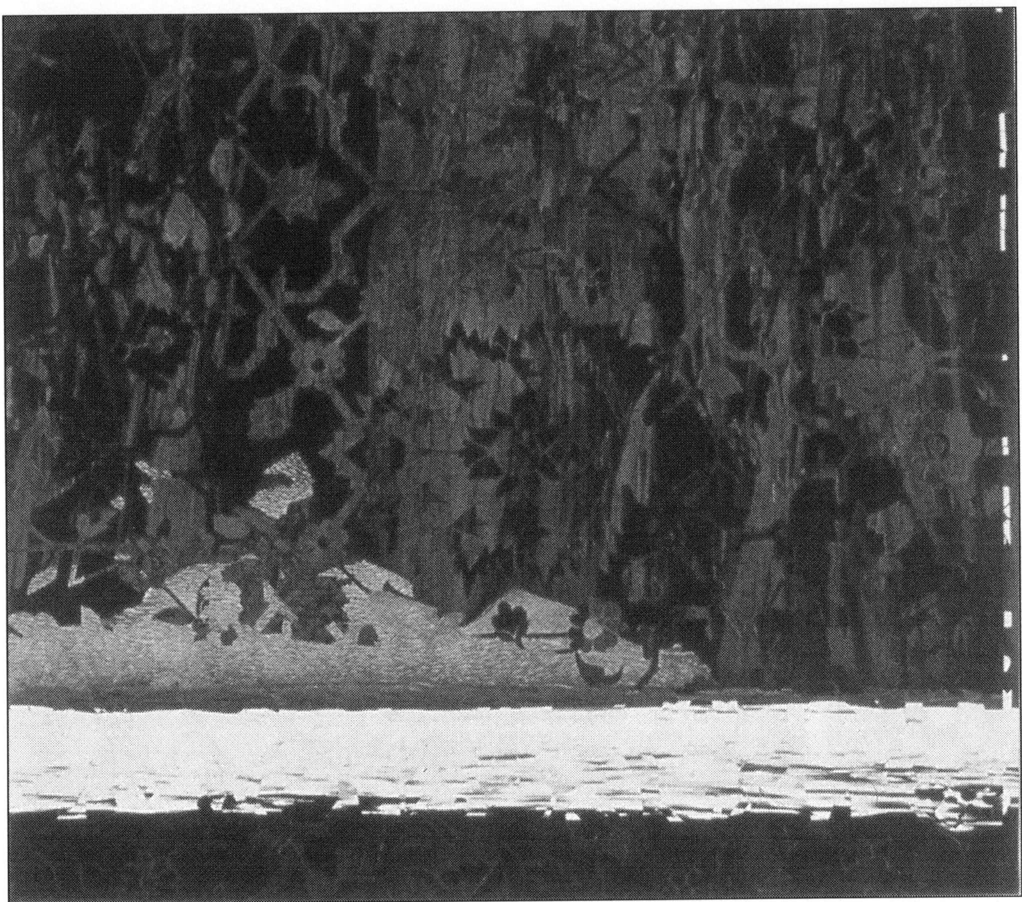

Figure 2. Henna Nadeem *Black and White Cliffs*, 2001, collage 41x46cm.

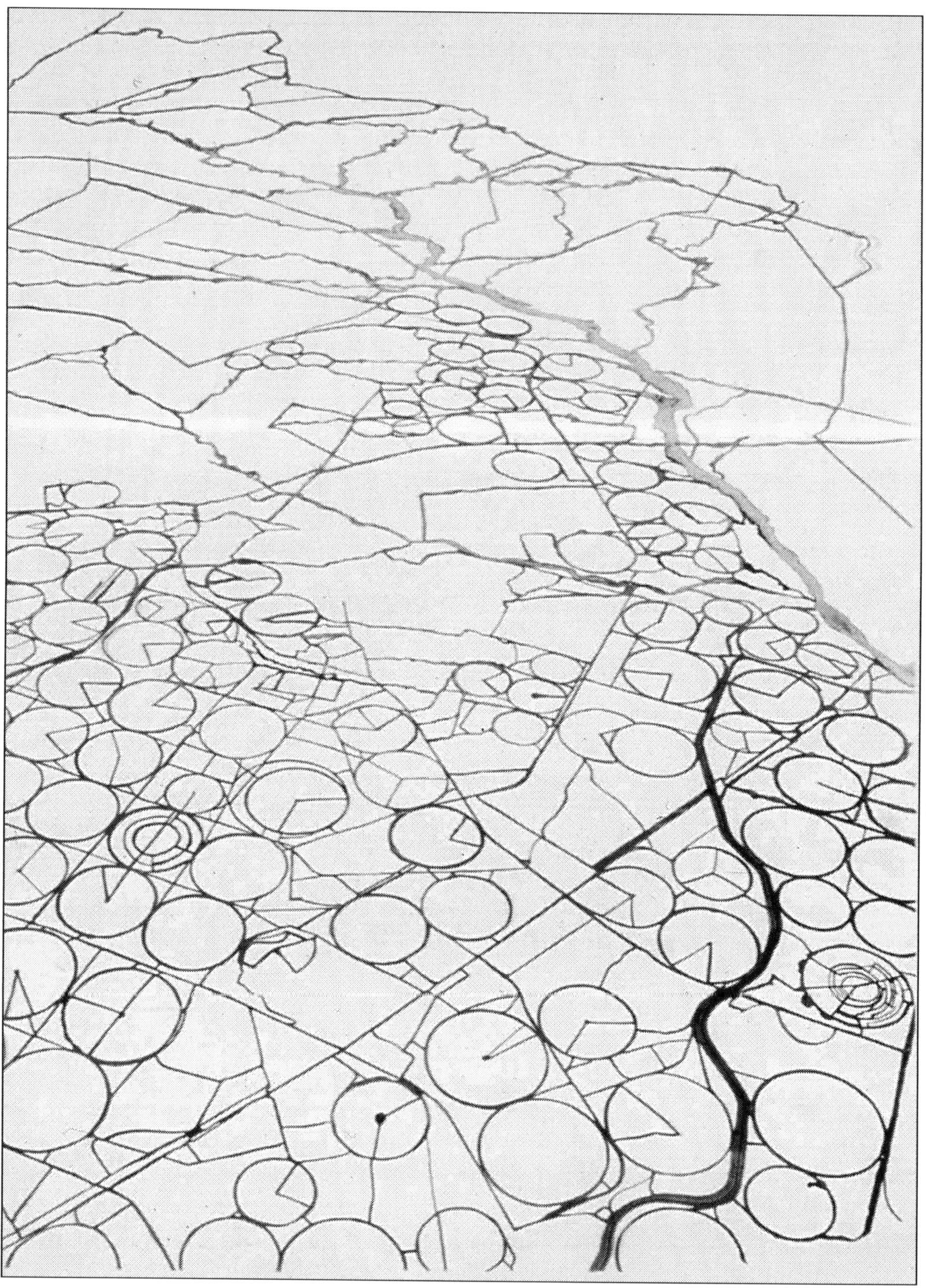

Figure 3. Annabel Howland *Cut Aerial I* 2001, lamda print 125x200cm.

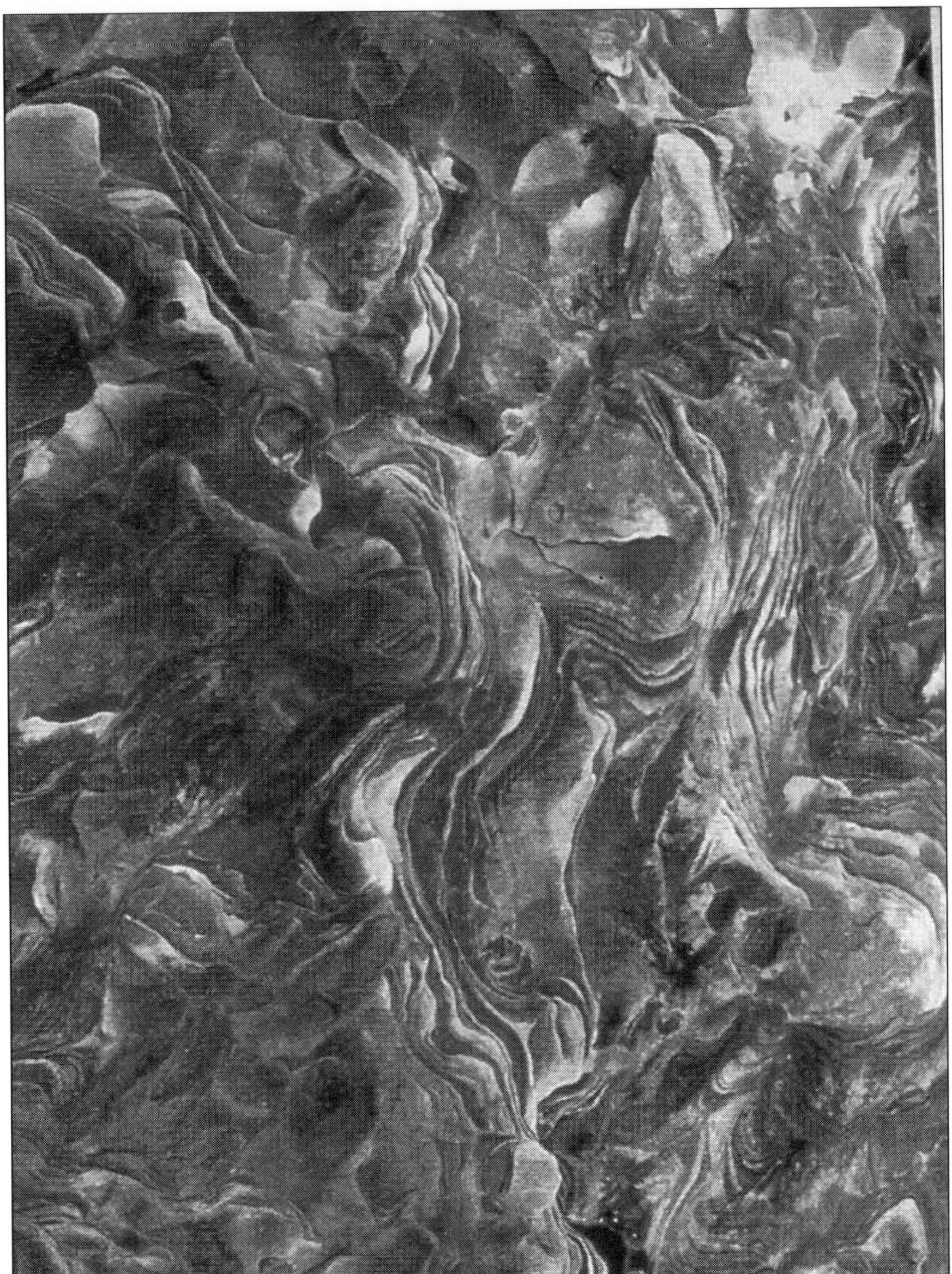

Figure 4. Ingrid Pollard *'Quondam-one that once had, but no longer'* 2001, digital print on vinyl 310x352cm.

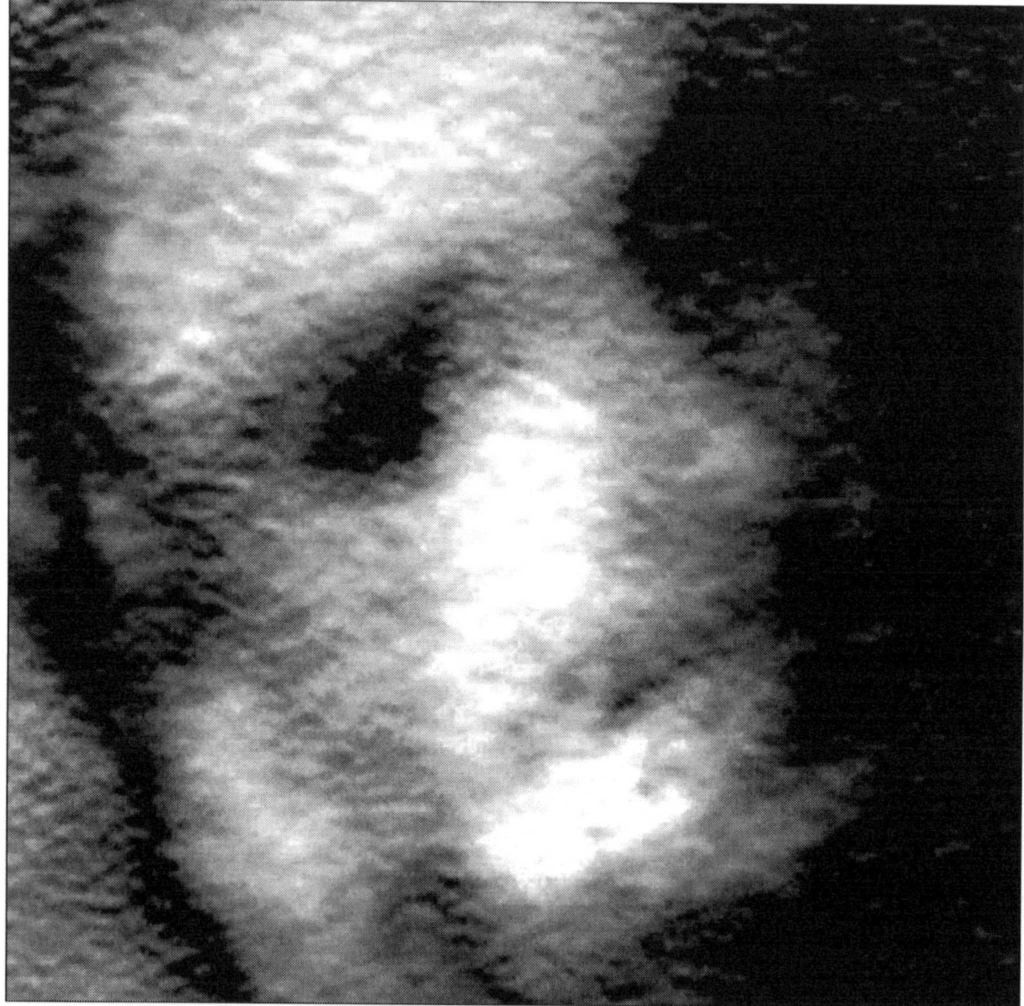

Figure 5. S.T.I. Narcissus *Movie [v1.0]* 2001 Frame # 00: 02: 08 digital video.

Prior to my arrival at Autograph, the organization had a tradition which leant towards projects mainly focused on photography and photographers. This work often focused on a 'Black' subject. With *Landscape Trauma*, I was interested in curating a show that would explore the notion of identity and self, not through the visualization of the figurative subject, but more so through the act of looking. Therefore, the 'subject' was not visible but was also, as suggested by much of the work in the show, as much to do with the viewer as it was to do with the *mise-en-scène*.

The best of Janette Parris

As a curator who works within the public sector and is therefore supported by public money, the notion of being critical or autonomous is arguably as fantastical as it is implausible. For better or for worse, I am locked into interdependency with public funding. Judith Butler (1997) refers to how power is paradoxical as both a subjugating force and the very force we seek in order to become subjects. This ambivalent relationship between the subject and subjection forms what Butler calls a 'bind of agency' and is the point at which power as subjection can be challenged. Butler states:

> Where conditions of...subordination makes possible the assumption of power, the power assumed remains tied to those conditions, but in an ambivalent way; in fact the power assumed may at once retain and resist that sub-ordination. (Butler 1997).

But I don't think that my 'curatorial strategy', if that's not too a grandiose term, was entirely obsessed with illustrating a sense of independence. Given the context I was working in, I wanted to explore the notion of what representation could mean. Therefore, the shifts in the reception of photographic institutions, coupled with a heady climate of inclusion, meant that Autograph's programme should not merely support the work of Black artists as a form of 'positive action'. For me, it had to challenge the assumptions about what such an organization should be doing rather than merely taking up the 'slack' of the mainstream. Therefore, the idea that Autograph was some sort of affirmative organization was for me very problematic. It was the over-affirmation of particular work (usually by white artists) in the mainstream that was the problem. There appeared to be a direct correlation between the trust in white artists' practice and distrust in Black artists' work.

What attracted me to produce a monograph on Janette Parris (Hylton 2002) was both the notion of failure which it seemed to explore through its use of narrative and its fearlessness in not being easily readable as 'good' art. This was particularly the case as Janette's work seemed to traverse not only different art forms, from cartoons and video to animation and performance, but also because it existed in different spaces, be it as animation on a website (*Fred's*, animation 1999); a musical in a theatre (*You're the One* 2001, musical commissioned by Artlab); or stand-up comedy (*Small Talk* 2001, commissioned by The International 3, formerly The Annual Programme, Work & Leisure International), scripted by Parris and performed by an actor in a gallery. For these reasons, although I could laugh at works like *Bite Yer Tongue* or Parris's *SE5* video series, it was also quite a difficult practice to locate. I also considered that Parris' practice was, because of its peripatetic approach to art form, a difficult one to sustain, particularly today when artists appear ever more aware and pressurized to commodify their art (Figure 6). This is not to say that Parris's practice is unambitious: quite the opposite. What I found interesting about her approach were both its unbridled ambition to stand out and how it cut through many of the traditional ways in which we might consider representation and identity to work in contemporary art. Her work is about failure, class, relationships and the artist's lot. Patricia Ellis has observed: 'Parris writes the most sincere scenarios, plagiarizing directly from real experience – her own, her friends, family and neighbours, etc, reweaving them into a believable fiction.' (Ellis 2002)

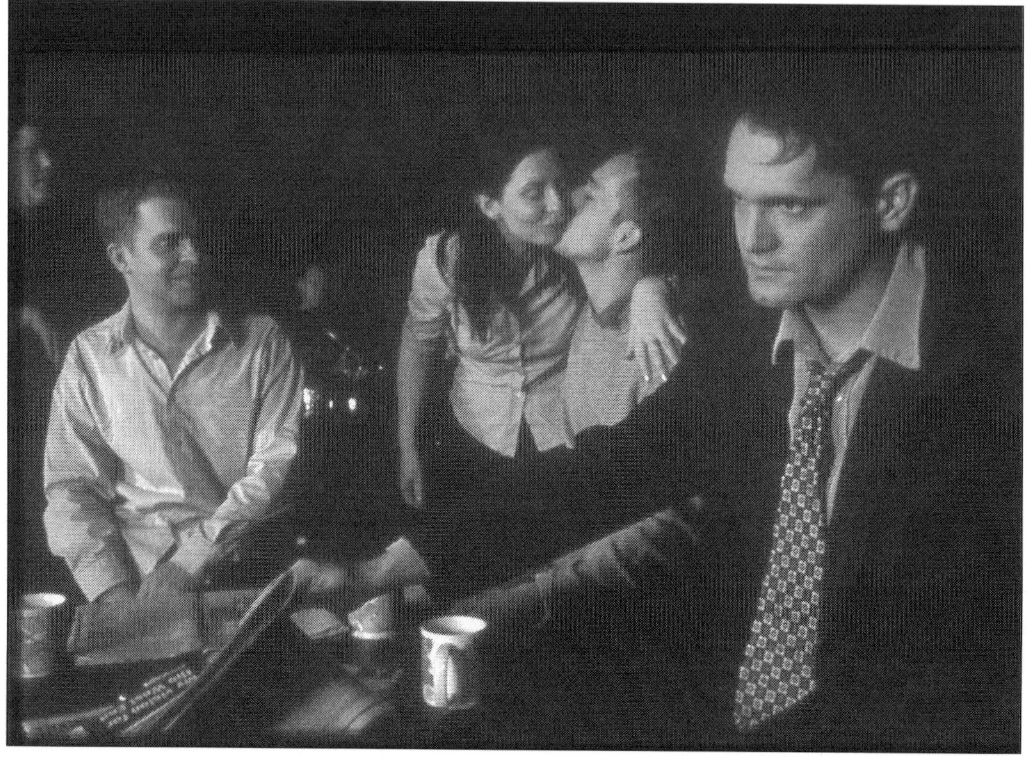

Figure 6. Janette Parris *If You Love Me,* 1999 musical, commissioned by Carolina Grau.

David Hammons: The Holy Bible: Old Testament

The Holy Bible: Old Testament (Figure 7) by the American David Hammons was co-curated with Virginia Nimarkoh. In some ways, this project was the complete antithesis to the other projects I have discussed, and even of anything else I have been involved with in the art world. For one, it brought together both the public and private sector, and secondly, it took seven years to complete from its inception in 1995 to its launch at Conway Hall, London, during December 2002. The project comprises a limited-edition artist book, the first to be produced by Hammons. Since the 1960s, Hammons has produced fascinating and compelling works in sculpture, installation, performance, video, multiples and photography. Often characterized, even caricatured, as a witty critique of race politics and its attendant histories, his work takes on far more complex readings which at their heart play with notions of the artist, art and visibility and, not least, the business of the art market.

It was the business of the market that came to encapsulate our project with the artist. However, given the longevity of the project, this took some time to materialize. Hammons has a reputation and mythological status and has also rarely shown in Britain. Whilst we attempted to persuade him to work with us on a project, we were also aware

that Artangel had been courting him for some time. To give an idea of the 'behind-the-scenes' nature of this project, I want to quote from one of a number of short narratives written by my co-curator Virginia Nimarkoh.
Gun (Nimarkoh 2003):

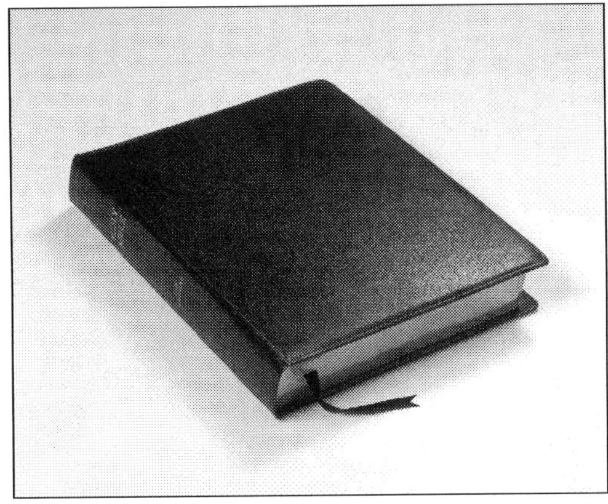

Figure 7. David Hammons, *The Holy Bible: Old Testament*, 2001 artist's book work.

> Thursday, 2pm. Hammons decides we should go and buy a gun. He wants to see what will happen. This is two days into his first research trip in London. I am less than enthusiastic. I am confronted by the reality that despite this being David Hammons, and us having worked for three years to get him over, I don't want to spend our project money on a gun.

Hammons is persistent. Each time he mentions guns over the course of the day, I try to look purposeful, but endeavour to let the matter drift into general chitchat. Yet I don't want to appear spineless, uptight or inefficient. I realise this is some kind of test. By the end of Day 3, he is still keen. Confrontation is clearly not an option. Richard tells me not to worry and that Hammons will eventually change his mind, as he has over just about everything else. So diligently, I do my research for the next day. Tomorrow, we will go to Catford Gun Company.

Saturday, 12.15pm. Richard calls Hammons to check he is up. We go and fetch him in the car. He is in good spirits. Our plan is to breakfast and then buy the gun. We set off. Within seconds, the journey is aborted. From a side street emerges a youth on a bicycle. Focused on friends gathered at the opposite corner, he crosses two lanes of oncoming traffic. I believe that he will stop. As we slow down, he hits the side of our car. Youth and bicycle somersault separately over the bonnet. They hit the ground. Strangely, the youth seems to bounce upright again. The youth is in shock. He is trying to save face, which makes him look much worse. I feel a compulsion to hug the youth, but decide that it would be inappropriate. I look at Richard and Hammons; both wear the same slightly dumb expression of concern and disbelief.

The youth is unconvincing in assuring us that he is OK. His arms are grazed and he is trying to disguise a pain in his side. His friends look afraid, more than he does. Collectively, we manage to persuade the youth to let us drive him to casualty. We set off again. Immediately in the car, the youth pulls out a mobile phone. He informs a friend that he will be 'about fifteen minutes late' and that he got 'mashup' – a term that implies more that he has been in a fight than road accident. The youth is in denial.

As I escort the youth into Kings College Hospital Accident & Emergency Unit, he assures me that 'nothing will come of this.' I take this to mean that he will not be suing us for the accident. The compassion I have felt for the youth is waning. I make sure that he signs in, get him to call someone to meet him, we swap numbers. I don't know what else to do, so I leave.

Outside Hammons is waiting. Richard is with the car. Hammons reckons that Richard deserves a gift. We track down the minuscule hospital florist shop. From a sorry selection, Hammons puts together a curious bunch of marigolds, carnations and Septembers wrapped in leopard skin paper. At the car, Hammons places the bouquet on the bonnet. He is not laughing. Hammons concedes that even thinking about guns can make bad things happen.

Over the course of five years, we visited Hammons and he made research trips to London. Numerous ideas and prototypes resulted from this work, much of which was aborted for various reasons. Whilst such stuttering progress made us believe that the project would never happen, we for some reason could not stop. On the one hand, it had all gone on far too long, without any product to show for our efforts, whilst on the other hand, it was too far gone as a going concern to let go. There was also an element of determination not to 'fail', as many people had come to know about our project.

Finally, Hammons came up with the idea of *The Holy Bible* in large part because his friend Delano Greenidge, a New York-based publisher, was about to publish a softback edition of *The Complete Works of Marcel Duchamp*. Hammons' view was that he'd made a good living out of Duchamp and this was a sort of crystallisation of this. For us it was an opportunity to fund other projects. For the Arts Council, who had funded part of the project, this became problematic. Despite the rhetoric of income generation, we were potentially being a bit too independent.

The Holy Bible: Old Testament is an appropriation of Arturo Schwarz's *The Complete Works of Marcel Duchamp* (softback edition), and was rebound to resemble a Bible: 1002 pages, 225 colour plates, soft cover, leather-bound, gilt-edged, gold tooling, plus slipcase. Approximately 30x24x2.5cm in size and weighs 8.6 kilos. It is produced in an edition of 165.

Interestingly, except for one sale to a private collector in London, this book has sold exclusively abroad, mainly in the US and Europe. This project has a different perspective on the art world, specifically the commercial sector. Much of our sales activity has been conducted via the Internet; we have only rarely met with dealers or potential collectors and transactions have been stunted by what some have seen as a prohibitive asking price. The experience of this project illustrated for me the limits of my entrepreneurial and curatorial drive – not everyone can or wants to sell art.

On one of the rare occasions that I took the book to a potential buyer, a major public institution in London, the curator was somewhat bemused by it. Having answered her questions about the project's genesis and attempted to gently point out that there was a dearth of Hammons' work in British public collections, she asked me, 'Where is the "Blackness" in the work?' I tried to reason that this was Hammons' first published artist book. Responding to what I believed to be a curious question about "Blackness", I implied that may be this was precisely the point of the work, in that one of its aims might be to question certain assumptions within the art world, in particular, the roles and positions we are (and are not) allowed to assume. Try as I might, my reasoning failed to convince the curator. Needless to say, this potential sale did not materialize. However, such an experience did put into perspective the current trends (in the English gallery system) towards a 'professionalised', and 'inclusive' art world. For if this candid exchange revealed anything, it was the extent to which such problematic and institutional mindsets appear to be untouched by prevailing policies towards 'professionalised' practice or 'inclusivity'. Alternatively, it could also be the case that, within the publicly funded arts sector, these policies are further compounding rather than challenging such attitudes making the art world ever more regulated and ever more regimented in its engagement with Black artists and curators. When would a curator ever be asked, 'Where is the "whiteness" in the work?' As 'cultural diversity' has come to play a greater role in arts funding, publicly funded art institutions have grown accustomed to exploiting their engagement with Black artists, as if to illustrate their 'inclusive' approach to programming. However, if 'professional' practice and 'inclusion' are really going to mean something worthwhile, then those responsible must start by doing away with laden and overly prescriptive policies, only then might there be a more fundamental change in attitudes within art institutions.

References

Bryson, N., 'The Gaze in the Expanded Field,' in Hal Foster (ed.) *Vision and Visuality* Seattle, Bay Press, 1988.

Butler, J., *The Psychic Life of Power*, Stanford University Press, 1997.

Ellis, P., *You and Me Against the World, The Best of Janette Parris*, London, Autograph (ABP), 2002.

Hylton, R. (ed.), *Landscape Trauma in the Age of Scopophilia*, exhibition catalogue, London, Autograph (ABP), 2001.

Hylton, R. (ed.), *The Best of Janette Parris*, London, Autograph (ABP), 2002.

Mercer, K., 'Ethnicity and Internationality, New British Art and Diaspora-Based Blackness', *Third Text*, winter, 1999–2000.

Nimarkoh, V., *GUN* 2003 (catalogue essay).

Schwarz, A., *The Complete Works of Marcel Duchamp*, revised and expanded paperback edition, volume one, (New York, Delano Greenidge Editions, 2000).

PART 4: EMERGENT PRACTICES: SUBVERTING THE MUSEUM

Oscillating at the 'High/Low' Art Divide: Curating and Exhibiting Animation

Suzanne Buchan

As a time-based moving image form, animation film is finding its way into what we can term 'serious' curatorial practice. The current proliferation of exhibitions featuring artists' use of animation that expands their oeuvre into time-based imagery attests to animation's increasing pervasiveness in other types of creative-making. As one of the intentions of this publication is to explore curating as a space for critical reflection and argument, here I take a specific attitude, perhaps an arts-political stance, towards the curatorship of animation films. I have been defined elsewhere as 'an activist for imaginative imagination'[1] and what I posit here is culled from my experience as an animation film festival director, a curator by experience, entering the practice obliquely (as distinct from one who has acquired curatorial skills and requisite methodologies via training) and as an academic. Some chapters in this book have dealt with curating the moving image, software art and video, and others have considered the material and virtual status of the work. With time-based art, there is often the reflection that these are emerging curatorial practices taking place in proper exhibition spaces as well as in what may be regarded as non-art venues. This chapter explores different approaches to curating and exhibiting animation as an extremely rich and artefact-based film form in a range of exhibition spaces, in terms of its interdisciplinary affinities with the arts.

Independent animation, that is, animation made without strong commercial backing or control, will be the focus of this chapter. The text's trajectory begins with various strategies of animation curatorship, from festival and cinema programming to gallery installations and museum exhibitions. It then poses some questions as to changing conceptions of animation as an art form, taking into account the diversity of fine arts, design and crafts media used in its production. These ideas are exemplified by a discussion of the *Spacetricks* animation exhibition, revealing the research-based nature of its conceptual development, selection methods, thematic refinement, adaptation and design of the exhibition architecture and publication. This should illuminate ways to mediate the relationships between pro-filmic artefacts as exhibition materials and the finished films for audiences. It will also address animation's technological shift from a fine arts base to a digital moving-image medium, and explores how, through curatorial and critical engagement, its singular status as both art (to which I hope to make clear why) and moving image can be retained.

Because animation is rooted in multidisciplinary arts practice before it is recorded as a moving image form, in contextualizing animation within curatorial activity, there are a number of issues worth reflection. These include: the phenomena of animation's historical exclusion from exhibition, the 'high/low' art divide, i.e. how animation figures as an art form; and how curatorial practice past and present has hindered understanding of animation as artistic practice. This is interwoven in the discussion to introduce animation into discourses of art and its relationship to both traditional and contemporary arts and crafts practice. We will see that animation's historical relationship to other media and its pervasiveness in contemporary artists' practice can allow surprisingly creative curating.

Animation film has many as yet unwritten histories and if we reflect on the abundance of films that have been made in the over 100 years of its presence as an art form, there is a vast potential for revealing the artistic nature and features of this creative form to audiences. The majority of these films are rarely seen outside of specialist festivals and art house cinemas. The Internet is, of course, changing that, but sites like YouTube or MySpace offer low-resolution clips that, whilst allowing an unprecedented access to films heretofore rarely seen, cannot provide the richness of image of a cinema screening situation, which is the locus most animation films are made for. Changes in audience access and receptivity to animation are effecting increasing curiosity about it.

Animation as a cinematic medium

The dominant outlet for curatorial practice for animation film remains programming for festivals and cinemas. Some festivals have a national focus as the central programming impulse, others a prevalent type or genre. The Holland Animation Film Festival (HAFF) spotlights Dutch and commissioned works, while the Fantoche International Animation Film Festival (Switzerland) privileges independent film-making and has developed a clear thematic framework over the years. Themed exhibitions that echo the film programme concept are consistently organized at Fantoche, and the inaugural Platform festival in July 2007 in Portland, USA, is promoting exhibition and installation to a greater degree, as does the recently renamed Aurora festival in Norwich, UK.[2] The Annecy festival in France is the largest, and with its increasingly dominant concurrent market event, its curatorial strengths have waned over the years. Specialist festivals thus remain the main dissemination point for independent animation, though there is a wide range of festival philosophies and thematic emphases, and it is the thematic programmes that exhibit curatorial ability and knowledge. Curated programmes are usually embedded within a main framework of competition, retrospective and other programme strands that are dictated by recent production, sponsorship or a festival's national or ideological priorities.

Animation curators come from a variety of backgrounds and range from freelance art historians to Film Studies graduates, festival programmers, film-makers and independent experts. Although wide-ranging and imaginative, their choices and preferences of which films to show have contributed to specific tendencies in corpus definition and assumptions, and, in turn, affects what gets shown. Some curators are passionate to provide access to little-known or hard-to-access films; others truly push conventional notions of the form. Edwin Carels, Curator at MUKHA (Museum of Contemporary Art, Antwerp), has done this to fascinating extremes. These are evident in his curated installations – most recently *Borderline Behaviour*, that 'regards animation more as a state of mind than a specific cinematic genre'[3] for the 2007 Rotterdam Film Festival – and his film programme curation like the *Not Done: Undone* and *Not Done: Overdone* programmes created for HAFF in 2002. Others perpetuate the canons that are found in academic writing about animation (or provide new ones), and still others, aiming to satisfy audience expectations geared to commercial productions, rarely venture outside what can be considered conventional animation. This has implications on how the form is received. Imaginative curating, that pushes questions of form and provides alternatives to the oftentimes self-ghettoizing canons, is relatively rare in the animation festival circuit, and a consequence of this has been the self-perpetuating notion that animation is, and can only be, popular entertainment.

Curating animation as an art form: current trends

Outside of specialist festival circuits, animation film enjoys regular inclusion in museum and gallery film programmes around the world. More recently, there is a growing interest in curating animation, but the tendency is towards presenting ways that artists, and I mean artists in the art world economies, are exploring their practice through animation tools and techniques. They are increasingly usurping the expressive possibilities of animation, especially digital process, but their work is regarded and presented in the first instance, as art, not as animation film. This brings me now to a recent phenomenon that can be observed with curating exhibitions dedicated exclusively to animation, in itself a good thing, but we will see that this is not necessarily benefiting independent animation as I have described above, but instead reveals symptoms of certain sectors of the art world's interest and engagement in 'high' art as distinct from 'low' animation.

Although exhibition and installation of conventional and commercial animation has persisted over the years – and the Disney exhibition at the Centre Georges Pompidou or the Pixar exhibition that is now travelling the world are two exceptions and examples of insightful curatorship that takes into account the material implicit in making these companies' films – less commercial animation has tended to be subsumed into larger thematic curatorial concepts. It also has been used to illustrate a particular expression of a movement (Dada, Pop Art, Fluxus), a technique (painting, drawing, digital media) or a political era (propaganda, information films). In the past year alone, there have been dozens of gallery and museum exhibitions with an especial focus on animation: some examples are highlighted here. The Museum of Modern Art's *Comic Abstraction: Image-Breaking, Image Making* (2007) explored how artists have abstracted popular imagery, which is deeply imprinted in our collective consciousness, and how it carries an extreme visual potency even when completely abstracted. At the San Diego Museum of Art (2007), *Animated Painting* presented intersections of time-based imagery and fine art techniques of drawing and painting: in curator Betti-Sue Hertz's words, 'artists use the playful possibilities of time and movement to extend the language of painting and drawing, to literally "animate" it, without releasing the work of art completely from painting's and drawing's static nature, visual codes and conventions' (Hertz 2007). *Animated Stories*, staged 2006–07 at the Sala Rekalde Gallery, Bilbao, took cause with artists who, in their works, were critical with the predominance of visual disinformation. The Parasol Unit's *Momentary Momentum* (Gavin 2007) included a dozen installations of one or more films in the different gallery rooms and a loop of films screened in a cinematic situation. The presence of artists, as distinct from animators, is the overriding emphasis, and I would suggest, art world rationale, for most recent animation exhibitions.

These exhibitions emphasize the qualities of 'art' in their concepts, eliding the fact that animation has been ubiquitous as an art form for over a century. In the visual surface of their films, independent animators can have as much, if not more to say not only about art, media and the moving image, but also through the ideologies, critiques and narratives that are embedded in their works. As artists (and the critics and curators who are receptive to this and analyse and contextualize exhibitions that are sensitive to these qualities), besides creating viable and often astonishing works of art, they often address contemporary issues and concerns, ranging from spatial politics and racial inequality to new modes of perception, cultural commodification and environmental issues. Because most techniques and styles of animation are not dependent on photo-representational imagery, i.e. use arts media in their making, their reception oscillates between perception as films, with figures, time-based narrative and other formal properties of film, and with the fact that these are created through an artistic intervention that has more affinities with fine arts practice. This allows a different freedom of expression not available in (pre-digital) photo-representational film. The 'worlds' they create, worlds that can represent thought, imagination and noumenal, or supersensible, experience can be abstract, figurative, impressionistic, highly stylized or utterly minimal. This is, indeed, one of the great attractions of the form for viewers. This is also evident in the increasing ubiquity of animation across a diversity of media platforms, from mobile telephony and game consoles, to LED advertising screens and the Internet.

It is worth asking the pertinent question at what point, and why, does an animator become considered as an artist. Jan Svankmajer is known as much as an artist, exhibiting sculpture, collage and other media, as he is as a film-maker. William Kentridge is one of the few animation film-makers to be given both solo shows and included in museum and gallery exhibitions. He is indeed a phenomenon, a polymath working across a number of media and disciplines, and he has made forays into exhibition curation himself: His *7 Fragments for Georges Méliès*, launched at the 2005 Biennale in Venice, was shown at the Museum of Contemporary Art at the Pacific Design Centre 2005–06 and is currently touring internationally. Other artists are seeing the potential for their works to be exhibited differently and, supported by funders and other patrons, they are taking initiatives, singly or collectively, to make their works available. Artefact-based exhibitions have tended to occur at the fringes and initiated by animators who are highly aware of the role of the artist in animation film – both in terms of process and finished result. These include radical artist-led installations (George Griffin in New York in the 70s), and others in which animation permeates what is generally regarded as experimental film as in the US West Coast psychedelic happenings and installations from the 60s onwards. New York artist Stan Vanderbeek, who organized multiple-projector shows for the Moviedrome theatre he created at his home in New York, worked extensively in animation as well. A selection of Vanderbeek's animation artwork, drawings and sketches were shown in the eponymous exhibition Guild & Greyshkul, New York, in 2003. Scholar and critic Mark Bartlett has begun exploring the philosophical implications of Vanderbeek's visionary thinking and making via Vanderbeek's agenda of a radical political aesthetic critique on communications systems.

Animation production: between art and moving image

Central to most of these artists is an interest in exposing the material base – the pro-filmic artefacts – used in the processes of making animation film. The Quay Brothers, known for their exquisite puppet animation films, and to a lesser degree for their stage and set design for theatre and opera, were commissioned by the Rotterdam Film Festival to create an exhibition, *Dormitorium*, with eighteen exhibition cases that presented reconfigurations of a variety of their puppets, film décors and fragments. As they work in puppet animation, these cases are tantalizing explorations and presentations of their work. But what is especially attractive is how different the works look on display compared to the lighting in the films. And screws are – well, just that – screws. The haptic becomes tactile. In 'Concrete Animation', an essay by New York–based film-maker, artist and author George Griffin, he addresses the fact that 'animation is more than the sum of its parts' and his argument aims 'to link "concrete" to actual materials, objects not just images, and the processes which cause them to spring to life. It would not then be tied to any particular rules of design or vanguard art theory. It would suggest the tactile, the tangible, the real, the stuff which is often forgotten in the river of illusion' (Griffin 2007). It is perhaps the film-makers who themselves are most aware of the value of the materials they use, that recognize they have a value in addition to the films, are the ones that are regarded as 'artists'.

It is this 'real stuff', the material used in making animation film, designed, crafted, created, that contributes to making a case for animation as 'art', and the film-makers who are aware of this are increasing. As a basis for single-frame recording, shooting, independent animators create complex paintings, detailed sculptures, astonishing cut-out collages, meticulous drawings, from dozens (object animation) to thousands (drawing and painting) for each film. Some of them could easily be compared with or brought into continuum with established artists: Paul Vester and Jeremy Blake; the Brothers Quay and Hans Bellmer, Joanna Priestley and Joseph Cornell, Norman McLaren and Jules Tanguy. In spite of the proliferation of digital tools, many artists choose to work with pre-production materials that can be used in future exhibits and some artists are aware of other forms of dissemination for the fascinating process imbued in their work towards a final film. Film-makers are also exploiting the Internet's resources to mount websites that can be regarded as self-curated online exhibitions. A fitting example here is Johnny Hardstaff, a hybrid artist who straddles the worlds of advertising, design and academia, and is best known for his Radiohead pop promos and Sony Playstation films. *Future of Gaming* (2001–02), the second he made for them, was highly political and critical of the impact and coercion of digital gaming. Although his films make heavy use of CGI, in his online archive, Hardstaff's sketchbook project and

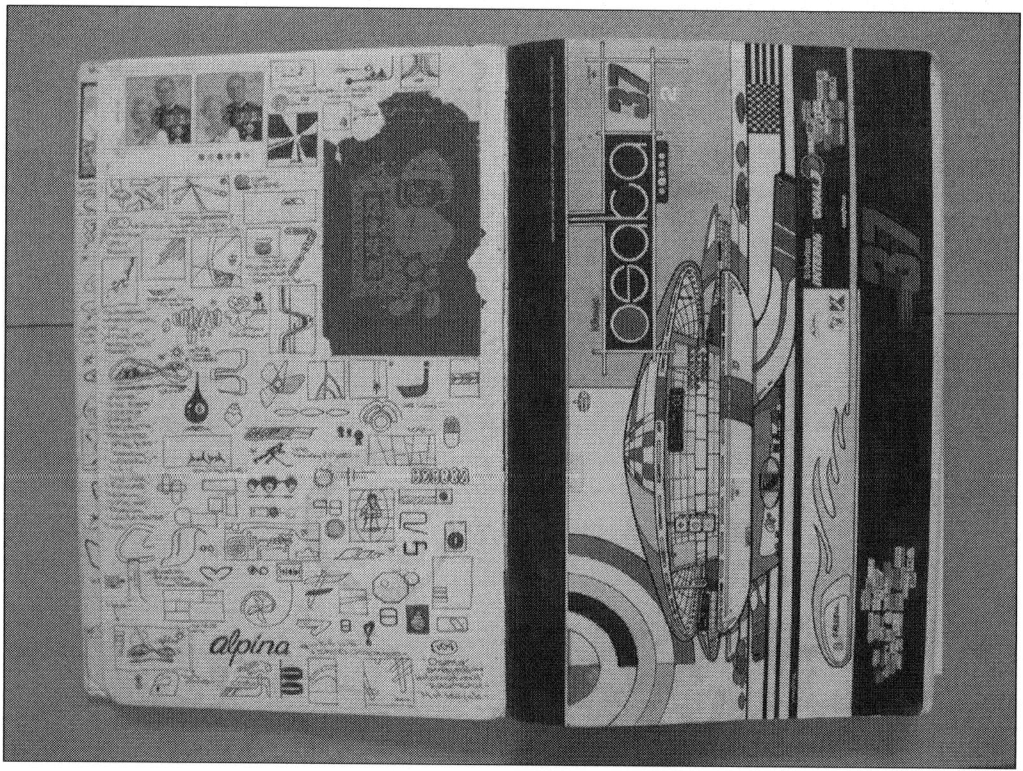

Figure 1. Page from Sketchbook 2, 1998–2002, © Johnny Hardstaff.

other images (Figure 1) unfolds the complex and creative design origins for his films, and many of the production materials for other works are available to help gain an understanding of the creative process from concept to finished film.[4]

As animation exhibition shifts from the festival screening context to the art world contexts of museums and galleries, there are some considerations that need to be made about this seepage into these exhibition spaces. After a discussion of content, it is now worth considering some of the formal challenges to curating animation. There are inherent problems in exhibiting animation film, as there are, indeed, for all cinematic works, as (pre-digital) films were made for a cinematic screening situation. In exhibition practice, where one of the intentions should be to allow visitors intimate access to original works of art, the common curatorial practice to install a monitor in a lit room achieves the opposite effect. Instead of the original artwork – an animated film – meant for a cinematic screening context, their experience is one of fragmentation, of the artwork being presented in an unsuitable environment, much like watching artist's film on a television monitor.

Curating animation for museums and galleries can require a sensitivity to the film's original intentions for viewers, and consideration for how a gallery space can best preserve this. These include suitable lighting, exhibition architecture, screen sizes and sound design. Dryden Goodwin's exhibition at the Chisenhale Gallery, London, in 2006 is an example of how it can be done well (Figure 2). Goodwin's film *Flight* (2005) was screened in a separate, dark room, and in another space the artwork from the film was presented in glass cases, showing the seriality of process, Goodwin's filigrane drawing technique and the origins of the images he used in making the film. In contrast, the 2007 *Momentary Momentum* at the Parasol Unit, London, presented a selection of films in empty white rooms, with reduced lighting, yet the experience of these works visually and aurally was not in keeping with the cinematic intent of some of them. Robin Rhodes' *Harvest* (2005), whilst more a series of dissolves than a traditional animated film, worked well. The works intended for cinematic screening fared better in the darkened cinema

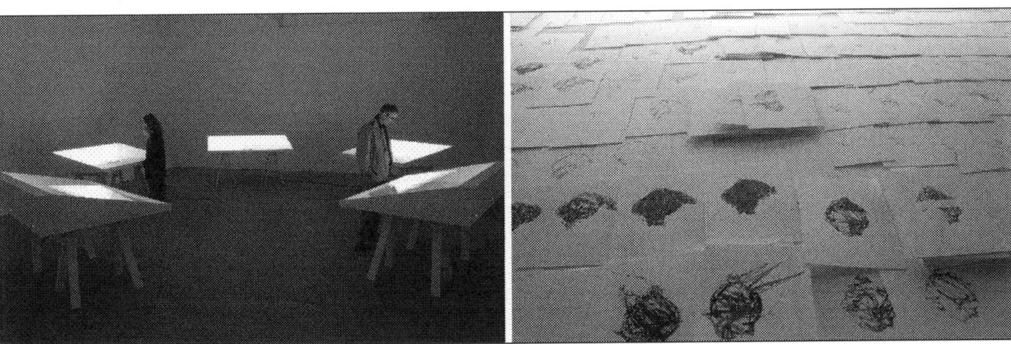

Figure 2. Dryden Goodwin's *Flight*, Chisenhale Gallery, London 2006. Images © Dryden Goodwin, courtesy Stephen Friedman Gallery, London.

setup where they were run on loops, and there were places to sit, and engage with the works, while in the other rooms people passing through added a particular distraction, as did the sounds they made. Artists making work for galleries are sensitive to the implications of this form of public presentation, whilst animation films belong in a viewing situation that allows the full experience of them, or, if not, curatorial explanation for the choice of installation mode and setting, and what it may imply in the viewer's experience.

Expanded visual languages of animation

The discussion up till now has focused on curating animation as a moving image form. Many years ago I visited a major Berlin museum and was transfixed by the framed artwork and designs of 'Absolute' film-maker Viking Eggeling's Horizontal-Vertikalorchester. This and other artworks provided insights into Eggeling's complex universal language of art and moving forms that inform his only film, *Diagonal Symphony* (1921). Esther Leslie suggests that the interrelationship of elementary forms and laws of perception tapped something universal. Eggeling's alphabet or lexicon of graphic forms was to provide the basis of a new visual language. This attempt rested on abstraction from nature, governed by a conceptual system based on polarities and analogies (Leslie 2004). Experiencing the original artwork not only changed my understanding and reception of Eggeling's film – it also got me thinking about the complex, rich relationships between animation artwork and the finished film. My point is that it wasn't just that it was a kind of storyboard or sketch. The figures and forms in Eggeling's film, and in most animation film, have their origins in artworks that can be accessed and engaged with, as was the case with Dryden Goodwin's exhibition described above. We can be in the presence of the pro-filmic phenomenal object that becomes the cinematic illusion as it appears in an animation film. Archives and private collections have a role to play here, as do institutional agendas and relationships between practice and theory that reflect on the materials of process as much as on the finished works.

It is only recently that, besides the trite commercial galleries selling animation cells as 'art' to wistful Disneyphiles and Tex Avery fans, the pro-filmic materials used to make animation: the artwork, drawings, sketches, paintings and even sculptures have found their way into larger galleries and public spaces. There are a number of reasons for this: the high/low art stigma that is attached to animation; the overtly commercial and popular orientation of animation art galleries, and both a lack of awareness of and difficulties in access to the notably few archives and collections of these materials. Perhaps the most relevant reason is that curators' understanding and treatment of the materials available to them varies widely, and it definitely is reflected in the art industry's relative distain for narrative animation as art. Happily, animation's range of techniques occupies an emergent, but growing, position in the art world and in its critical reception. Yet this position is not informed in the main by the rich histories of independent animation film production. It is predominately populated by artists considered in the first place as artists, with animation being subsumed to a formal medium means that established artists are using to expand their creative repertoires.

Animation and its artefacts

There is a crucial phase in the curatorial process that brings me to one of the concerns I have as director of the Animation Research Centre at the University College for the Creative Arts at Farnham, England, and its archive.[5] As an art form, animation is at a crossroads. Museums are increasingly including animation film in their acquisitions policies. But the artefacts – drawings, paintings, sketches, puppets, photography, sculpture – that reveal the fine arts base of works in time-based form and unique conceptual processes of animation film-making rarely figure in these acquisitions. In its pre-digital manifestations, animators have created an astonishing amount of materials using a variety of artistic practices to create their works in time-based form. With the increasing implementation of digital technologies, production artefacts and artworks that reveal the film-maker's creative process are becoming increasingly rare. As a moving image form, audiences will continue being able to enjoy animation, but if we reflect on animation as a multidisciplinary and multimedial art form, there is true cause for alarm. The 2005 fire at Aardman in Bristol that destroyed most of the studios' artwork and puppets was headlined in media around the world, and perhaps for the first time audiences have become aware of both the existence and the irreplaceable cultural value of such artefacts.

In light of its appropriation of fine arts and crafts practice and methods in its production, from painting and collage to sculpture, etching, drawing and even textiles and (ephemeral) rotting fruit, it is astonishing that curators have only now begun to also explore the richness of film-makers' archives and production materials as potential exhibition material. If these materials are to be available for future exhibitions, it is crucial that measures are taken to ensure preservation of, access to and awareness of, the enormous amount of artwork produced for every non-digital short film. If we recall the shift in Film Studies towards Early Cinema, and its relevance in understanding the histories and aesthetics of cinema back to its beginnings, it is in part the result of frantic searching for and rescuing of materials from studios, warehouses and of prescient collectors who systematically scoured the waste containers of production houses. Especially with the digital shift, which essentially means the disappearance of the tangible artefact, it is important that we search and secure animation production artwork where possible, especially as they are becoming increasingly rare. As animation is based on a multitude of art forms, its absence from galleries and most film archives is astonishing. Curators' understanding and treatment of the materials available to them varies widely, in part because there are very few archival holdings of animation artwork, and animation's range of techniques means it occupies a liminal position in the art world. There is an urgency for preserving artwork and other pre-production materials that can fill these gaps in knowledge and they may very well form the basis of future exhibitions.

Animation as exhibition: tricky spaces

Having explained why pre-digital animation offers curatorial opportunities because of its artefact-based production methods, I would like show how these thoughts can be manifested into practice. In August 2005, the *Trickraum: Spacetricks* exhibition opened at the Zurich Museum of Design and is currently touring internationally. It was, as the response from audiences and more critical reception can confirm, a highly successful animation exhibition. Three years ago I was approached by a curator and film and architecture historian from the Museum of Design Zurich, Dr Andres Janser, who asked me if I would be interested in developing an animation exhibition with him. The museum had presented one 20 years before, and as he and I had a shared interest in cinematic space and architecture, we agreed on a working concept. It loosely evolved around a concept I had developed earlier, that 'for an artist working in almost any medium, there is a fundamental element of the artwork that they cannot evade. Any narrative, object, relationship or action has to be or take place somewhere. This is so quintessential that it may not seem worth mentioning, yet there are artists that wilfully play with what these spaces can be. There are kinds of space that are not accessible in an immanent, physical way: metaphoric space, for instance, or space that diverges from Euclidean geometry and Renaissance perspective. In *The Logic of Sense*, Gilles Deleuze (1990, 2001) develops a series of paradoxes around the status of meaning and meaninglessness. One is "[the] paradox of the absurd, or of the impossible objects [...] – square circles, matter without extension, perpetuum mobile, mountain without valley, etc, – are objects 'without a home', outside of being, but they have a precise and distinct position within this outside: they are of 'extra being' – pure, ideational events, unable to be realised in a state of affairs".' (Buchan 2002). Inspired by Deleuze's paradoxes, that can be visualized in animation, my intent was to reveal the process of how animators created such 'ideational events', and spaces, with an emphasis on the creative process underpinned by tangible examples of each artist's materials, the 'state of affairs' coexisting alongside the films in the phenomenal world.

The exhibition's overarching theme illuminated the interdisciplinary relationships between and the expressive possibilities of pre- and post-digital animation and architectural space. Both an academic research project and a curatorial process, it addressed a relatively new and dynamic dialogue between architects, animation film-makers and scholars and their increasingly literate cinema audiences as well as embracing a wider public. As notions of space can be manifold and complex, to narrow our selection we developed a typology of four kinds of space: Narrative Space, Interior, or personal space, LandCityscapes and Architectural Space (Figure 3). The films were mostly from independent, *auteur* film-makers and ranged from popular and experimental works to narrative shorts usually seen only at festivals. Overall, the exhibition was aimed at a comprehensive target audience that included adults, children and teenagers.

We intended to engage the viewer/spectator, already enticed by the films' narrative and formal attractions, and by the powerful affects animation has on viewers, and then to fill in the gaps of knowledge of the process that takes place while conceptualizing an idea. Spaces and figures in Caroline Leaf's *Two Sisters* visually evolved from paintings by Frida Kahlo and photographs of an old house Caroline had photographed; Barry

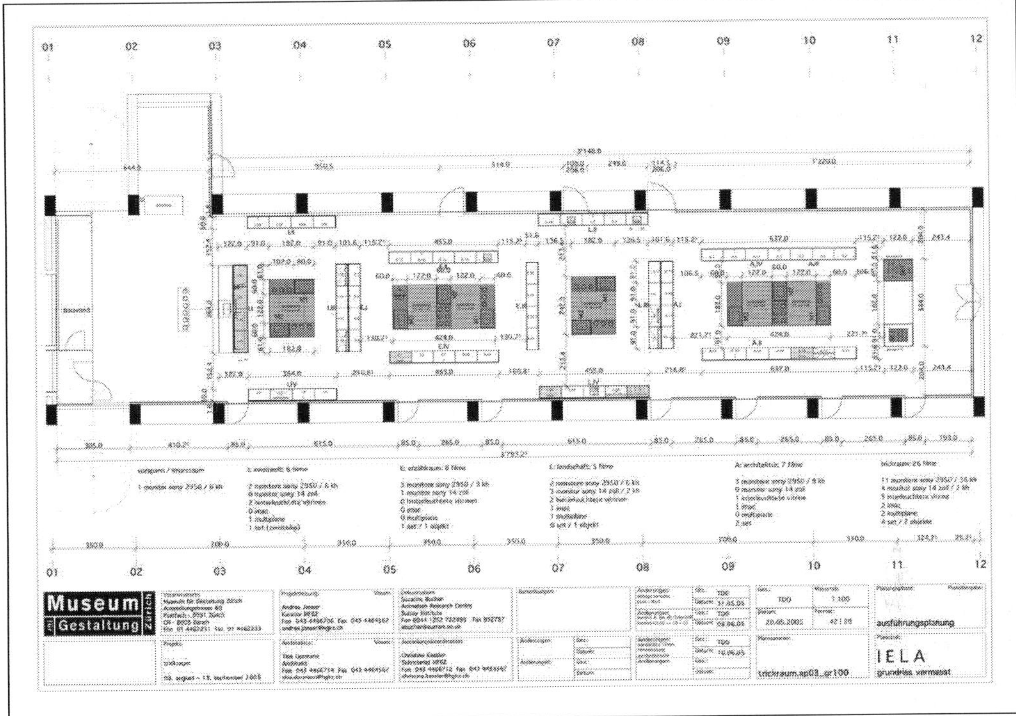

Figure 3. Exhibition, *Trickraum: Spacetricks*, Museum für Gestaltung Zürich 2005, plan.
Design: This Dormann. © Hochschule für Gestaltung und Kunst Zürich.

Purves' inspiration for the spaces in *Screenplay* was motivated by a Willow pattern china plate; Clive Walley's *Light of Uncertainty* originated in Heisenberg's Uncertainty Principle, and Stuart Hilton's *Six Weeks in June* was a merging of doodled drawings and an on-the-road documentary of his band's tour in the United States.

It became clear early on that the emphasis would be on process, not on result, i.e. not simply on the films, as is the case in most recent exhibitions. The essence of our strategy was to reveal the film-makers' artistic process through inclusion of a careful yet rich selection of artwork – exhibiting artworks as art alongside the films.

I began contacting film-makers to arrange visits to their studios to select suitable thematic materials, and it became apparent that there were disparate attitudes to the production material used for making their films. Some had saved all their work and it was catalogued in detail, others mentioned there might be a box in their attic, and still others were surprised at the question as they had binned all their work as they animated. Renowned Dutch animator Paul Driessen, for instance, had thrown away all his artwork for *At Land, At Sea and in the Air,* and we contacted the Netherlands Film Museum for the two remaining extant artworks for his film.

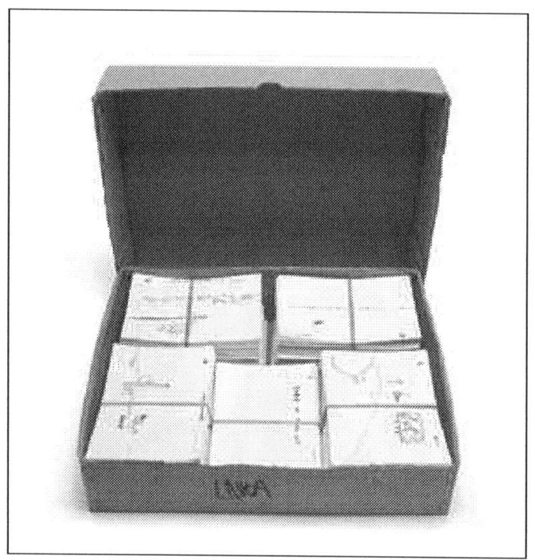

Figure 4. Stuart Hilton, *Six Weeks in June*, UK 1998 (all artwork used to shoot film). Photo: Regula Bearth. © Hochschule für Gestaltung und Kunst Zürich. In: Museum für Gestaltung Zürich/Suzanne Buchan, Andres Janser (ed.), *Trickrau: Spacetricks*, Christoph Merian Verlag, Basel 2005. © Museum für Gestaltung Zürich, 2005.

Besides the 26 films we chose, the exhibition was unique in that it provided insights into the expressive variety of both digital (dominant today) and traditional animation techniques (2-D, drawing, painting, sand, 3-D, puppet, textiles, etc.). It invited visitors to engage with the ways in which the manifold techniques of animation can explore and subvert ordinary perception of space in everyday experience. These were made accessible through installations, ten monitors, 66 exhibition cases containing hundreds of pieces of artwork and 3-D puppet animations sets, and four smaller monitors built into the cases that screened documentaries, works in progress and new works made especially for *Spacetricks* that embellished the artists' original films (Figure 5). Although we had originally planned to set up a small cinema, as the emphasis was on the artworks, and screening rights would have implied a different negotiation than showing films on monitors, we decided to integrate monitors and seating in the four thematic architectural sections. We privileged the artwork, and the films, while screened on decent-sized monitors, did not distract from this emphasis. Visitors could watch a film, peruse the materials used to make it, and watch the film again with an awareness of process. *Spacetricks'* emphasis was on what is considered by most as animation films, exposing relationships between text, artefact and moving image in exhibition and publication. We were also able to produce a richly illustrated book with essays to accompany the exhibition (Figure 6). Especially gratifying were the artists' very positive response to *Spacetricks* treatment of their work, and feedback from visitors who were artists working specifically in one of the media presented – drawing, sculpture, painting, graphic design – who found interdisciplinary assonances with their own practice.

'Just' animation, or art?

Besides the very real concern for locating and securing animation production materials for future generations who may never work with hands-on media, these artworks have a considerable role to play in our future understandings about the pervasiveness of animation in the development of moving image culture. But there is a long way to go to correct a common perception that animation is not 'art'. The BBC website reviewed

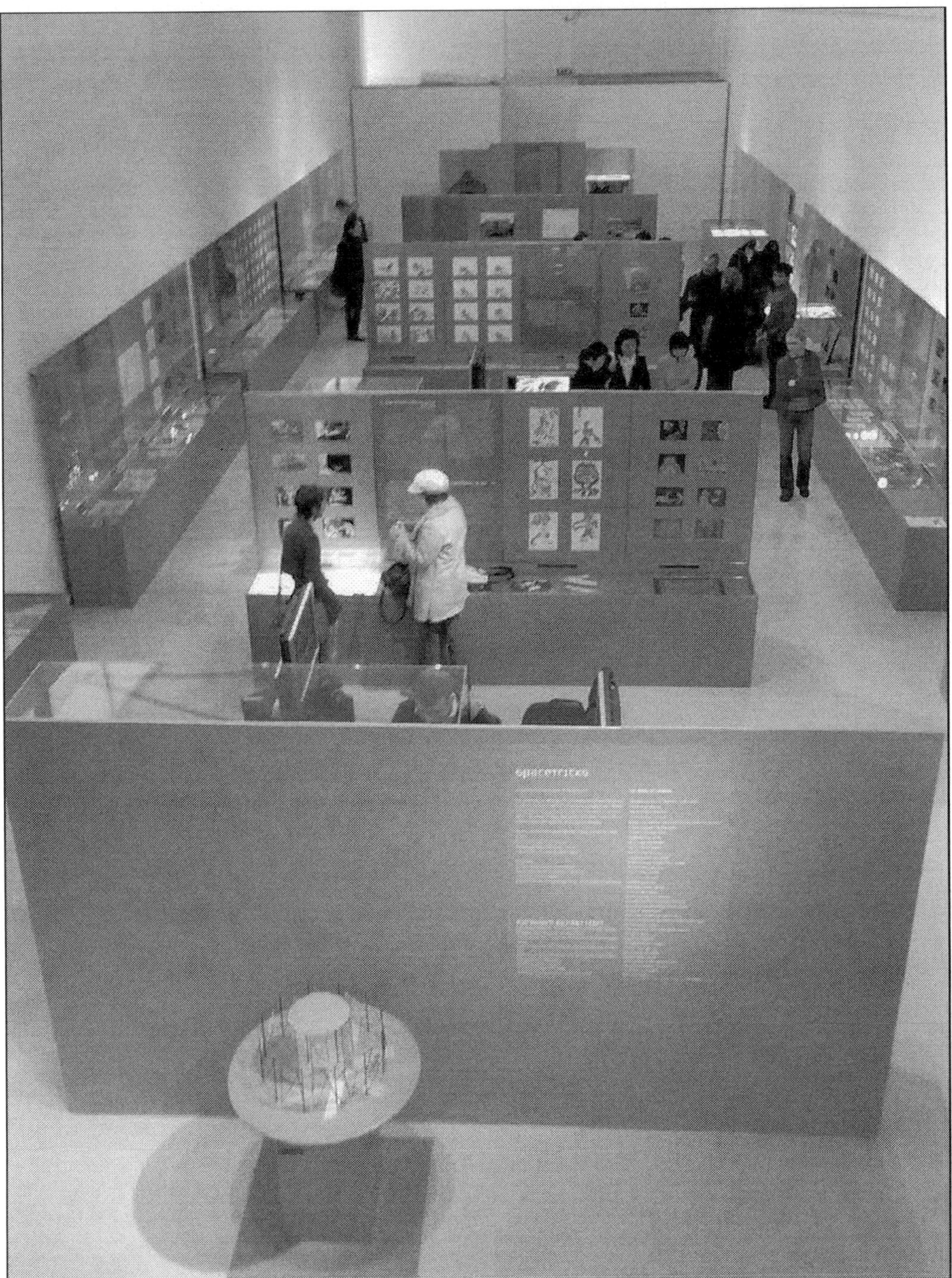

Figure 5. Spacetricks exhibition, James Hockey Gallery, University College for the Creative Arts, Farnham, 2006. Image © Suzanne Buchan.

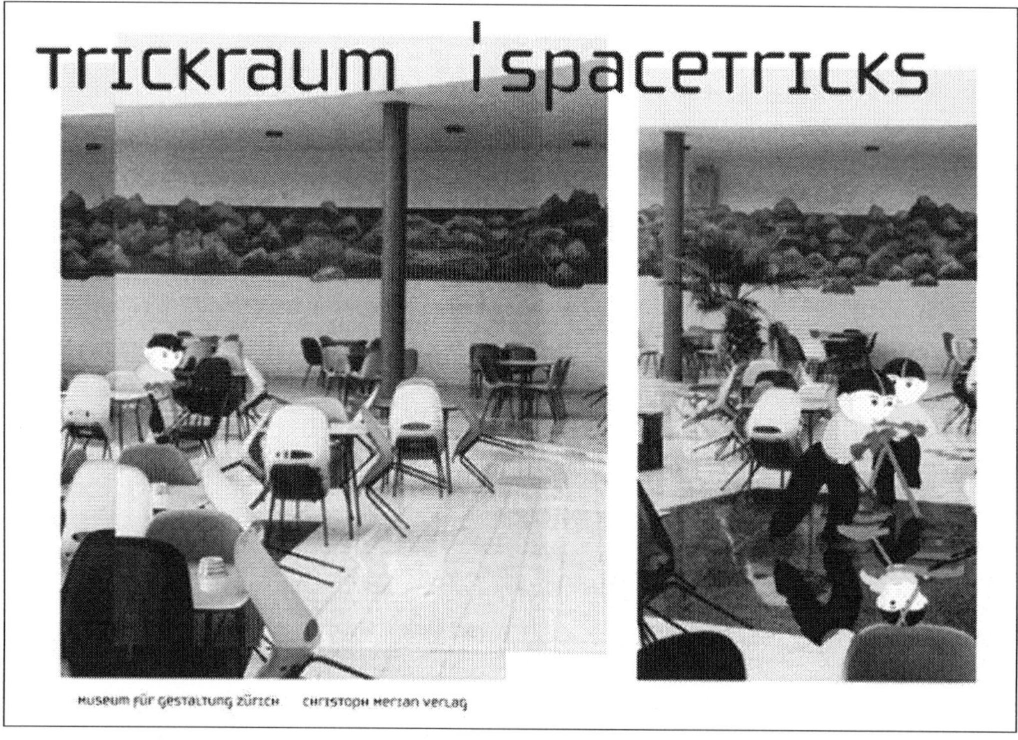

Figure 6. Cover publication, *Trickraum: Spacetricks*, Museum für Gestaltung Zürich 2005. © Hochschule für Gestaltung und Kunst Zürich

the London Parasol Unit Gallery's exhibition *Momentary Momentum*, that as well presenting artists from the arts economy, also included artists known, in the first instance, as animators: William Kentridge Robert Breer, Paul Bush/Lisa Milroy, Michael Dudok de Wit, William Kentridge, Jochen Kuhn, Georges Schwizgebel. The review stated that 'It would be wrong to refer to these works as just "animations".'[6] This comment is symptomatic of a number of common misconceptions of animation touched on in this essay that are perpetuated by media and academia, by 'safe' curating, and by corporate domination of dissemination platforms that offer no space for independent animation. As the Parasol Unit's selection of artists merges 'just' animation with art, perhaps, in reversal, in its own way it is challenging the high/low divide. Critic Adrian Searle had this to say about the exhibition: 'Like everything else in art, getting things right on your own terms is what matters.'[7]

I have tried to articulate what my terms are for sensitive curation of animation film and the relevance of including its attendant artwork. But to end on a hopeful note, perhaps it is as has often been with 'emergent' art practice: whilst many journalists and critics continue to propagate the misconception that animation is 'just' animation, others are engaging in its qualities as art, and it can be hoped that this will eventually have an effect on institutional and museum collections policies and curation strategies. Exhibitions give audiences opportunities to understand and engage with the overwhelming pervasiveness of animation in visual culture, and its breadth of inter- and multi-medial processes and techniques – as Griffin suggests, 'more than the sum of its parts' (Griffin 2007). Creative curating of animation exhibitions we are currently observing are revealing an expanding knowledge of the histories of animation, a growing sensitivity to the best methods of their presentation, simultaneously opening the doors, literally and figuratively, for animation in galleries and for a new paradigm for curation of animation as art.

Notes

1. http://www.vertigomagazine.co.uk/showarticle.php?sel=cur&siz=1&id=661.
2. www.fantoche.ch,/http://www.platformfestival.com/content/venue.aspx/ http://www.aurora.org.uk/.
3. http://www.tentplaza.nl/.
4. www.johnnyhardstaff.com.
5. See www.ucreative.ac.uk/arc for more information.
6. http://www.bbc.co.uk/dna/collective/A20531611.
7. http://www.parasol-unit.org/images/animation/Guardian%20Unlimited%20Arts.htm.

References

Bartlett, Mark, 'Stan Vanderbeek: Social Imagistics and the Culture-Intercom', in *Mainframe Experimentalism. Early Digital Computing and the Experimental Art*, Douglas Kahn and Hannah Higgins (eds., 2008, forthcoming).

Buchan, Suzanne, 'Uncanny Space, Narrative Place: The Architectural Imagination of Animation', in: *What is Architecture?/Text Anthology (Co To Jest Architektura?/Antologia tekstow)*, Adam Budak (ed.), Bunkier Sztuki Contemporary Art Gallery, Firma Wydawniczo-reklamowa RAM, Goethe Institut, Inter Nationes, Kraków, 2002.

Deleuze, Gilles, *The Logic of Sense* (Logique du Sens, 1969), Columbia University Press, 1990, 2001.

Gavin, Francesca, 'Moving Drawings at London's Parasol Unit', *Collective: The Interactive Culture Magazine*, 8 March 2007, http://www.bbc.co.uk/dna/collective/A20531611.

Griffin, George, 'Concrete Animation' in: *animation. an interdisciplinary journal*, vol.2.2, (forthcoming, November 2007).

Hertz, Betti-Sue, *Animated Paintings*, exhibition concept, unpublished, 2006.

Leslie, Esther, *Hollywood Flatlands: Animation, Critical Theory and the Avant-Garde*, London, Verso, 2004.

Searle, Adrian. 'Dirty Gritty Things' *Guardian*, 6 March 2007.

http://www.parasol-unit.org/images/animation/Guardian%20Unlimited%20Arts.htm.

GENERATOR: THE VALUE OF SOFTWARE ART

Geoff Cox

Practices that combine the fields of art and technology employ a contested range of terms. The term 'software art' has become popular to describe the contemporary artistic preoccupation with software production. Certainly 'media arts' is far too broad a description and one that would focus attention too heavily on the 'medium' and 'mediation' of software rather than emphasize its dynamic properties, processes and metaphors. Software art is clearly not just media art, as it expresses more complex processes than simply something mediated between sender, apparatus and receiver.

Software refers to a computer program and the resources related to it that act upon the hardware of the physical machine components and machine. In more detail, this means software includes not only the instructions written in a particular language as the program, but also the other materials required for it to run, that are usually combined for distribution. Hardware is worked upon, and software performs the work. This link to performance also clarifies something about the use of the term 'software art', in describing not merely software used to produce art, but the software itself as the artwork. In other words, the programmers put the pre-existing hardware to work, in a similar way to artists producing concepts and manipulating materials in more traditional forms.

There is little new in placing emphasis on process rather than end product in this way, but the assertion of this essay is that software art exemplifies process-orientated practice in a way that lends itself to critical work appropriate to contemporary conditions. Clearly there is a history to this, and there have been many previous examples of artists generating creative work in an algorithmic manner, using instructions and constraints, whether using computers or not. The older term 'generative art' is generally used in this connection, as well as 'computer arts' with reference to practices of the 1960s and 70s. A general view has emerged that older definitions associated with generative art stress the formal rule-based and syntactical properties of software, and thus do not place sufficient emphasis on semantic concerns and social context. Although, in general, this may be the case, formal concerns are essential to understand the more cultural aspects and the generative or transformative aspects of software. The chapter argues that taken together, the terms generative art and software art emphasize productive contradictions – inherent to both, and between the two.

Generator

There is broad agreement that generative art is a term applied to artwork that is automated by the use of instructions or rules by which the artwork is executed. The outcome of this process is unpredictable, and can be described as being integral to the apparatus or situation, rather than a direct consequence of the artist's intentions. But importantly, the description recognizes that other agencies are at work, including human agency as an integral part of the production process in setting the rules. It is this line of thinking that informed the curation of the touring exhibition *Generator* (2002/3),[1] presenting a series of self-generating projects, incorporating digital media, instruction

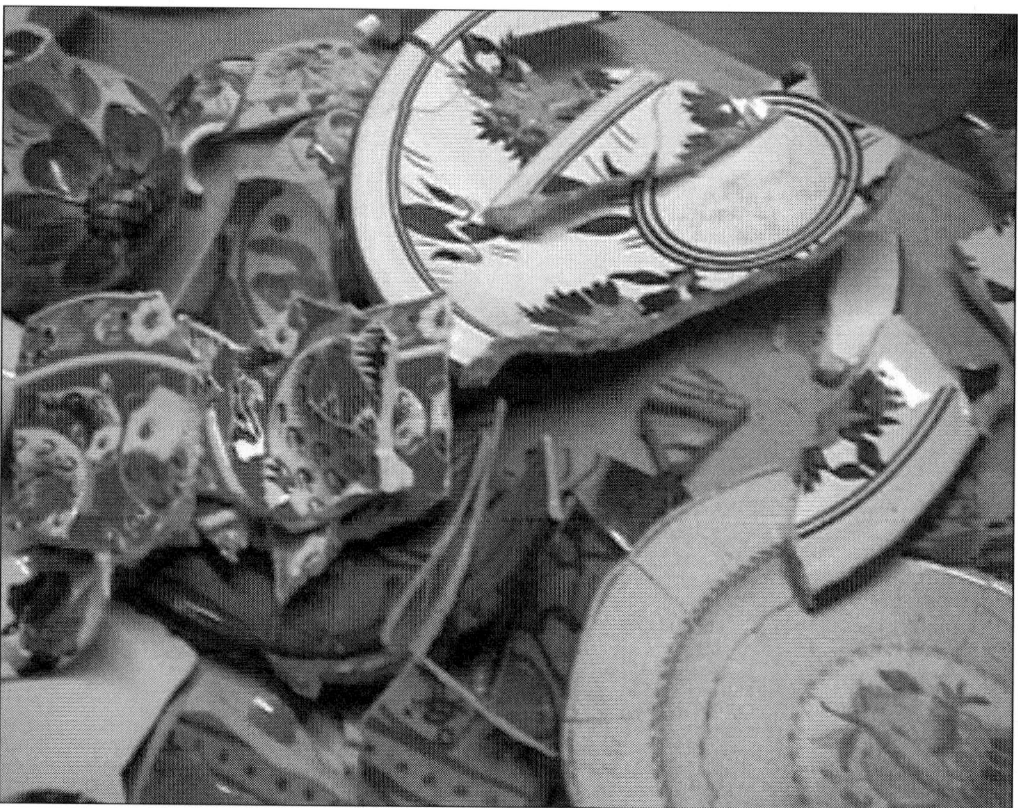

Figure 1. (detail, video still): Yoko Ono's *Mend Peace for the World* (2001).

and participation pieces, experimental literature and music technologies. The work of artist-programmers was combined with artists from a conceptual tradition who employ rules and instructions in their practice. For instance, the work of Alex McLean, Joanna Walsh and Adrian Ward were presented in parallel to Stuart Brisley, Sol LeWitt and Yoko Ono, amongst others (http: //www.generative.net/generator). All work was considered performative in the sense that the artwork was generated through a real-time process.

To stress the point about agency, two specific examples are offered: Ono's *Mend Peace for the World* (Figure 1) consisted of broken dishes from around the world and materials to mend them. The instructions, to be executed by those visiting the exhibition, were: 'Keep adding more crockery as it gets fixed. Keep wishing while you mend.'

In contrast, McLean's *forkbomb.pl* was a program script designed to take a computer to its operational limit. The program script creates new processes repeatedly using the fork system call, until the process table gets filled up and the system crashes. A computer system under such high load causes unpredictable results that pattern differently depending partly on the operating system it runs upon, in this case visualized as binary data.

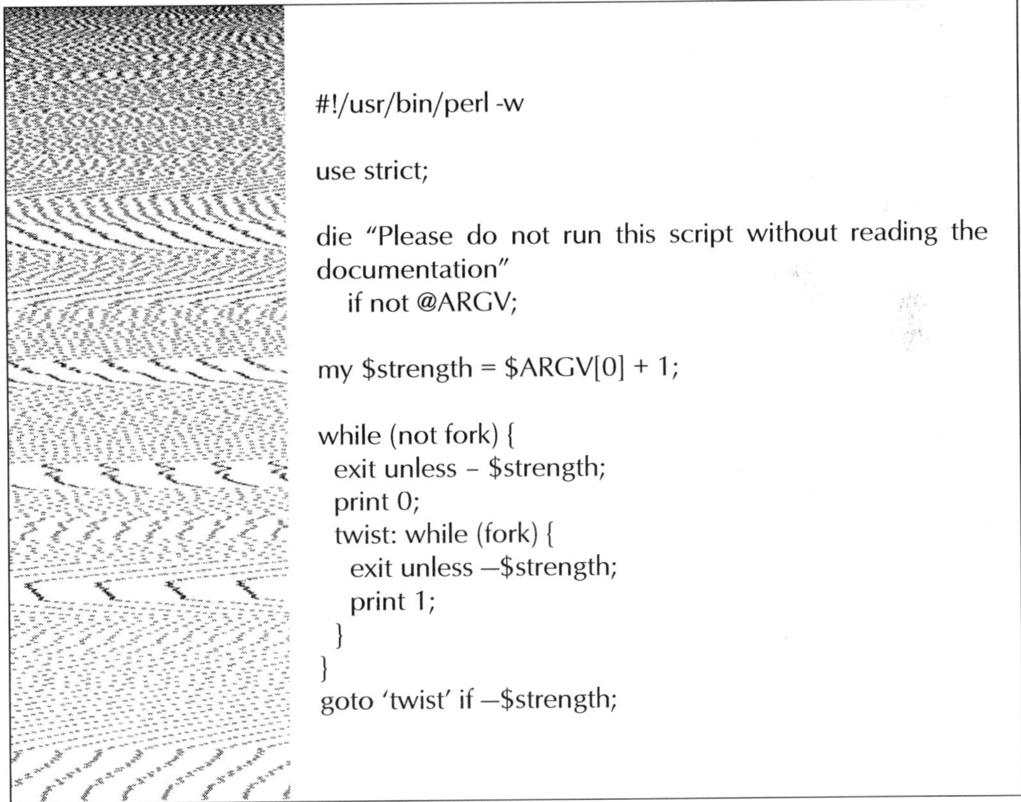

Figure 2. Output and program script from Alex McLean's *forkbomb.pl* (2001).

Both examples – one tending towards reparation or reconstruction, the other towards destruction – emphasize a rejection of what one might refer to as 'software-determinism'. They demonstrate how the producer can concede control to some extent – and this is an important qualification – over the production of the work but that human intervention is paramount to (software) production. In other words, the artwork is necessarily programmed – with or without the aid of a computer. Whether the artist was involved in the writing of the software or not is beside the point. Someone was.

Generative art

In contrast to what has been said about these examples from *Generator*, much of the work in the field of generative art stresses issues of unpredictability and autonomy rather differently. In seeking to clarify what constitutes generative art, Philip Galanter's definition is much cited and positions generative art as broadly rule-based:

> Generative Art refers to any art practice where the artist uses a system, such as a set of natural language rules, a computer program, a machine, or other procedural invention, which is set into motion with some degree of autonomy contributing to or resulting in a completed work of art. (Galanter 2003)

Also defining generative art, John McCormack adds the influence of biology and emergent behaviour and, in particular, the terms 'genotype' and 'phenotype'. He argues that software can be seen in terms of 'genotypes' (DNA in cells) as machine code, and 'phenotypes' (the higher level form of behaviour) as what happens when it runs. The programmer would set the parameters that defined the fitness, and the software would evolve 'autonomously'. Put simply, McCormack generalizes that the authoring process is directed towards a genotype as the specification of a process, and when this process is executed it generates the phenotype as the 'experience of the artwork' (in Brown 2003). It is worth noting the elevated position of the artist in this description as responsible for the DNA of the artwork in the perpetuation of a 'creationist' myth. Clearly, other external factors are at work in creative production in art and life.

In his essay 'What is Generative Art? Complexity Theory as a Context for Art Theory' (Galanter 2003), Galanter supplements his earlier definition by referring to generative systems as also displaying emergent behaviour. His definition of generative art is an eclectic one, contributing to wider discussions around cultural practices (and not just art) that allow for the inclusion of practices that do not necessarily involve computers at all. But to Inke Arns, this is part of the problem as the definition is far too inclusive, applied across many fields of practice that focus attention on the end product of a process. She quotes Tilman Baumgärtel's article 'Experimental Software' (from 2001) to stress the distinction between earlier work using computers and software art, where the latter is:

> ...not art that has been created with the help of a computer, but art that happens in the computer, software is not programmed by artists in order to produce autonomous artworks, but the software itself is the artwork. What is crucial here is

not the result but the process triggered in the computer by the program code. (Arns 2004)

Both Galanter and McCormack's statements do appear to verify an emphasis on end product as opposed to Baumgartel's emphasis on process. There is a danger of emphasizing the formal and syntactic aspects in using the term generative art. But in the case of software, it is not simply a choice of process or product but of the interaction between source code and its executed form. An example of this is McLean's *forkbomb.pl* (2001, described earlier) that demonstrates both the aesthetic appreciation of source code in parallel to a visualization of the process when run. This is, in fact, how it was exhibited as part of the *Generator* show, with the source code displayed as an integral part of the work. Nevertheless, the criticism Arns is making is that the privileging of execution, even if in combination with source code, avoids some of the contemporary practices associated with software art. She is thinking of programs that are not necessarily executable, or executable only on a conceptual level (often referred to as 'codework'). Perhaps it is simply a case of generative art requiring improved description to shift emphasis from the object generated to the process of generation. In this way, and quite literally, the term generator stands for: that which generates.

To generate something accounts for most creative activity in a very general sense. A more specific use in relation to arts practice can be traced to a lecture, 'Generative Art Forms' (presented at the Queen's University, Belfast Festival), in 1972, by the Romanian sculptor Neagu (who also founded a Generative Art Group). But a more common reference is Noam Chomsky's *Syntactic Structures* (1972), first published in 1957, often cited as the source of the concept 'generative grammar' (sometimes referred to as 'transformational grammar'). Chomsky assumes that somehow grammar is given in advance ('hard-wired') and, therefore, human consciousness contains innate grammatical competence that is pre-social (Chomsky 1972). This explains his interest in 'syntactic structures' by which sentences are constructed in particular languages to understand the properties that underlie successful grammars (ibid.). These concerns have also been the inspiration for much artistic experimentation using computers, as it lends itself to the procedural qualities of programming as an expression of transformative grammar.

Often cited in this connection is the 'Ouvroir de Littérature Potentielle' (OuLiPo), a group of writers and mathematicians founded in 1960 by Raymond Queneau and François Le Lionnais. Their concerns were syntactic rather than semantic, concerned with constraints 'brought to bear on the formal aspects of literature' (Le Lionnais, in Motte 1998). Rather than a chance operation (such as in the work of John Cage), Oulipean texts are generated through the use of constraints or rules, wherein any ideas associated with freedom of expression is undermined. An example that lends itself to computation is Queneau's *Cent Mille Milliards de Poèmes* [one hundred thousand billion poems] (1961) in which ten sonnets can be arranged according to formal rules. To each of the ten first lines, the reader can add any of ten different second lines, and so on. The sonnet has fourteen lines, so the possibilities are of the order of 10 to the power of 14, or one hundred trillion sonnets. Le Lionnais makes a claim for the significance of this in terms of technical superiority: 'the work you are holding in your hands represents, itself alone, a quantity of text far greater than everything man has written since the invention of writing' (Motte 1998).

Potential writing in this sense implies the impossibility of its potential reading – and both are exponentially bound. The full potential of this work lies unrealized for practical reasons, perpetually in a suspended state of its further reading. In an experiment to exploit the potential of the computer, Paul Braffort was commissioned to program some of the OuLiPo works, such as Queneau's *Cent Mille Milliards de Poèmes*. In describing this enterprise as 'algorithmic literature', Paul Fournel argues that the machine allows the author to dominate the existing relations of computer, work and reader in new ways (Motte 1998: 140–2). Inspired by such examples, for *Generator*, Joanna Walsh's *Oulibot* operated as a member of an active 'irc' (chat room) community (Figure 3). The program (bot) learnt from the channel and produced plausible utterances based on constraints, and other oulipean transformations of text; such as Jean Lescure's 'S+7' method in

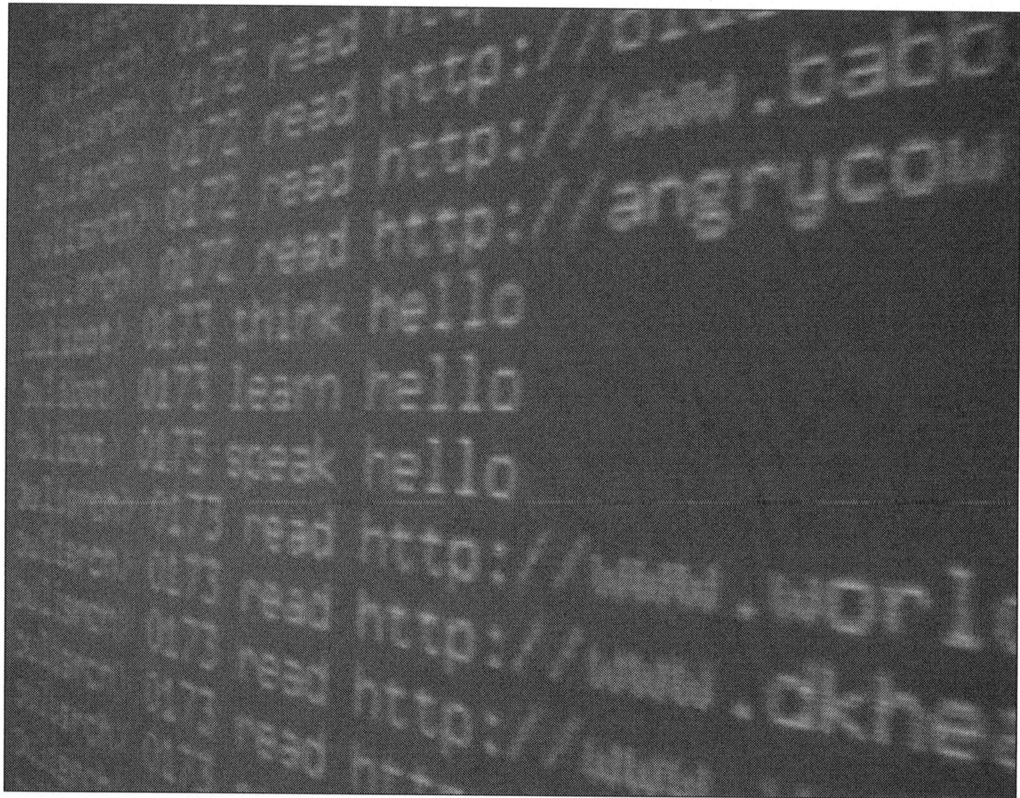

Figure 3. (detail, video still): Joanna Walsh's *Oulibot* (2002).

which a text is taken and each word ('s' for substantive) is replaced by the seventh following it in a dictionary.

Originality is clearly not the point in this work. Rather, creative endeavour is seen to be programmable and is considered in terms of its execution. But far from a deferral of authorship, the computer offers new potentialities in this way. What Le Lionnais calls a 'combinatory literature', is expanded greatly by the computer and its systematic compositional structure. The use of executable formal instructions makes explicit the idea of software as potential literature (or art), whether running on a computer or not. Indeed all conventions of writing and reading, of both text and code, have in common that they are part of a set of abstract (coded) systems of input and output.

Software art

In the many comparisons between contemporary software art and the older practices associated with generative art, McCormack explains one key difference was that in the 1960s and 1970s artists simply had to write (or ask someone to write) their own software in order to generate the outcomes (McCormack in Brown 2003). The now wide availability of authoring software has changed the conditions for the production of software art by the artist-programmer. It is with some of these issues in mind that Richard Wright traces the 'divergence between programmers and program users', based around the issue of whether a computer is considered a medium or a tool (Wright 2004). In a hierarchy of programming languages, Wright points out that not all programming practices are equal. He is thinking of the predominance of scripting languages such as Flash Actionscript (but also Lingo, Perl, MAX, JavaScript, Java, C++, as well as other programming and scripting languages) that use libraries of functions and a certain shared, if not prescribed, vocabulary of styles.

For Wright, this changes the terms of the discussion from a general issue of artistic programming to one of what kind of programming is being used. He cites the historical shift in Harold Cohen's practice from a painter to developing software to automate his artwork, through the use of what Cohen refers to as 'autonomous machine (art making) intelligence' (http: //crca.ucsd.edu/~hcohen/). Developed from 1973 onwards, the *AARON* program represents to Wright the historical transition towards contemporary culture, where the use of computers has become pervasive. As a result, the terms of practice have fundamentally changed for the artist-programmer. His argument is that 'Programming is not only the material of artistic creation, it is the context of artistic creation. Programming has become software.' (Wright 2004)

This refers to earlier practices that were characterized by artists working at the meta-level of programming. Despite this, programming in Cohen's work operates in a rather ambiguous relation to the overall artwork. Clearly in a general sense it is part of the artistic output but more in terms of a representation of his skills and technique, rather than as a constituent part of the artwork as such. In the tradition of generative art, the emphasis tends towards the completed work of art rather than the program or programming being a work in itself.

In contrast to Cohen's work, a more contemporary reference that situates software art overtly in terms of programming is the exhibition *CODeDOC* first for the Whitney Museum of American Art's 'artport' website (2002) and later at Ars Electronica (2003) (http: //artport.whitney.org/commissions/codedoc/index.shtml). The curator, Christiane Paul, set the invited artist-programmers an instruction to 'connect and move three points in space' in a language of their choice (Java, C, Visual Basic, Lingo, Perl) and to exchange the code with the other artists for comments. The viewers of all the works in *CODeDOC* were invited to first read the written code and then see the executed work. This raised some controversy on mail lists at the time, for deliberately obfuscating or aestheticizing code to non-programmers, rather than demystifying the creative process. Yet the significance is that code is taken to be part of the work and not simply meant to assist interpretation. The curatorial statement contains a number of useful comments

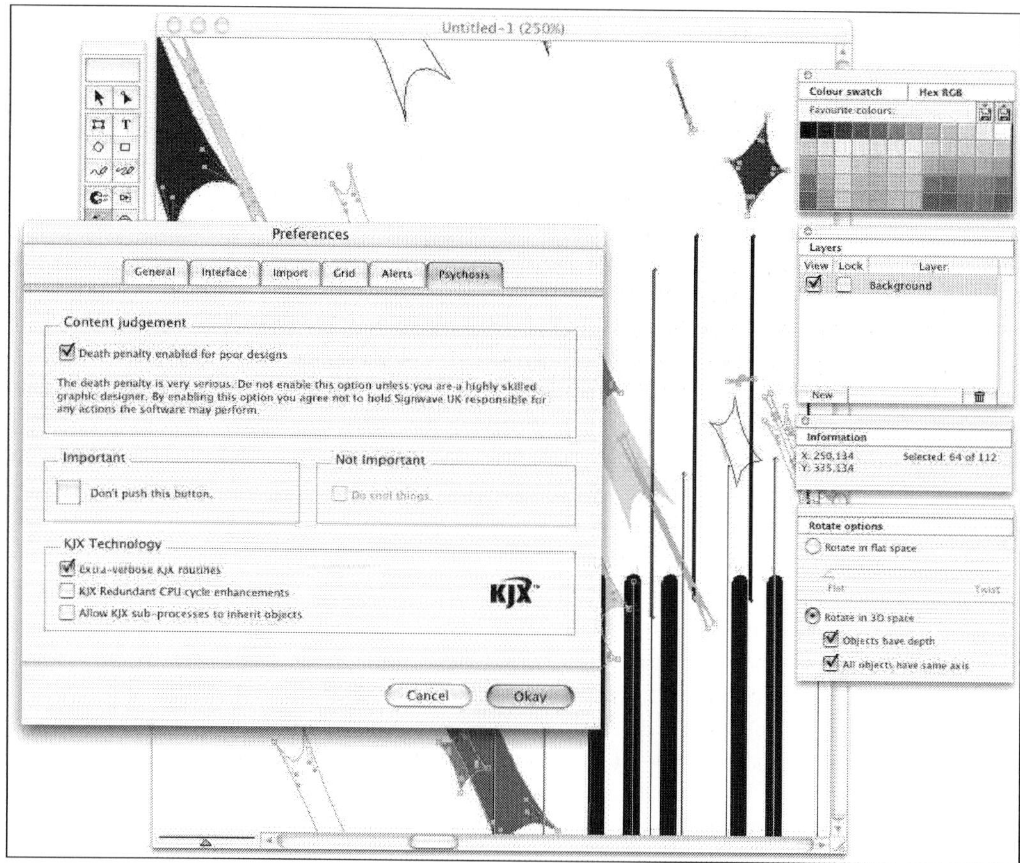

Figure 4. (screen grab): Adrian Ward's *Auto-Illustrator* (2000).

on the intentions of the experiment and reiterates the potential of software itself as artwork:

> In software art, the 'materiality' of the written instructions mostly remains hidden. In addition, these instructions and notations can be instantaneously activated; they contain and – further layers of processing aside – *are* the artwork itself. While one might claim that the same holds true for a work of conceptual art that consists of written instructions, this work would still have to be activated as a mental or physical event by the viewer and cannot instantaneously transform, transcend, and generate its own materiality. (Paul 2003)

This approach parallels some of the curatorial decisions for the *Generator* show, in particular McLean's *forkbomb.pl* where the source code was exhibited as an integral part of the artwork. Whereas formerly artists had to engage with programming in early computer arts practice, the lack of necessity now allows for other critical issues to be engaged (just as previously the invention of photography perhaps freed painting from figurative representation).

An example of critical software is Signwave's *Auto-Illustrator* that defies user expectation as a parody of the vector graphics design software Adobe *Illustrator*. It looks like and indeed works like conventional commercial software, but carries some extra auto-generative functionality that renders designs outside of the direct control or creativity of the user. Cheekily included in early releases was a license agreement that indicated that any designs were necessarily co-authored by the company Signwave who supply the software (aka Adrian Ward). Here, the parody operated particularly effectively, as some users were outraged that a company would insist on such a clause in a direct assault on their creative and intellectual rights. It highlights the issue that full authorship is rarely acknowledged in making art using software, as is the labour of all those involved in the process. The software was released as a boxed version for the exhibition *Generator* with a 'User's Manual' that contained both technical detail and critical essays. In this way, the commercial packaging added a further layer to its ironic critique of the commodification of art and software as art.

In linguistic terms, artist-programmers appear to have shifted their attention from an engagement with the syntax of programming to semantic concerns. This is, indeed, how Cramer makes the distinction between generative art and software art, by associating the former with syntax and the latter with semantics (2003). But this is not simply a shift from one to the other. Syntax, although not concerned with meaning in itself, certainly has implications for semantics, and both are required to inform an overall theory of language. Yet what Cramer is trying to emphasize is a shift in software art from 'pure syntax' to 'something semantic, something that is aesthetically, culturally and politically charged' (2003). It is not a choice of one or the other but a change of emphasis.

The apparent dualism between generative art and software art is also something that Mitchell Whitelaw disputes in questioning the binary relation of formalism (associated with generative art) and culturalism (associated with software art). Rather than seeing this as an impasse, Whitelaw suggests a 'complementarity' of positions that leads to alternative modes of being and relation (Whitelaw 2005). He calls this 'critical generativity' to stress the emergent and transformative properties that reflect social complexity and software's latent cultural agency (ibid.). This chapter also argues for new critical forms, but rather than seeking Whitelaw's complementarity or fusion, argues for a contradictory relation. That said, the competing definitions matter little in themselves but only in as much as they operate in terms of an overall contribution to a critical discourse around the practice of software art and culture. Software necessarily includes, if only on a conceptual level, a generative process in which something is always ready to come into being, however latent. It is for convenience only that this is referred to as software art.

The generative properties of software can be seen in parallel to the argument that art should now deal with the central issue of transformation rather than representation (whether software is used directly or not). On the surface this sounds like a very contemporary position, supported by the curator Nicolas Bourriaud's claim that the image is now defined by its 'generative power', and that art can be seen to be a program(me) for the generation of forms and situations (Bourriaud 2002). His term 'relational aesthetics' describes a practice that involves human interactions, social context and the new aesthetic and cultural concerns that arise from this. He is referring to artwork that is a programme to be followed, a model to be reproduced, or an encouragement to do something – and points to the parallel activities of artists engaging in ideas of interaction and sociability, set against the hype of interactive computer systems. To Bourriaud, artwork not using the computer has as much potential to make work about its effects. This may well be the case (as with many of the works selected for *Generator*), but this position is simply based on systems thinking, and the statement is consistent with Gregory Bateson's 1971 position on art (from *Steps to an Ecology of Mind*) that focuses attention not on the message but the code (Bateson 2000). Bateson considers the production of art, and art as product, in terms of behaviours or rules that are embodied in the machinery that then generates transformations (Bateson 2000). Software appears to characterize arts practices that privilege the idea, code, process, system and its transformational qualities. Whether using a computer or not, art has become ever more like software.

Software as cultural metaphor
Clearly there is a history to software art, and a canon appears to have emerged. Andreas Broegger is one researcher amongst many who situates the contemporary term software art in the historical context of the *Radical Software* journal published by the Raindance collective (launched in 1970, http: //www.radicalsoftware.org/) and Jack Burnham's exhibition *Software, Information Technology: Its Meaning for Art* at the Jewish Museum, New York (also 1970). Broegger describes the ways the term software was

used as a metaphor for arts practice at that time, to stand for the transmission of information using available communications technologies, in contrast to the 'hardware' of object-based art (Broegger 2003). Although any discussion of software requires an understanding of its relationship to hardware (even if it is accepted that software can exist without hardware), it is clear that the term software is being used in a rather different sense in the 1970s. In the field of art at least, the description runs in parallel to Conceptualism and its associated shift away from the end product at that time. A contemporary use of the term software reflects an emphasis on process, which has become the orthodoxy in contemporary cultural practices. Software is more than just art and expands an understanding of art's possibilities to engage wider social issues.

A statement from the first issue of the *Radical Software* journal gives a clear indication of its agenda: 'Power is no longer measured in land, labour or capital, but by access to information and the means to disseminate it' (Ross 2003). On a technical level, it was the widespread availability of the video portapak that inspired the belief that this could contribute to social transformation, through people gaining increased access to the means of production and becoming producers. In the context of its publication in the United States, the position of the journal was influenced by the rise of the civil rights movement, a general mistrust of the communications media on offer, requiring more independent and alternative media and cultural practices, combined with ecological concerns (according to Ross 2003). Those associated with this project 'imagined a world in which the contest of ideas and values could take place freely and openly' outside of the existing institutional and ideological frameworks of commercial telecommunications. They proposed 'a new information order in which the very idea of hierarchical power structure might be transformed or even eliminated' (Ross 2003). In this sense, what is radical about software is that it acts upon hardware. It operates as a metaphor for an emphasis on social processes that involve an engagement with relations of production and 'radical' transformation.

In parallel to the *Radical Software* journal, 'software as a metaphor for art' was explored in Burnham's *Software* exhibition. The show can be seen as a product of its times with its overt structuralist and conceptualist concerns, and its aim to focus attention on the technical apparatus. It corresponds to what has since become commonplace in looking to the 'dematerialization' associated with the conceptual arts tradition and the 'immaterialization' of information and communications technology. In his essay 'The House that Jack Built' (1998), Shanken traces Burnham's concerns with particular reference to his book *Beyond Modern Sculpture: The Effects of Science and Technology on the Sculpture of this Century* (1968) that ends with an account of 'systems aesthetics'. By an aesthetics of systems, Burnham refers to non-object–based art and time-based practices such as performance, interactive and conceptual art, but also public interaction that breaks down the false distinction between the operating systems of art and non-art. This is software metaphorically speaking, the abstract 'internal logic' of a program receiving feedback from human subjects. In summary, the exhibition *Software* was an attempt to reveal some of the contradictions between object and non-object, art and non-art, artist and non-artist, evident in art's organizational and systemic logic.

Conceptualism has been particularly influential in attempts to draw software art into an art historical register. Referring to Lucy Lippard's portrayal of dematerialization, software art is clearly both concerned with art as idea and action, which both on a conceptual and technical level describes source code and its execution. The generative approach of conceptual artist Sol LeWitt is evocative of software in this connection: 'The idea becomes a machine that makes the art' (in Lippard 1997). In LeWitt's work, instructions are provided for the production of artworks that are then executed by other people. For instance, in *Chicago*, a publication produced for *Generator*, a serial variation using nine found postcards was produced using a simple algorithm as follows:

```
1
2
1 2
3
1 2 3
4
1 2 3 4
5
1 2 3 4 5
6
1 2 3 4 5 6
7
1 2 3 4 5 6 7
8
1 2 3 4 5 6 7 8
9
1 2 3 4 5 6 7 8 9
```

The comparison of software art to earlier art movements such as Conceptualism, but also the avant-garde activities of the 1920s in Russia and Germany, provides an historical understanding of radical forms and strategies. But in the contemporary situation, it appears that many of the claims of the historical avant-garde have become:

> ...embedded in the commands and interface metaphors of computer software. In short, the avant-garde vision became materialized in a computer. All the strategies developed to awaken audiences from a dream-existence of bourgeois society [...] now define the basic routine of a post-industrial society: the interaction with a computer. (Manovich 1999)

The once radical technique of montage has become commonplace. On the surface, it seems that what was once a radical aesthetic vision to reveal the social structure behind

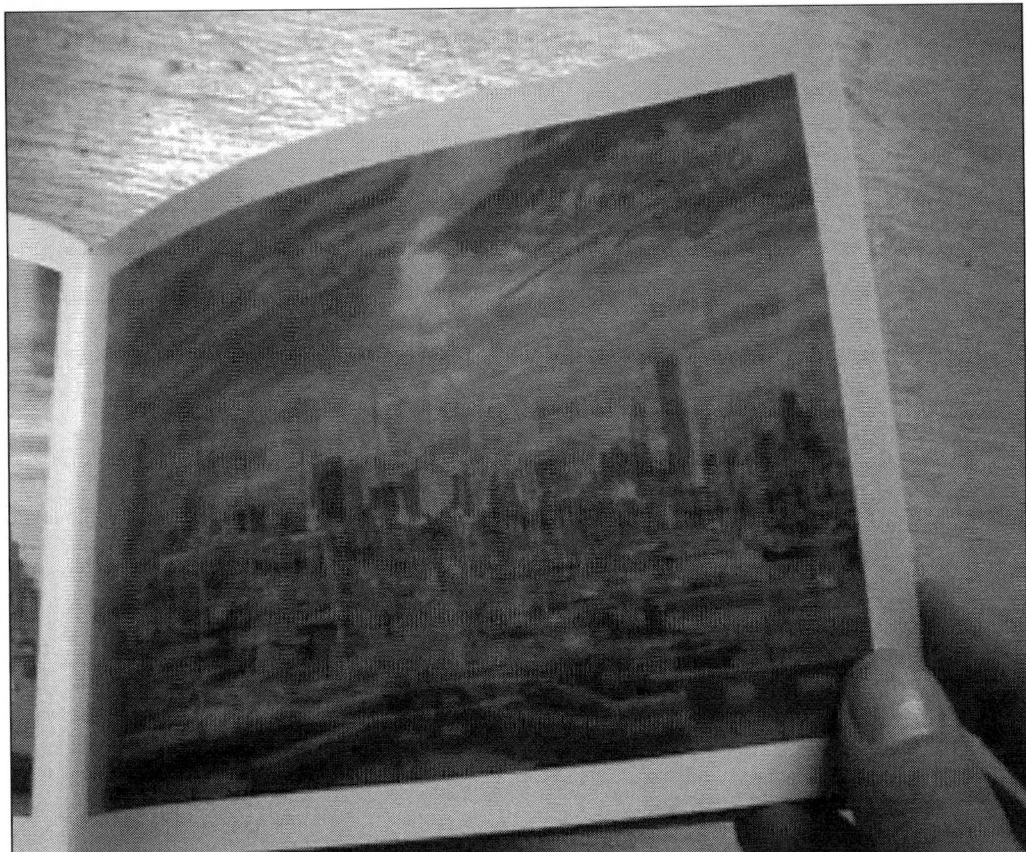

Figure 5. (video still): final page of Sol LeWitt's *Chicago* (2002), produced in collaboration with Alec Finlay of MorningStar/Pocketbooks.

the visible surfaces has become a standardized form through the use of computer technology. Lev Manovich discusses these perceptions of change and the ways in which ideology naturalizes these changes. This reflects contemporary culture's reliance on appropriation, wherein recycling, re-working, and re-combining media are the standard techniques. He concludes that 'the avant-garde becomes software' and that it continues to introduce revolutionary techniques but the terms are different:

> 'software does not simply adopt avant-garde techniques without changing them; on the contrary, these techniques are further developed, formalized in algorithms, codified in software, made more efficient and effective' (Manovich 1999).

If art holds radical potential at all in these post-political times, the issue remains how to produce art that resists its seemingly inevitable commodification and how to reconcile the apparent failure of the avant-garde to deliver its promises (evident in Conceptualism

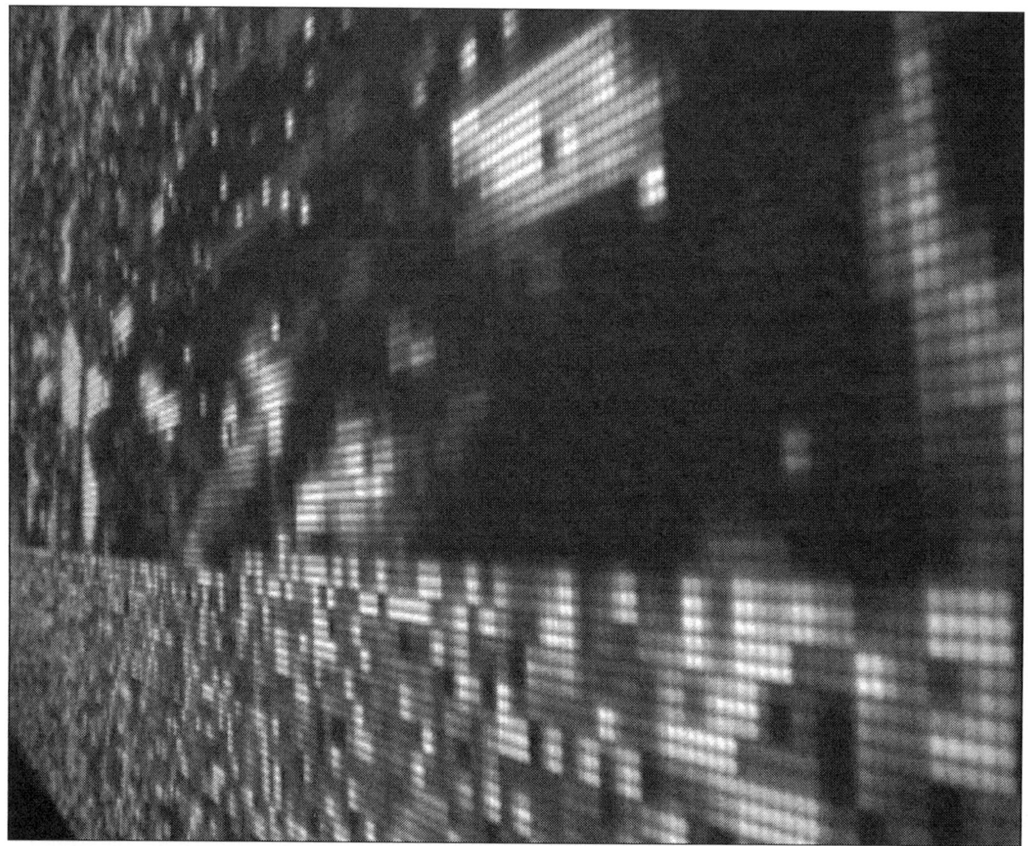

Figure 6. (detail, video still): Stuart Brisley and Adrian Ward's *Ordure: : real-time* (2002), courtesy of the UK Museum of Ordure.

and Dada). If, as Manovich thinks, software has naturalized montage techniques, how can software be further developed as a radical project in revealing the ideological processes at work?

Exhibited as part of *Generator* in the form of a large projection, Stuart Brisley and Adrian Ward's *Ordure: : real-time* is both a representation and a process of detritus that slowly 'corrupts' – pixel by pixel. The corruption is triggered by viewing the image. The more people that view the image, the more prevalent its decay. When the image is left alone, it rewrites itself anew. On one level, the resultant image with pixels moving incrementally out of order is the same as the first image where the pixels are in the correct order. The data is consistent, the pixels merely rearranged. The work demonstrates the dialectical play between two interconnected states of order and disorder, between generation and corruption, suggesting the potential for change built into any system. Indeed, complexity theory verifies that systems are not closed but can be seen to be also sensitive to small changes.

The challenge for a critical practice in software art is to maintain contradiction in the process of transformation, for this is where politics is evident and where re-invention takes place. In terms of the legacy of previous radical arts practice and some of the examples cited here, the lessons of art history exemplify the point that Lippard makes: that in a contemporary situation where conceptual strategies have become the orthodoxy of contemporary art and effectively recuperated, radical art can be found in social energies not yet recognized as art (Lippard 1997). Perhaps software art and culture represents such an instance – for now at least.

Note

1. *Generator* was a SPACEX touring exhibition, curated by Geoff Cox and Tom Trevor, with support from the National Touring Programme of the Arts Council of England. It was shown at Spacex, Exeter (2002), then toured to the Liverpool Biennial (2002) and Firstsite, Colchester (2003). Commissioned artists included emerging computer artist-programmers, as well as more established figures from a conceptual art tradition, all of who work with generative forms and ideas: Mark Bowden, Stuart Brisley, Angus Fairhurst, Alec Finlay, Tim Head, Jeff Instone, Zoë Irvine, Sol LeWitt, limbomedia, Alex McLean, Guy Moreton, Netochka Nezvanova, Yoko Ono, Organogenesis Inc., Jon Pettigrew, Colin Sackett, Sulawesi Crested Macaques from Paignton Zoo, Joanna Walsh, and Adrian Ward. http: //www.generative.net/generator/.

References

Arns, I., 'Read_me, Run_me, Execute_me: Software and Its Discontents, or: It's the Performativity of Code, Stupid!', in Goriunova, O., & A Shulgin, A., (eds.) *Read_Me: Software Art & Cultures – Edition 2004*, Ärhus: Digital Aesthetics Research Centre, University of Ärhus, 2004, pp. 176–193.

Bateson, G., *Steps to an Ecology of Mind*, Chicago/London: University of Chicago Press, 2000 [1971].

Bourriaud, N., *Relational Aesthetics*, trans. Simon Pleasance & Fronza Woods, Dijon-Quetigny: Les Presses de Réel, 2002.

Broegger, A., 'Gigliotti on "(radical) software"', as part of software art thread, *Rhizome* (via Andreas Broeckmann) 10 Oct 2003, http: //www.rhizome.org/.

Brown, P., (ed.) 'Generative computation and the arts', in *Digital Creativity*, vol. 14, no. 1, Lisse: Swets & Zeitlinger, 2003.

Burnham, J., *Beyond Modern Sculpture: the Effects of Science and Technology on the Sculpture of this Century*, New York: George Braziller, 1968.

Chomsky, N., *Syntactic Structures*, The Hague: Mouton, 1972 [1957].

Cramer, F.,'Exe.cut[up]able statements: the Insistence of Code', in Gerfried Stocker & Christine Schöpf (eds.), *Code – The Language of Our Time*, Ars Electronica, Linz: Hatje Cantz, 2003, pp. 98–103.

Galanter, P., 'What is Generative Art? Complexity Theory as a Context for Art Theory', *Generative Art 03*, international conference, Politecnico di Milano, Italy, 2003, http: //www.generativeart.net.

Lippard, L., (ed.) *Six Years: the dematerialization of the art object from 1966 to 1972*, London:

University of California Press, 1997.

Manovich, L., 'Avant-garde as Software', 1999, http: //www.manovich.net/TEXTS_04.HTM.

Motte, W. F. Jr (ed.), *Oulipo: a Primer of Potential Literature*, trans. Warren F. Motte, Illinois: Dalkey Archive Press, 1998.

Paul, C., 'Public Cultural Production Art(Software)' in Gerfried Stocker & Christine Schöpf (eds.), *Code – The Language of Our Time*, Ars Electronica, Linz: Hatje Cantz, 2003, pp. 129–135.

Ross, D. A., 'Radical Software Redux', 2003, http: //www.radicalsoftware.org/e/ross.html.

Shanken, E. A., 'The House That Jack Built: Jack Burnham's Concept of "Software" as a Metaphor for Art', in *Leonardo Electronic Almanac*, 6: 10, November 1998, http: //mitpress.mit.edu/e-journals/LEA/ARTICLES/jack.html.

Shanken, E. A., 'From Cybernetics to Telematics: The Art, Pedagogy, and Theory of Roy Ascott', in Roy Ascott, ed., *Telematic Embrace: Visionary Theories of Art, Technology, and Consciousness*, Berkeley: University of California Press, 2003, pp. 1–94.

Whitelaw, M., 'System Stories and Model Worlds: A Critical Approach to Generative Art', in Olga Goriunova (ed.), *Readme 100: Temporary Software Art Factory*, Dortmund: Hartware Medien Kunst Verein, 2005, pp. 134–153.

Wright, R., 'Software Art After Programming', *Metamute*, July 2004, http: //www.metamute.org/en/node/414.

WHO MAKES SITE-SPECIFIC DANCE? THE YEAR OF THE ARTIST AND THE MATRIX OF CURATING

Kate Lawrence

Context

This chapter constitutes a disciplinary act of trespass from dance studies into this collection of essays into the visual arts. I want to capitalize upon this incursion to consider site-specific dance works as performances that take place in non-theatre environments. Despite a mushrooming of locational dance works in Britain over the past fifteen years, fertilized in a large part by the Year of the Artist initiative in 2000, scholarly writing about site-specific dance is thin on the ground. Briginshaw (2001) has written about site-specific dance, but concerns herself almost exclusively with the use of space and site in dance on screen, with the exception of the chapter on choreographer Anderson's 1998 work, *Out on the Windy Beach* (2001: 59–74). Worth and Poynor's (2004) welcome recent publication about the life and work of North American choreographer Anna Halprin provides useful information on her seminal *oeuvre* in relation to site. Several texts address the postmodern era in dance – Banes (1977, 1987), Livet (1978) and Jowitt (1997) – providing a valuable resource for considering the non-theatre works of Judson Church dance artists, in particular Monk and Brown. Site-specific dance has also been discussed from the vantage point of other disciplines. From theatre, Kaye includes choreographer Meredith Monk in his interdisciplinary work, *Site-specific art: performance, place and documentation* (2000: 204–215) and Wilkie discusses my own work for the Year of the Artist and that of Seven Sisters Dance Company and Sirens Crossing (Wilkie 2004 and 2002: 140–160). From the visual arts, Goldberg discusses the work of Halprin and postmodern choreographers in her survey, *Performance Art* ([1979], 2001: 121–163). The work of recent choreographers is documented in reviews of the work published in dance magazines such as *Dance Theatre Journal*, *Dance Now* and *Animated*, as well as online resources. In contrast, the visual arts has a developed body of thought addressing site-specific art (Kester 2004; Kwon 2004; Lacy et al. 1995; Lippard 1997; and Suderburg et al. 2000).

Models of site-specificity in the visual arts

The main focus of this chapter will be on four dance events that took place as part of the Year of the Artist, an Arts Council of England-funded programme which ran from June 2000 to May 2001, and will consider the ways in which site-specific dance is made, experienced and valued. To provide a frame of reference for the discussion of the four case studies, I will propose models of site-specificity in the visual arts, focusing on the transportability of artwork and on community arts. The YOTA scheme has been pivotal in the recent development and understanding of site-specific dance in Britain and leads to my contention that a matrix of curating agents creates the outcomes. The potentially complex web of participants involved in the making of any given work leads to questions over whether the authorship of the choreographer is compromised or expanded. I also consider how the 'function' of art and its relationship with wider audiences might be expanded through the processes these works develop in new places with new communities.

While the focus here is on site-specific *art* practices, these practices intersect with the contexts, functions and peoples of the sites they inhabit, and diversify the values and meaning attributed to dance. Dance in the UK is, and has been, practised in many forms outside a theatre context; for example, in rituals, festivals and in social contexts, yet these wider cultural manifestations of dance have been separated from dance performed in theatres. Dance companies often undertake workshop programmes in various communities alongside their touring shows, often resulting in 'curtain-raisers', a short piece of dance choreographed by a professional company for a community group to be performed as a prologue to the company's work. There have been few attempts, however, to draw together social and art spheres to produce dance-as-art outcomes in new settings and contexts. I propose that site-specific dance provides such an opportunity as it has the potential to redefine notions of dance as art and integrate dance practices in a broader social and cultural context.

Stephen Hodge, of theatre company Wrights and Sites, proposes a consideration and classification of site-specific performance practices which include those both in and outside the theatre building (e.g. 'Shakespeare in the Park'). He cites 'site-sympathetic' (existing performance and text made visible in a selected site); 'site-generic' (performance generated for a series of associated sites); or 'site-specific' (performance specifically generated from or for one selected site) (Hodge, cited in Wilkie 2002: 150) This classification provides a useful framework with which to consider a range of site-specific performance works which I will refer to when considering the case studies. Its shortcomings, however, lie in its oversimplification of the actual practices of artists, which so often defy rigid classification.

The critical engagement of artists with location has led to what Kwon (2004: 26) terms a 'discursive' approach to site which further loosens the bonds between the art object and site, so that site itself might stand for subject matter or content manifested over a range of geographical locations. This allows artists greater freedom in interpreting site in their work, but, as Wilkie (2002) argues in her survey of site-specific performance in Britain, it raises fundamental questions about what the term 'site-specific' really means.

> For some, this kind of touring or relocating has an enriching effect on the work: it 'radically expands concepts' of site-specificity (Bobby Baker) and 'allows for a constantly changing dynamic in the performance' (Theatre Nomad)...if a performance is reworked, to what extent can it then be said to be the 'same' performance?...at what stage would we agree that a performance has been adapted enough to retain the label 'site-specific?' (Wilkie 2002: 150)

'New genre public art' (Lacy et al. 1997), arising largely from community art practices, is essentially art which is in the public interest: socially active, politically engaged and seeking to effect material or attitudinal change in particular communities through art practices that engage in a dialogue with communities. Kester characterizes this kind of work through a dialogical aesthetic, where artists

> ...begin their work not with the desire to express or articulate an already formed creative vision but rather...to listen. Their sense of artistic identity is sufficient to speak as well as listen, but it remains contingent upon the insights to be derived from their interaction with others and with otherness. They define themselves as artists through their ability to catalyse understanding, to mediate exchange, and to sustain an ongoing process of empathetic identification and critical analysis. (Kester 2004: 118)

Mary Jane Jacob suggests that 'the role of public art has shifted from that of renewing the physical environment to that of improving society, from promoting aesthetic quality to contributing to the quality of life, from enriching lives to saving lives' (1995, cited in Kwon 2004: 111).

The boundaries of understandings of site-specific art have been stretched by the conditions of production of the works and the intentions of artists. Works might be produced for a range of similar, generic sites, enabling a 'tour' of the work; or a range of dissimilar sites, approached with sensitivity and linked conceptually. In addition, a site might be understood *discursively* rather than primarily geographically constructed, whilst other works might develop content in dialogue with a local community connected to a site.

The Year of the Artist

The Year of the Artist (YOTA) was the culmination of eight festivals leading up to the millennium, launched by the Arts Council of England in 1990. These festivals were regional- and artform-specific, for example, in 1993, the East Midlands was designated

UK Region of Dance, and, in 1996, the North was UK Region of Visual Arts (Hutton and Fenn 2002: 1). YOTA, however, was a national programme delivered regionally, representing the first collaboration between all ten regional arts boards. One respondent to the report described the collaboration as a 'strange and fascinating structure that was evolving and emerging and only partly really being planned' (Hutton and Fenn 2002: 11). The focus on collaboration, process and uncertainty of outcome suggests that creative practices were involved at the institutional level of the project, as the Arts Council and the regional arts boards engaged with the challenges posed in delivering the project. This collaboration extended beyond the funding institution, to include Arts 2000 (a charity set up to 'lead, profile and co-ordinate YOTA at a national level'); Regional Artists' advisory groups; an artists' think tank; sponsors; national partners; and YOTA patrons (Hutton and Fenn 2002: 6). These separate partners brought different and potentially conflicting agendas to the programme. Regional Arts Boards (RABs) officers saw it as a marketing opportunity for the corporate identity of the RABs to increase access and audiences for the arts, whilst some artists saw it as 'a unique chance...to get involved at the heart of the decision-making process and to "make a difference"...to show that community art and art in rural communities can be cutting edge' (Hutton and Fenn 2002: 9). Other artists, however, 'opposed the idea of trying to make artists into social engineers or social workers...[they] saw community art as just one aspect of what artists do' (Hutton and Fenn 2002: 14).

YOTA invited artists to apply for funds to undertake residencies 'that take[s] the work of artists to new people, new places or new contexts'. The focus of the scheme based on a 'residency' model became a catalyst for dancers to make site-specific work, and, as a result, this work departed from established patterns of theatre dance-making and presentation. It also led to more complex notions of collaborative practice and authorship by engaging a wide range of agents in the making of new dance work.

Case study one: *Plastic Chill*
Choreographer Maxine Doyle's project was linked to a Southern England Touring Agency (SETA) theatre tour of an existing dance work, *Plastic Chill* (2001), which 'fused aspects of club culture with Mike Leigh's 70's play *Abigail's Party*' (Doyle 2001: 7). Doyle was to make a new dance work to be performed in a nightclub, 'a high-energy, site-specific work with a group of young people, which will act as a prologue to the narrative of *Plastic Chill*' (Doyle 2001: 7). Her decision to present the work in a nightclub was driven by a need to contextualize the first section of the work, in which she attempted to recreate the 'the illusion of a hot, sweaty and crowded club' (Doyle 2001: 7). This relocation of an existing dance text suggests a 'site-sympathetic' approach (Hodge 2001, cited in Wilkie 2002: 150), alongside an established model of touring dance practice. The original site, The Shuttle Nightclub, and participants, Generation Arts Project, for the residency were chosen through discussion with the arts development officer for Eastbourne Borough Council. The final outcome was achieved through a range of creative and 'functional' collaborations between Doyle and the range of agents and participants which radically affected the form and content of the

performance in several ways. The project received less than fifty per cent of the funding required, so the number of professional dancers was reduced from two to one. The original site had to be changed to a nightclub at the end of Eastbourne Pier and the constituency of the community group changed entirely, shrinking the number of participants to six. Health and safety considerations, the state of the dance floor and the furniture and design of the club placed further restraints upon the choreography: trainers had to be worn, floor work was omitted and movement that involved 'climbing and hanging off the podiums' had to be jettisoned (Doyle 2001: 9). Doyle's stated aim was to give her original work 'context, to go beyond conventional theatre spaces...shifting between moments of improvised vernacular movement language and choreographed phrases', to produce 'a performance event that integrated professional and community practice in a socially inclusive context' (ibid., 2001: 7/8). Her final evaluation of the experience – 'overall the project consolidated my commitment to the value of dance within a structured outreach programme and its potential to develop confidence and self worth within young people' (ibid., 2001: 9) – suggests that she saw this work as having contributed to their creativity and well-being. Whilst she is keen to blur the boundaries between art and social spheres, from the outset to the completion of the project she appears to see her work with GAP as outreach work, linked to and providing a 'prologue' for the work of art (*Plastic Chill*) rather than as a work of art in its own right. She reflects that the effects of the reduction in budget upon her artistic vision were frustrating, and that 'the theatrical subtleties of the [original] work were lost in the space and at times the dancers looked exposed and vulnerable' (ibid., 2001: 9). It is possible that the loosening of artistic control over the outcome necessary to realize the performance in a non-theatre environment led to a perception that what was produced was not a work of art, but community dance, or social work. But Doyle's choreographic vision was 'contingent upon the insights to be derived from [her]... interaction with others and with otherness' (Kester 2004: 118). This project bears not only her signature and that of the professional dancer with whom she worked, but also those of the participants, the nightclub owners and workers, the borough council officers, the SETA director and the audience/clubbers.

Case study two: *The Bunker Project*

In *The Bunker Project*, collaborators Sandiland, a multi-media artist, and Thomas, choreographer, were commissioned by essexdance to make a work for the secret nuclear bunker/museum at Kelvedon Hatch. The site, masquerading as a family bungalow in a bluebell wood, was chosen by the producers, Fleur Derbyshire and Kari O'Nions of essexdance. Derbyshire states that 'it was the uniqueness of the location, that proved the catalyst for the invention of what was to become a multi-strata project...anchoring...arts activity to "place"' (Derbyshire 2001: 23). It was the particular contrast between the idyllic rural countryside and the cold underground bunker that would house a select few in the event of a nuclear explosion that inspired both the producers and the artists. Thus, this site became the original creative impulse of the work and the artists were part of a web of partners associated with and crucial to the making of the work. This 'anchoring' of the work to 'place' is echoed by the artists' reflections on their aspirations for the project that it should be 'ultimately a direct response to the uniqueness of the site' (Derbyshire 2001: 25). The notion of place includes not only the site itself, but the local community, and this was developed through a cross-generation Easter course in which the artists replicated processes that they were using in making the work of art, including visits to the site to collect materials to be worked into the performance. The final work created a 'performance trail' through the underground maze of the nuclear bunker, using 'dance and technology to enhance the physical experience' (Derbyshire 2001: 23). In pairs, audience members entered through a dimly-lit entrance tunnel in which their footsteps triggered lights. In a boiler room flooded with blue light, text compared a nuclear reaction to the colour of bluebells, providing a link to the outside world. Images of nature were further juxtaposed with the concrete underground environment in a 'tying pool', where a woman attempted, 'with bird-like movements', to build herself a 'nest' under a table, surrounded by lifeless dummies, phones and tele-printers (Derbyshire 2001: 25).

Project manager Fleur Derbyshire describes her role in the project in artistic terms as 'a creative one, a delicate choreography of inter-personal relationships between the project manager, the site owner, the artists, partners, community and the audience' (Derbyshire 2001: 25). Her use of the word choreography attaches the qualifier 'artistic' to the labour of the matrix of agents involved in the project and amplifies the authorship of the work of art. This expansion of the number of authors active in the work does not belittle the role of the artists; it is rather a testament to their ability to listen, 'catalyse understanding' and 'mediate exchange' in order that the final product is a result of a shared artistic process (Kester 2004: 118).

Case study three: *A Space in Place*

The director of Colchester Arts Centre, Anthony Roberts, acted as a creative producer/curator for the artists (Roberts 2001: 10–11) in another project. His creative input was in choosing the artists who would collaborate, namely, the art and architectural practice muf and the aerial dancer Isabel Rocamora. Like Derbyshire, Roberts also sustained an ongoing involvement with the creative and logistic processes involved in making the work. Finding and gaining permission for a site proved very difficult for this project and shaped the final outcome, which was to make an itinerant work. The group purchased a van from one of the sites with which they developed a relationship, a second-hand car auction in Essex, and then incorporated aerial dance on a ladder welded to the back of the van and video projections. This construction was made in residency at the second-hand car auction, where a dialogue developed between the artists and the dealers:

> ...this intervention created a great deal of interest – and became a talking point between the regular dealers, who we began to know, and ourselves. What we found is that people would start by talking about the van, the performance etc....and then move on to talking about themselves, their families and the artistic things that surrounded their lives. (Roberts 2001: 11)

They then took their work to a range of different locations where the relationship between the van as work of art and the site was foregrounded. The car park of Rollerworld allowed the work to be seen from the windows of passing trains – in this instance the experience of the work lasted approximately fifteen seconds. At St Mary's graveyard in Colchester the work lasted from dusk to dawn, and from 2am the only 'audience' was the dead. The work, which was about presence and absence of the body, entered different relationships with each site in which it was displayed. At the car auction an empty dress was hung instead of the usual flag, 'a bizarre unexplained intrusion into a male world' (Roberts 2001: 11). In the graveyard, TV monitors screened a busy rush hour scene from Liverpool Street station, 'the anonymity of long dead people set against the representation of other anonymous people, their images stolen and represented in their absence' (Roberts 2001: 11).

This work, set in motion initially by Roberts as the creative producer, was the result of a series of creative collaborative engagements between the artists and creative producer/curator, various sites and communities of people. It would be impossible to ascribe a single author to this process-based collaborative work, and its deliberate avoidance of permanence is highlighted by the absence in Roberts's article of a name for the project (the name of the project, *A Space in Place*, is provided on dancer Rocamora's website, (http: //www.isabelrocamora.org/magnoliaPublic/home/Biog/C-V.html, accessed 19/7/06)). Furthermore, Roberts suggests that the theme of the work 'emerged' from the process rather than being present before the project began (Roberts 2001: 11). The theme of the work was constructed in its relation to sites and collaborative partners; rather than taking place in one site, or a series of similar sites, and being tied to a fixed notion of site, the work and its concerns were fluid and able to be reconstituted to reflect the artists' sensitivity to the different sites chosen. The artists were also able to listen to each other, and to the 'otherness' of the environments they found themselves in, placing themselves in a dialogical relationship with the process of art-making and sustaining 'an ongoing process of empathetic identification and critical analysis' (Kester 2004: 118).

Case study four: *Apart from the Road*

Apart from the Road (2001), directed by choreographer Rosemary Lee, was a dance, film and poetry installation in Barking Central Library, arising from a year-long residency at Marsh Green Primary School. Unlike all of the previous projects, Lee chose her site of residency and her artistic collaborators, film-maker Nic Sandiland and poet Chrissie Gittins. The work was commissioned by East London Dance, who, according to Laraine Fisher, general manager of East London Dance, 'were required to take a back seat during the creative process'. She describes the institution's role as one of brokerage of 'connections, partnerships and dialogues where none existed previously' (Fisher 2001: 26/27). Lee's initial vision was to explore themes of home and 'belonging' in an 'alienating environment' (around the A13 trunk road), but says that 'these ideas had to be radically rethought once the children became involved' (Hale 2001: 27). There was a shift away from physical place to the identity of the children involved as it became clear that many of these schoolchildren were displaced and already leading transient lives, and that the idea of home was a site of potential trauma to them. Thus, the artist's vision was challenged and changed through her collaboration with the children. Lee developed filmed miniature movement portraits of the children and, at the end of each,

> ...hesitantly, they walk right up to the camera and sign their name, as if on the lens, with their noses. Their gaze – curious, bold or coy – pierces through that of the camera. They become subjects claiming authorship, no longer the silent, nameless recipients of a 'welfare state' (Hale 2001: 28).

Lee was forced to make concessions and changes, as her work became 'a tissue of quotations drawn from innumerable centres of culture' (Barthes 1977: 146). Hale notes that Lee was 'reluctant to claim authorship' of the project, but she claims 'its careful elicitation of a heightened reality and its concern for authentic representation make *Apart from the Road*, a highly crafted and compelling piece of art' (Hale 2001: 28). Hale recognizes the power of art practices to affect changed perceptions amongst community groups when expertly directed by experienced artists and she is also clearly calling the products works of art.

Who makes site-specific dance? A matrix of curating

My incursion into visual arts necessitates a return to the subject of this volume: curating. In *Art in Question*, academic and curator Martin Kemp calls artists and curators 'stagers of visual events' (Kemp in Raney ed. 2003: 197). The words 'stager' and 'event' imply action, moving visual art towards the condition of performance and, simultaneously, blurring the boundaries between curator and artist and between arts disciplines. Karen Raney comments that curating is often described as a form of research, 'an endeavour that is exploratory, collaborative, dynamic' (Raney 2003: 5). Under this formulation, art as research, rather than (or as well as) art as expression, might pervade all aspects of life, ceasing to retain its differentiating features as a discipline and as a practice. Artists and curators potentially face redundancy as art is open to everyone, yet it is precisely artists and art practices that are able to create the environments in which 'exploratory, collaborative, dynamic' endeavours might flourish.

Curating is not a term generally applied in dance in Britain; the nearest equivalent might be 'programmer' or 'producer'. Pauline Johnson, creative producer of music and dance events, understands curating in the visual arts sense of 'bringing together a collection', comparable to bringing together a group of artists for a curated evening of performance (Johnson, interviewed by author, May 2006). The producer is not 'totally creating an artistic product, but manipulating its coming together' (Johnson 2006). Programmers and producers are usually attached to arts centres or theatre institutions, programming seasons of performances, with no direct role in the creative processes employed in the making works of art. They may, however, exert significant influence over the artistic output, and they certainly employ creative strategies in devising seasons and programmes of work which reflect the programming policies of their institutional framework and of the funding body that supports them. When a work is commissioned, producers are likely to play a greater part in the creation process with the artists. Where a site-specific work is commissioned, they might, for example, choose the site for the commission, placing physical parameters around the artist's creative work. Johnson, who refers to herself as a 'creative producer', sees her position as a collaborator within the artistic team when working on site-specific projects. She emphasizes the role of logistics in the creative development of a locational project, saying that it is impossible to separate practical and artistic ideals and that sometimes it is difficult to identify who has originated an idea (Johnson 2006). Therefore, where site-specific dance is concerned, the notion of a creative producer resonates as someone who may contribute significantly to the creative labour that gives rise to an artistic event without, however, being identified as the leading or named artist/s or as a member of the artistic team. According to the Arts Council of Scotland,

> Experienced creative producers, with vision and a deep understanding of performance can play a crucial role in the development of high quality performance work. (http: //www.scottisharts.org.uk/1/latestnews/1003259.aspx accessed 21/5/06)

The choice of a physical site might lead to the involvement of other bodies who can alter the shape of the final dance work; for example, communities, local authorities, businesses, residents, landowners and institutions. The role of the choreographer as author of the dance as work of art is therefore challenged by these inputs. In dance, the notion of an authorship is already disrupted by the interpretations of dancers (except in the case of solo performer/choreographers) and collaborations with other artists (lighting, costume designers and composers), prior to being interpreted by audiences. Furthermore, many choreographers utilize improvisation as a choreographic methodology, so the movement content might be created by the dancers and organized by the choreographer. In the case of site-specific dance, I consider that not only is the authorship of the choreographer challenged by the creative and interpretative inputs of dancers, collaborators and audiences: it is also further challenged by a range of other bodies and stakeholders involved and who might shape the producing process significantly. These bodies might include institutions, landowners, business proprietors, producers, critics, educationalists and funding bodies, who operate within particular established relational configurations. Through the Year of the Artist programme, the Arts Council of England actively sought to change its position in relation to the value of the arts in society by requiring artists to work in unfamiliar surroundings. Consequently, participating artists, producers and a range of other bodies within and without the field of dance (if such a field can be clearly marked out) were forced to collaborate to produce artistic outcomes. These collaborations redefined notions of how dance as art is produced and called into question some established boundaries within and without the discipline of dance (for example, between choreographer, producer, community, business and funding organization), around the notion of creative labour. It follows, therefore, that in the case of site-specific dance, a range of bodies play a significant role in the creative processes that shape the final dance work.

A way of understanding how different bodies are connected creatively in the making of site-specific work is perhaps offered by Raney's discussion of Sadie Plant's work in *Art in Question*. Raney suggests that in her search for ways to avoid binary oppositions and hierarchical forms, Plant uses the metaphor of weaving, 'where patterns emerge from a matrix of overlapping threads' (Raney 2003: 27). This metaphor allows a non-hierarchical, decentralized picture to emerge on how works of art are made. I would like to propose curating as a process of creation in which a multiplicity of bodies are engaged. This process may be understood as a matrix of overlapping positions, in which any position may be seen as important or crucial to a particular project as any other.

Conclusion

Through my examination of these four projects in the Year of the Artist programme, I wanted to try to understand how these site-specific dance works were made, and whether conclusions might be drawn about the making of site-specific dance works in general. The four works articulate different relationships with their sites of 'residency', displaying a range of interpretations of site-specificity. The troubled boundaries of site-specificity evident in the visual arts appear to also operate in dance, highlighting a need for more scholarly attention to consider how these categories have expanded since 2000.

References

Banes, S., *Terpsichore in Sneakers: Post-Modern Dance*, Hanover, Weleyan University Press, 1977, 1987.

Barthes, R., 'The Death of the Author' in Barthes, R., *Image Music Text*, London, Fontana Press, 1977.

Briginshaw, V., *Dance, Space and Subjectivity*, Basingstoke, Palgrave, 2001.

Derbyshire, F., 'Sssh! The Bunker Project', *Animated*, summer 2001, pp. 23–25.

Doyle, M., 'Plastic Fever', *Animated*, summer 2001, pp. 7–9.

Fisher, L. and Hale, C., 'Apart from the Road', *Animated*, summer 2001, pp. 26–28.

Goldberg, R., *Performance Art: from Futurism to the Present*, London, Thames and Hudson, 1979, 2001.

Hutton, L. and Fenn C., Year of the Artist – Evaluation of the programme in England, Research report 26, Arts Council of England, 2002.

Johnson, P., interview conducted by the author, 3rd May 2006.

Jowitt, D. (ed.), *Meredith Monk*, Baltimore, Johns Hopkins University Press, 1997.

Kaye, N., *Site-Specific Art: performance, place and documentation*, London, Routledge, 2000.

Kester, G. H., *Conversation Pieces: community + communication in modern art*, Berkeley, University of California Press, 2004.

Kwon, M., *One Place After Another: site-specific art and locational identity*, Cambridge Massachusetts, The MIT Press, 2004.

Lacy, S. (ed.), *Mapping The Terrain: new genre public art*, Seattle, Bay Press, 1995.

Lippard, L. R., *The Lure of the Local: senses of place in a multicentred society*, New York, The New Press, 1997.

Livet, A. (ed.), *Contemporary Dance*, New York, Abbeville Press, 1978.

Raney, K. (ed.), *Art in Question*, London, Continuum, 2003.

Roberts, A., 'Target Audience: The Dead', *Animated*, summer 2001, pp. 10–11.

Suderburg, E. (ed.), *Space, Site, Intervention: situating installation art*, Minneapolis, University of Minnesota Press, 2000.

Wilkie, F., 'Out of Place: Out of Place: the negotiation of space in Site-specific Performance', unpublished thesis, 2004.

Wilkie, F., 'Mapping the Terrain: a survey of site-specific performance in Britain', *New Theatre Quarterly 70*, vol. XVIII, part 2, May 2002.

Worth, L. and Poynor, H., *Anna Halprin*, London, Routledge, 2004.

Websites

http: //www.isabelrocamora.org/magnoliaPublic/home/Biog/C-V.html (accessed 19/7/06).

http: //www.scottisharts.org.uk/1/latestnews/1003259.aspx (accessed 21/5/06).

THE MOVEMENT BEGAN WITH A SCANDAL

Alun Rowlands

The video *Do you really want it that much? – More* by Volker Eichelmann, Roland Rust and Jonathon Faiers is an ongoing, crash-edited montage of the fleeting visits Hollywood film pays to the museum. The artists have assembled countless hours and sequences, taped off-air or from pre-recorded video, to construct alternative narratives. Studying these sequences in juxtaposition we accumulate characteristics of how the museum is represented within fiction. What does cinema want to tell us about the function of these spaces? For example, in the familiar 'heist' movies, the museum is represented as an impregnable, glittering fortress only to be reduced to a self-service shop window for the master criminal's pickings. These films subvert the museum's function as custodian of the priceless cultural artefact. The museum as a place of order and clarity is rendered chaotic and obscure open to a strong range of emotions from love and jealousy to loss and melancholy. In many films the love of art is intermingled with the love of flesh. Galleries and museums are charged to provide the perfect cruising ground stimulated by the act of looking. With art spaces transformed into meeting places, the love of the object and the object of love become irretrievably blurred. The municipal formality of the gallery becomes a site for clandestine meetings, scandal, crime, action, daring, theft, murder, forgery and corporate parties. The video *Do you really want it that much? – More* utilizes the filmic representation of art spaces and transforms their narrative structure. By reassembling these narratives, the work proposes intriguing outcomes and endless formulations for art spaces. Why does the cinematic representation of museums and galleries differ so much from the real? The result is suggestive that, perhaps, the fictional representation of the museum can inform the organization, running and our behaviour within the real institutions themselves. This fiction projects the museum or gallery as a transformative space; an active progressive arena.

In *Prisms*, Theodor Adorno observed, 'museums are like the family sepulchres of works of art. They testify to the neutralisation of culture'. The museum still dominates the horizon of our material culture, legitimizing cultural form and expression. The institutional practices of selection, presentation and historiography deploy value that control and decipher our past. These governing practices, the ruling force of political and economic factors, reveal the museum as subject to the shifting associations of authority. They, also, exert and reflect specific contradictions in society. The museum's position as the most authoritative art institution may allow it to govern the construction of our present and also our hallucinatory future.

Institutional critique from artists such as Hans Haacke, Michael Asher, Daniel Buren and Dan Graham aggressively desired to affect change. For these artists the institution is both subject and object of their work, or 'both target and weapon' (Foster 1986). For some, museums were depicted as asylums. The works of art they housed appeared to be going through some kind of 'aesthetic convalescence' (Smithson 1972): separated from society they were politically lobotomized, inanimate invalids ready for consumption. Alan Kaprow's disdain towards institutions extended to the opinion that museums should be converted to a more actively pleasurable use of space such as swimming pools or nightclubs. Yet, contemporary art's critique of the museum, even if reluctantly, still 'belongs' to the museum: critiques are offered as services, invitations encourage absorption and are legitimized by the institution. Here, it maybe similar to Herbert Marcuse's idea of 'repressive tolerance', that these tenable positions form part of a liberal toleration of dissent as a symptom of relativism or perhaps disorientation. Broadside attacks, nevertheless, recognize that the museum was, and still is, an arena in which power is secured, acknowledged, underwritten, disputed, confronted, lost and gained.

The exhibition *The movement began with a scandal* was born out of discussion. It formed part of *hosted by....:* , a series of interventions organized by the Kunstraum, Munich. The Kunstraum is a city-funded collective of artists and curators who are essentially nomadic – moving from space to space in constant negotiation with the city and responding with a flexible programme of exhibitions and events. The Kunstraum brokered the opportunity to curate a show that would thread itself through the various permanent collections within the Lenbachhaus Museum. The exhibition sought to consider the conventions and effects of the museum, its forms of definition and its dissemination of social and political values; by inserting twenty contemporary artists in amongst one of Munich's major historical collections. The attempt was to open up patterns of aesthetic and ideological consumption within and around the museum for critical examination.

The Lenbachhaus Museum is a collage of collections housed within and extended from the original villa of the painter and philanthropist Franz von Lenbach. Its international reputation is based on its unique collection of works by the Blue Rider group. In addition, the museum offers insights into nineteenth-century Munich painting and has a policy of purchasing works by significant representatives of more recent art during the last twenty years.

Like a number of museums, Lenbachhaus has become more than the sum of its collections. As an institution, it recognizes that it is not a unitary entity. By moving outside its four walls it has disseminated itself through various media into the broader social realm. Deploying a range of promotional activities, in competition with a burgeoning tertiary sector, the museum has extended its civic duty through publishing, corporate functions, tourism, websites, education, temporary exhibitions and café culture. The proliferation of these educational and promotional activities has increased visitors. These audiences are a mixed constituency of people with varying interests, demands and expectancies from the museum, whose agenda has shifted from being merely a representative building towards a highly specialized space for communication and presentation to an increasingly heightened interpretative role, through co-operation and communication, allowing the museum to understand itself as a living organism.

It is within all these dispersed, interlinked and interpretative structures that the discourse of art is fashioned and regulated and it is within such an interpretative web that the exhibition sought to intervene. Broadly speaking, two approaches here were put into play: a reinvigoration of the historically important works that the particular collections comprised and a broadening out of how the museum might today be perceived, utilized and evaluated. The fact that these two strands were not mutually exclusive was demonstrated by Kaye Donachie's contribution to the exhibition, *Enlightenment* (2002), a compact installation of six small canvases depicting the esoteric spaces of Masonic ritual and exchange. The central painting reproduces the pose in a well-known photograph showing Paul Klee and Wassily Kandinsky in a double handshake that is a restaging of Schiller and Goethe's act of kinship, while other paintings similarly record recognizable aspects of the Craft. Freemasonry underpins the original formations of bodies such as the museum and artistic movements that reveal their secrets through the very fabric of their architecture.

The image of complicity, co-operation and scheming within institutions is heightened through these imaginary covert meetings. A dominant culture is perhaps being manipulated, reinforced and sold through a series of power relations and Kaye Donachie's paintings delve into the formal and informal spaces where such decisions are made, bound within conspiratorial origins where agreements are reached. Donachie's provocative tableau suggests that the gallery and work surrounding it, by Klee, Kandinsky and their contemporaries, should be reconsidered in a more questioning light. In presenting Freemasonry as an elitist discourse ghosting that of modernism Donachie reminds us that, while art is frequently regarded as an enlightened occupation, its most celebrated practitioners often rise to prominence through clandestine but influential networks and connections.

Sometimes networks allow a forging of space. Interventions can occur: an opportunity, an invitation, a moment of slippage or a temporary shift in focus where something unexpected is allowed to happen. People meet, ideas are exchanged and perhaps scandals are plotted. Movements gain momentum, plans put into action, documents are written and intentions displayed all in the name of what happens next. *The movement began with a scandal* evolved through such a network – a relay of communication and exchange formed the foundations of the show's construction where artists were invited to respond to a number of scenarios. Its curation was a collaborative venture and each collection and each room came with its own curator to be consulted. The curatorial role was one of filtering information and intentions to all those concerned in an attempt to produce something more solvent. The series of relations constructed allowed the host museum to evolve heterogeneously and become more elastic.

Liam Gillick responded with his text for *Winter School* (1996): he recounts the story about a 'Winter School' set up in Kassel in 1971 before *Documenta V*, in order to challenge the structure of expansive international exhibitions. There was no record of this meeting and no record of the school, but Gillick imagines the scenario – the creation of an alternative structure, to place action into action, a projection into the future, changing everything. He envisages discussions, agendas being drawn, disputes, reorganization of crises and reclamation of the near future through an understanding of the middle ground. This middle ground offers a pre-representational social area that foregrounds the executive decision-making. Of course, this is all presupposition, with no records filed, no evidence of the school's activities, *Documenta* continues pretty much as it began. Also aware that the Lenbachhaus boasted a recreation of the coloured walls of the original Blue Rider salon, Gillick issued a directive for the museum's technicians to attempt to paint the wall of its reading room the colour and hue of Coca-Cola. *Inside now, we walked into a room with coca-cola walls* (1998) proposed a shift in environment that leaves its test marks on the wall. The act reflects a reference to a passage in Gillick's book *Discussion Island: Big Conference Centre* (1997) where one location has walls the colour of Coca-Cola. Within the context of the Lenbachhaus, perhaps big brands have almost acquired the aura of universal abstract truth – the 'real thing'.

The museum as a site for corporate play was previously the domain of chairmen and their wives. Now through the emerging influence of promotion and association the museum has become a more formidable culture broker. It is here we find the Szuper Gallery where artists are seemingly involved at boardroom level. The Szuper Gallery was founded in Munich where a number of artists were working as assistants dealing in East European modernist painting but the business was failing. Under a cloud of fraudulent suspicion of money laundering, the gallerist fled overnight leaving the assistants to run the gallery whilst it was being investigated. The artists developed an exhibition programme that performed the procedures of a commercial gallery, demonstrating a fully functioning gallery to the outside world but filling the formal elements with different narratives. It showed work by different artists often in collaboration, in this way the commerce of the Gallery became the project itself. The space closed after two years as part of the bankruptcy but the name was appropriated for future collaborative practices.

Sited within the preserved apartment of the benefactor Franz von Lenbach, *Good Morning Mr. Bloomberg* (2000) unveils a business deal, recorded on video, which is being celebrated between the artists and a collector. The camera focuses on gestures, ritual actions, artificial friendliness and smart dress. From these details the viewer begins to sense that here the art world and economics are meeting in a lavish environment. The collection and acquisition of artworks, the clinching of a deal, all begin to display the overlap of culture and corporate economy. The artists here, perhaps, are entering into a partnership in which they are both complicit in their manipulation of symbols and representation. Is this a scandal? Or maybe Szuper Gallery just recognize that power lies within the process of mediation and contextualization.

Salon de Fleurus is an anonymous endeavour in the form of a long-term exhibit whose subject is the collection of modern art assembled in Paris by Gertrude Stein and her brother, Leo. Housed in a small apartment on Greene Street, New York, this strange incarnation of a salon is not a museum, a gallery, a residence or sacred space, yet it suggests all of these. There is not an 'official explanation' or 'manifesto' that would elucidate to the visitors what this place is, what they are looking at and what might have been the intentions of its 'authors'. All interpretations (statements, articles) of this place so far have been external and they are all considered to be 'legitimate'. Its caretaker, Goran Djordevic, explains to visitors that the collection of African sculptures, antique curiosities and reproductions of modernist paintings constitutes a contemporary exhibition of anonymous artists. He reveals that reproductions relate to Gertrude Stein's art collection at her apartment on Rue de Fleurus, Paris. It is as if this place is a Proustian return to the realm of memory and an evocation of the modernist spirit of the early twentieth century through an imaginary re-staging.

At the Lenbachhaus Museum we encounter artefacts from the collection 'on tour'. Sited in the Blue Rider Gallery these facsimiles relate to Kandinsky et al.' search for original expression that included plundering non-European cultures. The objects and paintings are, themselves, a negation of authenticity, authorship and even historicity. The salon is a healthy antidote to the museum's demand for clear and easy boundaries. It recaptures something of a bygone experience of art viewing, forging a critique of contemporary museum presentation imbued with a shifting modernist revisionism. What is apparent is that artists, their work and practices exist and are claimed under the banner of a larger economy of culture. The show as a whole, although decentred, attempted to incorporate practices that are interested in working alongside all of the institutions that manipulate the exchange of values between people and things. At times these activities are a search, resistant to, and therefore reclaimable from, the dominant culture.

Flatpack, a fluid collective of artists, designers and architects, presented *Presence: cultural mining excavation No. 5* (2002). They attempted to solicit the museum visitors to offer up interpretations for a dark and mysterious abstract silhouetted form found on the cover of Led Zeppelin's seminal 1976 album, *Presence*. They connected Munich, the city where Led Zeppelin recorded the album, and Birmingham – both Hypnosis', the designers of the album sleeve, and Flatpack's home city. The object appears without any explicit function and allows speculation for possible use or meanings for its existence, its dark form appeared within various parts of the museum from centrepieces within the museum café to billposters around the museum and was a visual reminder to jolt the audience into investigation. Posters were printed packed with suggestions as to the work's meaning, consisting of a spiral of text, projecting various meanings. Speculating on interpretation of popular culture within the confines of the museum implied that the museum must be open to values and agendas quite distinct from those that informed it during the eighteenth and nineteenth centuries.

Collaborative enterprises such as Inventory, Flatpack and others engineer a state of affairs or new constellations that are at once contradictory and apposite. Shifting between disparate venues, subjects and forms of engagement there is no object, text or image held in higher esteem than the other. Allied variously to institutional critique and activist and political documentary traditions as well as to post-studio, site-sensitive or public activities, these practices do not necessarily share a thematic, ideological or procedural basis. What they do seem to share is the fact that they all involve a concern with asserting a material and political relation of affect with their social context. In each of these examples, shared communal and functional space is created as the literal location of (and means for) the artwork's realization. The exhibition is revealed as just one way amongst many of working with and letting art exist.

The movement began with a scandal sought to be a field for discursive formations inside which the protagonists engaged in a process of temporary positioning. Curatorially, it mirrored the collaborative groups who foster a collective approach in order to blur traditional hierarchies and did not seek to construct a closed narrative around curating. Rather it attempted to open up a divergent space where fractures, conflicts and interruptions are all key to enquiry. This fluency of collaboration was not only in the work contained within the show, but between the exhibition and its host. Self-institutionalization allows for a moment of convergence before disappearing to follow a new constellation. The appeal, perhaps, is to plot against the compliant filling of gallery space and the time frames that currently shape the life of institutions. Instead of bolstering exhibition routines, which limit certain practices, emotions and activities there is an increasing need to introduce different rhythms and narratives that promote a continued questioning of the institutional and ritualized exhibition forms. The impetus stems from piggybacking institutions temporarily. There are not really any supply lines that need to be cut off or borders that have to be established; it is more a matter of testing the agonistic resistance that art proffers within the field. This subjunctive proposition within curating could foster a solvent flux between the created and the re-created through interstices that function differently, opening up discourses in which the exhibition, as a form, forges the elision of documentary with fiction that promotes speculative thinking.

References

Adorno, T. W., *Prisms*, trans. Samuel and Shierry Weber, London, 1967.

Foster, H., *Recoding: Art, Spectacle, Cultural Politics*, Seattle, Bay Press, 1986.

Holt, N. (ed.), 'Cultural Confinement', *The Writings of Robert Smithson*, New York, University Press, 1979.

Marcuse, H., *A Critique of Pure Tolerance*, Boston, Beacon Press, 1969.

CONTRIBUTORS

Suzanne Buchan is Professor of Animation Aesthetics and Director of the Animation Research Centre at the University College for the Creative Arts at Farnham and editor of *animation. an interdisciplinary journal* (Sage). She is a founding member and artistic director (2003) of the Fantoche International Animation Film Festival, Switzerland. Her research explores interdisciplinary approaches to animation, film, theory and aesthetics and she is also active as a curator and consultant. Publications include *Trickraum: Spacetricks*, Christoph Merian (Verlag, 2005); *Animated 'Worlds'* (Libbey Publishing, 2006); and *Metaphysical Playrooms: The Films of the Brothers Quay* (University of Minnesota Press, 2007/8 forthcoming). She is currently writing a book on animation spectatorship.

JJ Charlesworth is a freelance critic who has written widely on contemporary art for publications such as *Art Monthly, Third Text, Modern Painters, Flash Art, Time Out* and *The Daily Telegraph*, with a focus on art's relationship to contemporary politics. He has published numerous catalogue essays on contemporary British artists and is a visiting tutor at the Royal College of Art; the Royal Academy Schools and the University of the Arts, London. He is currently the reviews editor for the UK-based magazine *Art Review* and works with the campaign network *The Manifesto Club*.

Dr Geoff Cox is an artist, teacher and projects organiser as well as a lecturer at the University of Plymouth and at the Transart Institute, Donau University, Krems. He has a research interest in 'software art' expressed in various critical writings and projects, such as the co-curated touring exhibition, *Generator* (2002/3), and in his (unpublished) Ph.D. thesis, *Anthithesis: The Dialectics of Software Art* (2006). He co-edited *Economising Culture* (2004) and *Engineering Culture* (2005) as part of the DATA browser series (Automed). He is also a trustee of the Kahve-Society (with Hatice Abdullah and Victoria de Rijke) and (with Stuart Brisley and Adrian Ward) of the Museum of Ordure. He is on the council of management of Spacex Gallery, Exeter.

Chris Dorsett is Reader in Art School Practices at the School of Arts and Social Sciences, Northumbria University. His curatorial practice is at the interface of contemporary art and traditional museum display; natural history; scientific objects and examples of vernacular architecture. His curated projects include *Divers' Memories* (Pitt Rivers Museum, Oxford) and *Resurrection Shuffle: A Story of Storage* (Cheltenham Art Gallery).

Catherine Elwes is Reader in Moving Image Art at Camberwell College of Arts, University of the Arts, London. She is a video artist and writer whose most recent book is *Video Art, a guided tour* (I.B. Tauris, 2005). Her recent curatorial work includes ANALOGUE, an international selection of pioneering video, and *Figuring Landscape*, a series of screenings of film and video work from the UK and Australia on themes of landscape. She is currently writing a book on installation art with Susan Lawson.

Richard Hylton is a curator and writer of art criticism. His international exhibitions include *Imagined Communities* (1996) and *Landscape Trauma in the Age of Scopophilia* (2001). He has edited monographs on artists Donald Rodney and Janette Parris and co-curated (with Virginia Nimarkoh) *The Holy Bible: Old Testament* (2002) – an artist's bookwork by David Hammons. His book, *The Nature of the Beast: Cultural Diversity and the Visual Arts Sector, a study of policies, initiatives and attitudes*, to be published by the University of Bath's Institute of Contemporary Interdisciplinary Arts (ICIA) in 2007.

Kate Lawrence trained at Laban Centre, London, and is a lecturer in the Department of Dance Studies at the University of Surrey where she teaches on the first British undergraduate module in Vertical Dance. She was director of the feminist dance company Nomads during the 1990s and her research focus engages with site-specific practices, particularly the relationships between rock climbing and dance. Her recent projects include *St Catherine's Chapel* (2001), funded by the Year of the Artist and *High Art* (2002), a vertical dance performance.

Paul O'Neill is a writer, artist and curator based in London. He has curated over 40 exhibitions and projects in Britain and Ireland. He was gallery curator of the London Print Studio between 2001 and 2003 and is co-director of Multiples X. He is editor of *Curating Subjects* (De Appel and Open Editions, 2006), an anthology of new curatorial writing and a contributor to *Art Monthly, Cica* and *The Internationaler*.

Sophia Phoca is Course Leader in Video Media Arts at the University College for the Creative Arts at Maidstone. She is a writer and critic in time-based media and post-feminism and has contributed to *Third Text* and *Contemporary*. She is the author of *Introducing Post-Feminism* (Icon Books, 1999) and co-curator of *Europa: Film and Video at the Centre of Europe* (Tate Modern, 2005).

Dr Jane Rendell is Reader in Architecture and Art and Director of Architectural Research at the Bartlett School of Architecture, University College, London. An architectural designer and historian, art critic and writer, she is author of *Art and Architecture* (2006), *The Pursuit of Pleasure* (2002) and co-editor of *Critical Architecture* (forthcoming 2007), *Spatial Imagination* (2005), *The Unknown City* (2001), *Intersections* (2000), *Gender Space Architecture* (1999), *Strangely Familiar* (1995). She is on the editorial board for *ARQ* (*Architectural Research Quarterly*) and the *Journal of Visual Culture in Britain* and is a member of the AHRC Peer Review College.

Alun Rowlands is an artist and curator and has collaborated with institutions, artists and museums internationally and in the UK. He is the author of *Three Communiqués* (Bookworks, 2006) and is the editor of temporarysite.org, an occasional archive of transient events, curatorial initiatives and writing. He is based at the University of Reading.

Dr Judith Rugg is Reader in Fine Art Theory at the University College for the Creative Arts at Canterbury. She is an artist, writer and critical theorist and co-editor of *Advances in Art and Urban Futures: Recoveries and Reclamations* (Intellect, 2002) and has written and published widely on issues of space, gender and contemporary art. She is currently working on a book for I.B. Tauris on issues of contemporary art, site and space.

Michèle Sedgwick is an employment lawyer with an interest in cultural theory and discourse. She is co-author of 'Budapest's Statue Park: Memorial or Counter-monument?' (*Soundings Journal of Politics and Culture*, issue 17, spring, 2001) and 'A Place in the Sun: Repression and Desire in Andalucia' (*Soundings Journal of Politics and Culture*, issue 28, winter, 2004).

Liz Wells is Reader in Photographic Theory at the Faculty of Arts, University of Plymouth. She curated *Uneasy Spaces*, contemporary British photo/video (New York, 2006), *Facing East, contemporary landscape photography from Baltic areas* (UK tour 2004/7) and co-curated/co-authored *Shifting Horizons: Women's Landscape Photography Now* (I.B. Tauris, 2000; UK tour 2000/1). She is editor of *Photography: A Critical Introduction* (Routledge, 2004, 3rd ed.) and of *The Photography Reader* (Routledge, 2003). Her study, *Land Matters: landscape photography, culture and identity*, is due for publication in 2007 (I.B. Tauris).